NEW BRADWELL

BRADWELL

REMEMBER WOLVERTON, STRATFORD & BRADWELL

FRONT COVER: The Wolverton town parade on Jubilee Day, 1935.

The district's first motor 'buses at their terminus outside the Cock Hotel, Stony Stratford in 1914 — the link between the three places.

REMEMBER WOLVERTON, STRATFORD & BRADWELL

The story of three towns
in a council 1919-1974

BY

BILL WEST

BARRACUDA BOOKS LIMITED
BUCKINGHAM, ENGLAND
MCMXC

PUBLISHED BY BARRACUDA BOOKS LIMITED
BUCKINGHAM, ENGLAND
AND PRINTED BY
THE DEVONSHIRE PRESS LIMITED
TORQUAY, ENGLAND

BOUND BY
CHARLES LETTS LIMITED
EDINBURGH, SCOTLAND

JACKETS PRINTED BY
CHENEY & SONS LIMITED
BANBURY, OXON

LITHOGRAPHY BY
DEREK CROXSON LIMITED
CHESHAM, ENGLAND

TYPE SET BY
HARPER PHOTOTYPESETTERS LIMITED
NORTHAMPTON, ENGLAND

© Bill West 1991

All rights reserved. No part of this publication may be reproduced, stored in a retrieval system, or transmitted, in any form or by any means, electronic, mechanical, photocopying, recording or otherwise, without the prior permission of Barracuda Books Limited.

Any copy of this book issued by the Publisher as clothbound or as a paperback is sold subject to the condition that it shall not by way of trade or otherwise, be lent, re-sold, hired out or otherwise circulated without the Publisher's prior consent, in any form of binding or cover other than that in which it is published, and without a similar condition including this condition being imposed on a subsequent purchaser.

ISBN 0 86023 474 6

Contents

ACKNOWLEDGEMENTS (AND GLOSSARY)	8
FOREWORD BY THE REG WESTLEY	9
INTRODUCTION	10
THE FURTHER PAST	11
HARD TIMES	16
GETTING ABOUT	48
MAKING IT WORK	62
THE HOME FRONT	75
SAY IT WITH MUSIC	85
THAT'S ENTERTAINMENT	106
COMMUNITY SPIRIT	131
MIND AND SOUL	140
NEW TOWN BLUES	150
INDEX	159
SUBSCRIBERS	163

ENDPAPERS — FRONT: Street map of Wolverton Urban District, c1955. BACK: Map of WUD in 1919 (with Haversham Estate and houses built up to 1950 of Wolverton, Bradwell and Stratford added).

Acknowledgement

I wish to thank all those who gave me so much help, general information and advice in the writing of this book. First and foremost is Audrey Lambert for her contribution on Guides and for her interest and help throughout the compilation of this book; she was kind enough to read the manuscript. Bill Coxhill supplied information, photographs and co-operation on the local Scouting scene. I am greatly indebted to Tom Wilmin and Frank Atkins, two old school pals, for the use of their large collection of local photographs and for their expertise in copying them for this book and for their tolerance towards my never-ending requests. I make grateful acknowledgement to Arnold Jones for use of his material on the Wolverton Light Orchestra and his notes on Mr Lunn and the Choral Society; to Doug Dytham and Tommy Clarridge for information on their band experiences and to Sheila Tomkins, Sarah Haycock and Yasmin Goodman, who made a fine job of typing the manuscript, I am most grateful. My sincerest thanks go to Reg Pateman and his wife Dolcie, Frank Atter, Vic Davis and Bill May for their valuable information on fêtes, carnivals, football and cricket events.

Finally I wish to express sincere gratitude to Clive Birch, my publisher, for the care and attention he has given to this book.

Glossary

ARP	—	Air Raid Precautions
L & B	—	London and Birmingham Railway
LCM	—	London Central Meat Co.
LDV	—	Local Defence Volunteer
LNWR	—	London & North Western Railway
LMSR	—	London Midland and Scottish Railway
MARMY NIGHT	—	Traditional bath-night (usually Friday), originally the trade name of a shampoo
NFS	—	National Fire Service
PH	—	Public House
RAF	—	Royal Air Force
RFC	—	Royal Flying Corps
RNAS	—	Royal Naval Air Service
WAAC	—	Womens' Auxiliary Air Corps
WUDC	—	Wolverton Urban District Council
WVS	—	Womens' Volunteer Service

Photo Credits

ILN — *Illustrated London News*
JT — John Toogood
GC — Graham Crisp
RW — Roger Warwick
JS — John Starsmore

Foreword

by Reg Westley

With the inception of the New City of Milton Keynes it became imperative that the local history of our district should be chronicled so that future generations should know what it was like before this event took place. The author of this book has attempted this successfully.

The period of the Wolverton Urban District Council from its formation in 1919 to its demise in 1974 is probably the most colourful of our history.

Here we have the three separate towns of Stony Stratford, Wolverton and New Bradwell and the village of Calverton, all with their own particular interests, working together for the good of the whole district.

I can remember many of the characters and episodes mentioned, in particular the St Giles Choir Outing in the early thirties. I was one of the choir boys on that 'bus. The District can be proud of its achievements over the years. It has produced excellent skilled engineers and craftsmen due to the facilities of the Railway Works and other companies.

Education had always been a top priority. It was also noted for its fine musicians, bands, orchestras and choirs.

There were fine sportsmen and women in all aspects of sport, but I think the most successful community effort was during the last War. Its serving men and women were among the first in action. The district was also among the first to receive evacuees. A big effort was also made to sustain the needs of our fighting men in raising money and producing the goods and materials needed to bring the War to a successful conclusion.

There have been numerous changes during the post-war years. Many new houses were built, and this helped the district to become more prosperous. It was with regret that the Railway Works had to be slimmed down but unfortunately it was inevitable. Many of the skilled trades that the district was noted for were no longer needed: progress always brings its casualties.

All those who lived through the period of the Wolverton Urban District should enjoy this book and will be able to tell the present generation how they took part in many of the episodes mentioned.

Reg Westley

Reg Westley was born in Stony Stratford in 1919, attended the Church of England Boys School at Stony Stratford, and served in the Fleet Air Arm and the Royal Air Force, 1943-47.

Elected a Director of Wolverton Co-operative Society Ltd in 1947, he continued this service when the Society amalgamated with the Bletchley Society in 1967 to form the Milton Keynes Co-operative Society Ltd, and retired as a Director in 1990 after 43 years of continuous service, five of them as President.

Elected to the Wolverton Urban District Council in 1958-74, he was also a member of the Northampton and District Hospital Management Committee 1968-74, and for a number of years Chairman of the former Wolverton and District Trades Council, a keen local historian and a rare book collector.

Introduction

The Urban District of Wolverton was constituted in April 1919 by the amalgamation of the townships of New Bradwell, Stony Stratford, Calverton and Wolverton by order of the Ministry of Health. Previous to this, the civil parish of New Bradwell was in the Rural Area and Union of Newport Pagnell and those of Wolverton, Stony Stratford and Calverton in the Rural Area and Union of Potterspury. (For a short time before WUDC the parishes of Wolverton and Stratford formed the Wolverton Rural District Council.)

The new Urban District was the largest in the county, extending over some 4,699 acres with a population of around 13,000. It was governed by a council of twenty-one members, divided into four wards: New Bradwell — five, Calverton — one, Stony Stratford — five and Wolverton — ten.

Services administered by the Council included sewerage and its disposal, refuse collection and disposal, highways, street lighting, recreation grounds and open spaces, burial grounds, allotment gardens, water supply and housing.

The badge of office worn by the Chairman of this body, and its coat of arms, was a shield with two navy blue lines to symbolise the River Great Ouse, which passes through every part of the old urban district, on a white background, with the initials WUD. Surrounding the shield were three equi-spaced circular panels depicting, for Wolverton, the railway viaduct over the River Ouse; for Stony Stratford a star, the badge of De Vere who was Lord of the Manor of Calverton including Stony Stratford West side; and for New Bradwell a hand, the badge of Manfelin who, as Baron of Wolverton, founded Bradwell Abbey.

WUDC crest.

Dedicated to the Memory
of my Mother, Father
and two brothers, Bob and Gerald

The Further Past

New Bradwell or Stantonbury was born with the first expansion of Wolverton Works in 1849 when more men were engaged to cope with an increased workload. It was essential to provide facilities for their accommodation so the company had to see where they could best erect houses. The railway company's first thought was to enlarge Wolverton, but the Ratcliffe Trustees, who owned the greater part of the land immediately surrounding Wolverton, refused to sell, so obliging the company to look elsewhere.

The railway company looked a little to the east of Wolverton, a mile distant from the Works, and that was the start of New Bradwell or Stantonbury.

In early 1854, the site consisted principally of old gravel pits on the edges of two old Parishes, Old Bradwell and Old Stantonbury, hence the dual name. There was not much there — Stonebridge House, the old toll-gate house on the Newport Pagnell road at the junction of Old Bradwell and Shenley and Loughton road, the wharf alongside Bradwell bridge, the wharf house by the side of the Grand Union Canal at Stanton Low, and the old Smock Mill.

The old parish of Stantonbarry was a mile and a half away; William the Conquerer had bestowed the Manor of Stantone with several others on Milo Crispin, whose heir was Ralph. His descendants took the surname Barré and so Barry was added to Stanton. In 1296 Sir Robert Barré represented Bucks in Parliament and twenty two years later, Northamptonshire. The last male heir was William Barry, who held Stanton-Barry in 1376. Through his only child, Petronilla, it went in marriage to Hugh Boveton of Yardley Gobion, and until 1735 passed through several families, when the Duchess of Marlborough settled it on John Spencer, her grandson and it became the property of Earl Spencer of Althorpe in Northamptonshire, through whom the L & NW Railway Company was able to create New Bradwell or Stantonbury.

Sir John Whitlewrong, who sold the estate in 1725 to the Duchess of Marlborough, built a large mansion here, rebuilding the old Manor House; the remains are still to be found. Here also are the ruins of the parish church of St Peter, still in reasonable condition until after the war (1945) but since then much decayed. Sir John barbarously murdered Joseph Griffith, a mountebank, at the Saracen's Head Inn at Newport Pagnell and fled the country, but later fetched up in Fleet Prison, dying there in 1743 of wounds he got in a drunken brawl with a fellow prisoner.

Old Bradwell, with which New Bradwell or Stantonbury was closely identified, was listed in Domesday as 'Bradennell' and also belonged to Milo Crispin; in the reign of Henry II it was given to the Keynes family for taking King Stephen prisoner. About 1315 it passed, through the marriage of Margaret, daughter of Robert de Keynes, to Philip de Aylesbury. As early as 1189 Nigellus held the Priory of Bradwell and the last prior was John Ashby in 1515. It was converted to a mansion, then degenerated into a farmhouse in the possession of the Adams family.

In early 1854, the L & NWR Co purchased a portion of the Stantonbury and Bradwell estates and a poster was circulated: 'An estate purchased on the Newport Pagnell road, March 20th 1854. Plans and specification at the Racliffe Arms' (Wolverton). Here the railway company erected about

200 houses, ranged in parallel streets almost midway between the Grand Union Canal and the Newport Pagnell main road. Built of white bricks, they were soon occupied by mechanics and other railway employees; a new settlement was quickly established. Then private enterprise generated additional houses beyond those of the railway company and within three years this new place had grown so rapidly that it was decided to form a new parish of 904 acres by lopping off a portion of Old Bradwell. Like Wolverton, it grew as the Wolverton Works developed, and expanded again in the early 1930s.

The manor of Calverton, which included Stony Stratford, West Side was held in 1086 by Hugh de Bolbec as part of the Barony of Bolbec. About a hundred years later it passed by marriage, along with the manor of Whitchurch, to the De Veres, Earls of Oxford. Stony Stratford became a separate manor in 1257. On the death of John, fifteenth Earl, in 1540 his widow was granted the manor of Calverton-cum-Stony Stratford with other properties for life. When his nephew Nevill, Lord Latimer died in 1580, Calverton-cum-Stratford was assigned to Katherine Nevill, wife of Henry, Earl of Northumberland and in 1616, Katherine's sons sold it to Sir Thomas Bennett, Alderman of London. The latter's grandson, Simon Bennett, added to his fortune by enclosing common arable lands and converting them to pasture. Through the marriage of one of his daughters the manor passed to James Cecil, Earl of Salisbury. A later James, Marquess of Salisbury, sold it in 1806 to William Selby Lowndes of Whaddon Hall. The manor included a fishery on the Ouse and several mills on its banks, including one at Stony Stratford, as well as the fair and market dues of the town.

Calverton from 1919 to 1974 was a peaceful district consisting of Upper, Middle and Lower Wealds, where church, farm and cottage seemed to have grown up naturally among the woods and streams.

Wolverton (*Wolverintone* in Domesday, *Wolfrington* in the twelfth century, *Woolverington* in the seventeenth and *Woolverton* in the eighteenth) takes its name from Anglian chieftain Wulfhere who, according to legend, probably settled in the area sometime after Cuthwulf's invasion of Buckinghamshire in AD571. Wulfhere's *ingtun* (farm) by the end of the eleventh century consisted of most of the land within the Watling Street on the west, the River Ouse to the north and a stream now called Bradwell Brook on the south and east, more or less the area that was later administered by WUDC.

Wulfhere's settlement was also positioned astride the highway between Bedford and Buckingham. For a time it was under the control of the heathen Kingdom of Mercia and in the reign of Edward the Elder (AD901-925) was an outpost of the Danish fortress of Bedford.

At the Norman Conquest, Wolverton was divided among three thegns, Godwin, Tore and Alvrie, all supporters of Harold. They were dispossessed and their land given to Maigno the Breton. His barony consisted (with Wolverton at its head) of Little Loughton, Stoke Hammond, Padbury, Thornborough, part of Lamport in Stowe, Choulesbury, Helpasthorpe in Drayton Beauchamp, Aston Sandford, the Vache and Isenhampstead Chenies, Chalfont St Giles and one half of Ellesborough, all in Buckinghamshire; to which was added in 1190 Simpson and, around the same time, Wykhamon, Maidwell and part of Thenford, Cold Ashby and West Haddon in Northamptonshire.

These vast territories were all governed from Wolverton, where Maigno erected his castle on rising ground away from the river, with the township at the foot of the hill. The keep of Maigno's castle is in the grounds of Holy Trinity Church.

The Domesday Survey states 'Wolverton answers for twenty hides, land for twenty ploughs; in lordship nine hides; five ploughs there. Thirty two villagers with eight smallholders have ten ploughs; a further five possible. Ten slaves; two mills @ 32s 8d; meadow for nine ploughs. Total value £20; when acquired for £15; before 1066 £20.'

After Maigno's death his son Manfelin became lord of the Manor c1110 and in 1125 he was Sheriff of Bedfordshire and Buckinghamshire. Manfelin was a religious man and founded a small Priory of Benedictines at Bradwell. Hamon, Manfelin's son, succeeded him as the third Baron and had a reputation as a great huntsman and poacher — in 1176 he was fined £100 for trespass in the King's forest. Hamon was succeeded by a son and grandson of the same name. The third baron Hamon, dying without an heir, was succeeded by his brother William in 1211. He also died without an heir and was followed by his brother Alan in 1246. Alan was the first baron to style himself 'de Wolverton'.

Alan's grandson, Sir John de Wolverton, was the last eminent member of this baronial house. He was born about the year 1268. In 1324 he was called to Parliament, and he died in 1342. After the death of Sir John's grandson, Ralph in 1351, the manor ceased to be a barony and passed through the female line into the de Longueville family.

The de Longuevilles held Wolverton for three hundred and fifty years, during which (1654) the parish was enclosed and the open field community swept away. The big arable fields and common land were carved into farms and the park of the Longuevilles remained for many years as evidence of the family's greed and tyranny. This led to the decline of the village and the depopulation of the locality. What was left of the community moved to houses adjoining the church. In 1713 the Longuevilles also departed, when Sir Edward, a spendthrift, was forced to sell up. The buyer was Dr John Radcliffe; he paid over £40,000 and when he died, left Wolverton to University College and other institutions at Oxford. Until the coming of Milton Keynes, the Radcliffe Trust was the largest landowner in the Urban District.

The rural peace of the second Wolverton was shattered in the late 18th and early 19th centuries by an invasion of huge armies of 'navvies', constructing the Wolverton section of the Grand Junction Canal.

The railway came to Wolverton in 1837, the line entering the parish near the site of the old Bradwell Abbey, travelling along its eastern side for around two and a half miles, and leaving it after crossing the Ouse on its northern boundary. This heralded the coming of a new third Wolverton. Here was built a 'Grand Central Depôt' of the L & B Railway. An engine house was erected to meet the needs of the engines of the day and around this workshop sprang up cottages to house company servants. The expansion of New Wolverton reflected the development of the workshops, and the establishment, in 1878, of a new factory by printers McCorquodale & Co. The population increased from 1,261, after the workshop had been established, to some 6,197 in 1921.

The ancient market town of Stony Stratford is on the banks of the Ouse near where the stream is crossed by the old Roman road the Saxons called Watling Street. There is no evidence of a township before the Normans but there was probably a Roman resting place near the approach to the river. The crossing provides the name. The spelling of Stony Stratford has changed little through the years: *Stoni Strafford, Stani Strafford* and *Stony Stretteford* all appear in thirteenth century documents.

From Norman times the Watling Street, the town's High Street, divided it into East and West Sides. The road also formed the boundary between the manors of Wolverton and Calverton. The town never received a charter and few records of its early history were kept.

In 1257 Hugh de Vere, Earl of Oxford, the then Lord of the Manor of Calverton, obtained from Henry III the grant of a fair to be held at West Side, Stony Stratford, on the vigil, feast and morrow of St Giles (1 September). Soon after that, a market was also granted. In 1290, the same Hugh obtained a grant from Edward I of a second fair on the vigil and feast of St Mary Magdalen (22 July).

A bridge existed over the Ouse before the middle of the thirteenth century, and at Stony Stratford a home of rest for diseased and infirm paupers was founded on the causeway to the north of it, as the Hospital of St John the Baptist without Stony Stratford; it was there in 1257, and probably even before 1240, when William de Paveli, one of the family that gave its name to Paulerspury, bequeathed 12 pence 'infirmis de Stratford'.

Watling Street has perforce brought English monarchs to Stony Stratford. It was one of the places where the cortège that accompanied the body of Eleanor of Castile, Consort of Edward I, from Harby to Westminister, stopped to rest. In 1291, an Eleanor Cross was erected.

Nearby Whittlebury Forest was a hunting ground visited by English kings. In 1464 Edward IV arrived, making one of the inns of Stratford his HQ. Here he met his future Queen, Elizabeth Woodville, then Lady Grey, widow of Sir John Grey of Groby. Their meeting place of an oak tree is still known as the 'Queen's Oak'. One morning he rode out to Sir Richard Woodville's house at Grafton Regis where they were married.

Edward IV died in 1483; his elder son by Elizabeth Woodville was Edward V. Travelling from Ludlow Castle to Westminster for his coronation he was seized at Stony Stratford by Richard of Gloucester (afterwards Richard III) and the Duke of Buckingham. The end of the young prince's journey was not at Westminster Abbey, but the Tower of London and a secret death by violence. In Shakespeare's Richard III, the Archbishop says:

> 'Last night, I hear, they lay at Northampton
> At Stony Stratford they do rest tonight'

According to tradition the inn where the young King lodged was the Rose and Crown (now 26-28 High Street) but according to Brown Willis, the antiquarian, it was the Swan.

During the Civil War, the Earl of Cleveland maintained a station for the King at Stony Stratford. In 1644, he defeated a small Parliamentary force near Newport Pagnell; Charles Rex passed through on his way from Aylesbury to Woburn. The only violence was the destruction of the Eleanor Cross and some damage to the bridge by Roundhead troops two years later.

In the mid-16th century, lace-making was introduced by Flemish refugees from Mechlin, who fled Spanish persecution on the invasion of the Netherlands. These refugees settled mainly at Cranfield, Bedfordshire (Bedford was then an inland port), and spread to Olney, Newport Pagnell and Stony Stratford. Huguenots of Lille, Lyon and Rouen also sought refuge in the area after the massacre on the feast of St Bartholomew on 24 August 1572. During the next 200 years, Stony Stratford, along with Newport Pagnell, Olney and Bedford became one of the country's leading lace towns. In fact, the economy of the district was geared to it.

From the mid-18th century Watling Street brought stage coaches and prosperity to Stony Stratford. At its peak some 40 coaches per day passed through. Added to this were waggons, carriers' carts, pack horses and private vehicles. This had a knock-on effect for services such as smiths and wheelwrights and, of course, more inns for travellers. The boom continued for some 50 years.

In 1801, the Grand Junction Canal arrived at Old Stratford, becoming the main source of outside supplies. This same canal took with it most of the freight traffic that had passed through the town, so its fortunes declined.

Stage coach traffic continued until the coming of the railway in 1838. Then the town really suffered — inns were closed, as were the stage coach trades of shoesmith, saddler and wheelwright. Stowell Brown describes it in 1840 as a 'dull dead and alive place'.

Then, as Wolverton Works developed, so too did Stony Stratford, both economically and materially, due mainly to the workers who made their homes there. E. Hayes opened a foundry to make agricultural implements in the early 1850s, developed and later produced marine engines, tug boats and various launches. The town remained dependent on the prosperity of Wolverton Works until the Watling Street came back into its own with the development of the motor car and lorry, just after the 1914-18 war.

ABOVE: The Queen's oak tree at Potterspury is allegedly over 600 years old. It stands by the overgrown bridle path on Queens Oak Farm. Under its branches, it is said Elizabeth Woodville first met King Edward IV. Hearing the King was hunting nearby she waylaid him and begged for the restoration of her lands, seized after the death of her husband, Sir John Grey, at the second battle of St Albans in 1461. Elizabeth not only received her lands but on 1 May that year, 1464, she was secretly married to the young King at Grafton Regis. The following year she was crowned Queen at Westminster. After the King's death at 41 in 1483 her sons, the ill fated princes, were seized at Stony Stratford and perished in the Tower. Elizabeth Woodville, of Grafton, Queen of England, grandmother of Henry VII, great grandmother of Elizabeth I, died in 1492, 28 years after that meeting beneath the 'Queens Oak'. BELOW: The Stratford Ambulance returns home from Mesopotamia in 1919, marching to the Square at Wolverton for the stand-down parade. The unit was not reformed.

LEFT: Archie Sayell in his Austin Seven, off for the day, the first working man car owner in Bradwell. RIGHT: Cosgrove, showing the tunnel entrance beneath the canal southern side. BELOW: Canvin's, the Stony Stratford butcher, delivering meat at Cosgrove to the Plough Inn.

Hard Times (1919-1938)

The 1914-18 war had been over just a few months when the WUD was first formed. Everyone looked for a change for the better: full employment along with better housing, while preserving the more pleasant aspects of the pre-war era. Yet 1921 was one of the worst years of depression since the industrial revolution. The General Strike started on 3 May 1926 and lasted until the 12th.

The railwaymen at the Carriage Works and the printworkers in the main answered the call, but there was contention between the few that went to work and the strikers. Charges of intimidation against Wolverton Works strikers were brought before Stony Stratford and Newport Pagnell magistrates. Trouble had brewed at Castlethorpe where volunteer platelayers were working. There were disturbances outside the Carriage Works, outside the non-strikers' homes or *en route*. Some who went to work were threatened with a ducking in the brook at New Bradwell. 24 were charged with intimidation, one was sent to prison and the others paid fines varying from £2 to £10.

Mainly through causes outside the region's economy, the 1920s saw two local firms fail: E. Hayes of Stony Stratford and E. & H. Roberts of Deanshanger. This same period saw the development of a local omnibus service, and long distance 'buses began operating services through Stony Stratford, bringing back some of the prosperity of the old coaching days. Both Midland Red and Black and White stopped at the Cock and at the Bull for luncheons, dinners and teas and to pick up and set down passengers.

Between the wars many plied the streets, dealing from horse-drawn vehicles or handcarts; Amos Bull pushed a perambulator selling sweets and small grocery items. At Stony Stratford there were Tom Worker and Bert Payne, greengrocers; Clarke of Church Street with his hand cart traded grocery and 'Coddy' Jones hawked wet fish. At Wolverton and Bradwell street vendors like Busby sold wet fish, Clarke grocery. Nigger Brown of Cosgrove was another familiar sight, selling wild rabbits in season from his horse-drawn cart, skinning the product on the tail-gate when requested. The price ranged from fourpence to sixpence depending on how prolific the coneys were. W. Howe, fishmonger of 24 High Street, Stony Stratford, ran mobile fish and chip vans, which operated daily from the old tram shed yard. There they stoked up their coal-fired chip fryers before working the locality and surrounding district, summoning customers with handbells. Likewise Sarah Sayell's fried fish shop of Spencer Street, New Bradwell, gave a service to the surrounding villages on Saturday evenings. Her ordinary van had hay boxes fitted to carry the fish and chips, returning to the shop to replenish them as necessary. There were also the numerous milk and bread roundsmen, delivering daily, or even twice daily by ladle from the churn.

In the Wolverton Road, Stony Stratford, lived a Mr Yates, his wife and handicapped daughter. Mrs Yates ran a small business from home — home-made crumpets. Mr Yates, affectionately known as 'The Crumpet Man' would go around the town on Saturday nights with a tray calling 'The best crumpets in town'. Many a time local youths, having a drink at the other end of town, say at the Barley Mow public house, would look to see how many he had left, then order and pay for more than there were. Yates would obligingly walk home, (nearly a mile) and then retrace his steps to deliver the odd crumpet. During the week and Saturdays, orders for crumpets were taken at Mrs Yates' door for delivery at specified times. Daughter Connie would then deliver dead on time.

On Sunday mornings 'Cinder Billy' Alderman of Stony Stratford always dressed in a corduroy suit, with leather 'yorks' just below his knees and a red bandanna around his neck, touring the town selling watercress and crying, 'Watercreasy, tuppence a plate'. His product was freshly picked from the wild beds that abounded at the source of Gorricks Spring (the Lion's Mouth), along the Calverton Road. At noon, any crop left would be soon disposed of at the local hostelry.

Around the streets one could witness errand boys galore, darting round on their trade 'cycles delivering produce to households. The wages averaged eight to ten shillings per week for up to 60 hours, six days a week. Even then mishaps occurred. One butcher boy's 'cycle fell over, tipping joints all over the pavement, along with their weight and price tags. The boy hastily gathered them up and, not realizing what he was doing, haphazardly replaced the tags. Subsequently, customers who required a beef joint received pork or lamb, along with other permutations. Some looked at the price and thought they had a good deal and others were grossly overcharged. Within an hour the shop was full of irate customers, but the errand boy was absent, out with another basket for delivery.

Derek Smith, who worked for Roberts the ironmonger, was ordered late one Saturday afternoon to take the trade tricycle with 18 gallons of paraffin to a farmer at Nash. He was advised not to ride the loaded tricycle down hill, but to push it. Ignoring this advice, (he wanted to go to the cinema) he rode down the hill out of Upper Weald, Calverton. At the bend at the bottom, over he went, skinned knees, paraffin spilled all over the road and a damaged tricycle. There were no pictures for Derek that night. But worse still, Roberts charged him for the spilled paraffin, deducting it by weekly instalments from his meagre wage. He then sent him back to complete his errand, which took until 8 o'clock that night.

Charging boys for damaging, breaking or spilling goods was not out of the ordinary. Pete Martin, as a boy, worked for Cox & Robinson, the chemist. He accidentally dropped a carton of Dettol, smashing the contents. He was just going about his duties moving the cartons and other goods to the warehouse after delivery by the LMS dray. Pete swiftly cleaned and mopped up the mess, but did not report his misdemeanour. Philpotts Snr soon found out, reprimanded him, and told him that he would deduct the cost by weekly instalments from his ten shillings per six day week.

Throughout the district there were take-away food shops: faggots and peas and fish and chips. Stony had four fish and chip shops, Bradwell two and Wolverton two. Faggots and peas could be obtained from Porky Green's of Stony Stratford and from Amy Compton of High Street, New Bradwell. A like service could be procured from Mrs Goodridge of Aylesbury Street, Wolverton every Saturday dinner time, sold from her private residence by knocking on the front door. Fish and chips were threepence (tuppence for fish and a penny per portion of chips), faggots and peas, a penny per portion (2½p = 6 old pence). Porky Green, whose slaughterhouse was in the yard of the Shoulder of Mutton at Calverton, was established in Stony Stratford in 1908. All his products were home-made or home-produced like potted meat (now called paté), hams, brawn, lard, dripping, polony, sausages, chitterlings, black pudding, all cuts of pork, beef and lamb. These products, all made on the premises, were in the first instance cooked at Yates' bakery on the corner of New Street and from around 1934 until after the 1939-45 war, at Haseldine the bakers. It was a familiar weekday lunchtime scene to see one of the Green family walking down from the bakers *en route* to the shop with a cloth-covered tray of cooked pies or pasties balanced on his head. Then, for the last few years that pies were produced, they were cooked in ovens on the premises. These products were also taken to the surrounding villages during the inter-war years by horse-drawn cart. A permanent stall at the Wolverton Friday Market was manned, as it still is. Besides this Dennis, one of the sons, attended the Winslow Market on Mondays and the Buckingham Markets on Tuesdays and Saturdays, carrying the produce on the local 'bus.

E. Wickens of Stony Stratford, tailor, outfitter and draper, advertised his merchandise as 'Strong and Hard Wearing'. Outside the shop hung hobnail boots while corduroy trousers stood up on their own, the material was that stiff. He also employed a man who travelled around surrounding villages running a tally book, customers paying, say a shilling a week on a card, for goods received. Calladine, of Stony Stratford and Bradwell, boot and shoe repairers ran a boot club on similar lines, delivering by horse-drawn van. Wells outfitters of Loughton had and continue a similar service around the district.

Wickens also used the services of Teddy Ratcliffe, the last carrier in the area. Teddy lived in lodgings at Potterspury and operated between the village and Stony Stratford six days a week. The seventh day he pumped the organ at Potterspury Church services.

Teddy had a charge list: 'Penny for small parcels and tuppence for big cases'. He would remember most of his orders, repeating them to himself as he travelled along. Occasionally he would make notes on scraps of paper. Each day he left 'Pury at 11.30am, placed his orders at shops in Stony, collecting between two and four in the afternoon. This regular service went on until the late '30s.

One day Teddy's donkey lay down in York Road and refused to get up. Teddy went into the chemist's shop and asked Mr McLean if he could see what was the matter. After examination, McLean explained — 'I'm afraid it's dead Teddy'. Teddy looked thoughtful, then commented 'That's funny, it's never done that before'. Because he was held in such esteem and affection Stony Stratford tradesmen paid for a hand truck, to be made by Ted Yates. Teddy continued as a carrier until just after the war, when ill-health forced his retirement. He died at 'Pury soon after.

Many 'diddlem clubs' (loan and divi and farthing clubs) were managed by social clubs and individuals and were used to pay bills such as rates, electricity and gas and to assist with holidays, with the emphasis on Christmas. Shares were issued at the beginning of the year worth sixpence each. Members could have as many shares as they liked. All monies were banked to earn interest. Each member could borrow up to the equivalent of his shareholding *ie*: one share value = sixpence × 52 weeks = £1.6 shillings. Therefore, a holder of ten shares could borrow £13 0s 0d. On obtaining a loan, one paid a levy of tuppence per share borrowed and tuppence per share when paying back. If you did not borrow at all, you were fined tuppence per share per annum.

A club with such rules was run at New Bradwell for over 50 years. Initially its HQ was at the Morning Star. After closure, it transferred to the New Inn. After a short time there, it moved to the Workman's Social Club where it remained until it packed up in 1985. Throughout its existence, no one ever defaulted. At the end, its total annual payout some two weeks before Christmas was between £8,000 and £9,000. The club ceased when the government said it would tax interest.

Farthing clubs were organised on similar lines except that these were purely savings clubs for Christmas and ran for a twelve-month. Members had ¼d shares, as many as they wished, and paid on each share — ¼d the first week, ½d the second week, ¾d the third week and so on for fifty-two weeks which, for one share, came to £1 8s 10d. From this the organiser, generally a private individual, deducted an agreed fee for time and trouble. Usually these ran trouble-free but, on rare occasions, human nature being what it is, temptation stepped in and the money went missing.

For the two decades before the Second World War, local life more or less returned to pre-1914 normality. Sundays were days of complete rest. Even the Radcliffe Trustees did not allow any work on the allotments except feeding animals and fowl. Sunday schools, whether Church of England or Chapel, were well attended. At eleven o'clock the majority of the male population trekked to various bakers, taking the Sunday roast and Yorkshire pudding to be cooked. Then they would go for a stroll, weather permitting, at 12 noon calling at their respective local or club for an aperitif, and at one o'clock collecting their cloth-covered baking tins to take home.

In the winter and late autumn, Sunday afternoon family walks were the norm. Around Stony Stratford, crocodile columns of orphanage boys could be seen, snaking in various directions.

During the early spring and summer people turned out in the evening. Most promenades would be across the field footpaths to a nearby village, arriving at an inn at opening time (seven o'clock). These family rambles incorporated nature study and local history lessons. Birds would be noticed building nests one week, then laying and hatching. Father would pick out old man's beard, lady's smock, shepherd's purse, fleabane and fat hen, and explain how, years ago, the seeds of the latter were gathered for food and the leaves harvested, boiled and eaten as a green vegetable. Rotation crop growing would be explained, and at harvest time, how the stooks of corn were so arranged to run in rows north to south to allow full exposure to the sun.

A Bradwell family had a choice of many walks, all with circular routes, to Old Bradwell, Loughton, Linford, Haversham or Wolverton. To Haversham the path would be along the canal towpath to Stanton Low, across the fields, passing the site of the old Rifle Butts. Here it would be made known to the children that these were built in 1879 by the L & NWR Co for use by the Wolverton Works companies of the Rifle Volunteer Corps, later the Territorials. These were pulled down c1926 by Taylor's steam traction engines of Little Linford. Perhaps a few minutes would be spent in probing the soil to retrieve a spent bullet. Next to the Butts stands the Norman church of St Peter (now in ruins). Up to the late 1940s a church service was still held here once a year. There was, at one time, a large mansion and quite a substantial village surrounding the church, and a (legendary) secret passage from church to mansion. The last house here was occupied by a Mr Fowler until around 1946. At one time the river was crossed by a ford, a crossing in use in Roman times, for Romano-British remains have been found on both banks of Hill Farm, Haversham and also at Stanton Low. The Roman engineers who built what we term the Watling Street disregarded this and other easy passages like the Beachampton crossing, and pushed their alignment straight from *Magiovinium* near Fenny Stratford, to *Lactodorum* on the site of modern Towcester. The walk continued to the gated road to Carrs Mill, through the village of Haversham, calling first at the Greyhound, before returning to Bradwell *via* the Haversham Road.

Another favoured walk was from Bradwell to Old Wolverton along the canal towpath. A cast-iron railway bridge crossed the canal at Wolverton Works; built in 1834-5 it was the stuff of legends. The ironfounder's name of Butterly was cast on the girders, there was ornate panelling and once four ornate bronze lions were mounted on each corner. The 'Battle of Wolverton' between R. Stephenson's railwaymen and Lake, the Canal Company's engineer and his navvies took place on 30 December 1834 when Stephenson built a bridge across the canal against the canal company's wishes. Lake marched on Wolverton with some 2,000 men. Stephenson with a like number tried to defend his works. Lake succeeded in demolishing the structure, but the railway company won the day in court in January 1835 and the bridge was completed without further interruption from the canal company.

The Locomotive Inn (re-named the Galleon in 1939) recalled the infamous Culworth Gang's attempt to rob a Mr Eaglestone — before the coming of the canal or railway. On 23 November 1783, five members of the notorious band tried to rob the house of Mr Eaglestone in the Parish of Wolverton — Turrell, Bowers and three named Smith. They put on smocks, blackened their faces and, having met one of Mr Eaglestone's servants near home, led him to the house and threatened to murder him if he refused to knock at the door. When it was opened, they rushed in. Mr Eaglestone and two of his servants immediately attacked them and would have secured them all but, in the confusion, one of his men received a terrible blow from his fellow servants which almost disabled him. The robbers had got so much the worst of it they were glad to make off empty-handed. Later they were caught and hanged at Northampton for this and other crimes.

Then, perhaps, the traditional stimulant at the Loco preceded the walk back along the 'Old Road' to Bradwell.

A popular walk for Wolverton families was across the fields to Calverton and the Shoulder of Mutton. This path was part of the old Southern Ridgeway Road which ran from Oxford to

Cambridge. Locally it wended from Beachampton to Calverton, up Gib Lane, crossing the Watling Street by the gibbet tree, thence to what is now Green Lane, down to 'Stonebridge' and *via* Stanton Low to Newport. This course was followed, in reverse, from Wolverton to Calverton, all across fields with well-worn paths and pleasant scenery, on weekend evenings.

Drawing near Calverton, the walkers might make for the stone wall at the back of the church to inspect the stone carving in the wall which outlines two gibbets with crows flying around and the date 1693. Legend has it that it marks the site of the old gibbet and the hanging of the murderer of Mrs Bennet. Mrs Bennet was the wealthy widow of Symon Bennet, of Calverton manor. She was mean, so mean she would not pay her poor rates, and unpopular.

At Stony Stratford, butcher Adam Barnes was a man of some standing for he was involved in many local transactions between 1680-93 as an Overseer of the Poor. Barnes lived in a small house in the High Street on the site of the old Post Office (No 58 High Street). In some kind of financial predicament, he set out to rob Mrs Bennet, who was known to keep a large sum of money and valuables in the house.

Caught in the act by the old lady, he killed her. He was arrested and held in the Old Cross Keys, a public house in the High Street. Here he was tried, found guilty and condemned to be hanged. According to local tradition his body was exhibited there until the rooks came and pecked every morsel of flesh from his bleaching bones. 'This was done as a lesson to men not to murder'.

From there, local families would call at the Shoulder of Mutton before making their way home past Gorrick's Spring, renowned for its healing qualities. The ancient verse might be quoted as they wended their way back to Wolverton *via* Stony Stratford:

> 'When 'Gorrick's Spring' flows fast and clear
> Stoop down and drink for health is here.
> If 'Gorrick's Spring' should e'er run dry
> Beware for pestilence is nigh.'

One of the favoured walks for Stony Stratford families was to Cosgrove across the fields *via* Wolverton Mill (Woods Mill), passing the site of the old Roman villa to one of the three hostelries of the village. For the return journey, there were three ways home: by road through Old Stratford, by the main canal towpath, over the aqueduct to Old Wolverton, or along the Old Stratford section of the Buckingham arm of the canal to Old Stratford. The length to Old Stratford was built in 1800 to the main line dimensions and was 1 mile 2⅜ furlongs long.

At Old Stratford were the remains of the old wharf and warehouse. They were later taken over by E. Hayes, boat builder of Stony Stratford, as his launching site and fitting-out yard. The wharf and warehouse were used as a workshop and store.

The entrance to this large basin was crossed by a large swing bridge, connecting the end of the Old Stratford branch towpath and the commencement of the Buckingham Arm path. The Buckingham Branch was of smaller dimensions than the main canal, 9 miles 4⅜ furlongs long with a rise of 13ft 9 ins, and restricted to boats of 7ft beam. It was built in 1800-01 in eight months, commencing September 1800 and opened for traffic on 1 May 1801. It had two locks, twenty-nine bridges, one tunnel (under Watling Street) and six wharfs: Deanshanger, three; Leckhampstead, Maids Morton and Buckingham.

Unless going through Old Stratford, walkers would bear south-west at the end of the Old Stratford Branch and cross two fields to the Stony Stratford river bridge on the way home.

Another well-trodden path was that from Stony Stratford Mill (Rogers Mill), crossing the mill meadow (Shoulder of Mutton Field) and the long plank into the Windmill field and on to the Passenham Lane. South along the lane and past the tithe barns and church, past the stone cross built into the church-yard wall, locals recalled one of the many ghost stories about Passenham —

maybe that of Bobby Bannister, the curate and the organ or of Nancy Webb. Of the latter, it was said for years that her ghost was to be seen on the night of Deanshanger Feast, the nearest Sunday to 11 October, on or before, but never after that date.

She lived in Deanshanger, a good-looking girl. At the feast she met a soldier and they were married at Passenham Church. Her husband went to war and was killed. A child was born but that died a few months later. The mother stayed at her child's grave night after night and her mind became unhinged. One night, as people were returning from Deanshanger Feast, she was heard screaming along the road. Before they could catch her, she leapt into the Mill stream and was crushed in the mill wheel. Her body was recovered in the morning and laid in the churchyard by that of her child, but not to rest, for every night the feast came round, her white-clad ghost could be seen flitting beneath the tall trees by the churchyard round to the watermill. Again and again she went to her death, but now with her child in her arms. Nancy's shrieks mingled with the crushing of bones and the cries of the child. Thereafter it was 'Don't come to Passenham at midnight on the day of Deanshanger Feast'.

Past the mill, walkers joined the Beachampton Road, down the hill and into Stony Stratford.

The end of the 1920s and the start of the '30s saw hard times. 29 October 1929 was Black Tuesday, the day of the Wall Street Crash. In England a Labour Government met the full brunt of the worldwide slump. Two million unemployed by 1930 became three million in January 1933. Hunger marchers passed through the district, many of them ex-servicemen from the depressed areas of the north of England and Wales, who marched on London to demonstrate their discontent at the country's failure to find them work. Soup kitchens were set up and overnight accommodation found for them in local schools and halls.

There were many other men from all over the country who struck off on their own to look for work, coming through the district, knocking on doors to ask for hot water to make tea. Locally, some 800 men in the three communities were unemployed out of a population of around 16,000. Many of these sought work in the car industry at Luton, Oxford and Coventry. Although this trade was depressed, some were lucky and never returned.

One circumstance which eased the local situation was the construction of airship R101 at Cardington. Many men from the area had experience of this type of work, having served in the RFC (later RAF) and RNAS airship sections during the war. Local 'bus proprietors organised trips on Sunday evenings to view progress and, on one occasion, the arrival of the German airship *Graf Zepplin* in 1931 during its tour of Great Britain.

Test flights of the R101 began in October 1929 and it became an accustomed sight, flying over the area. The R100 built at Howden and the R101 were committed to a conspicuous inauguration. At the end of July 1930, R100 set off for Montreal, managed it easily, and returned two weeks later, flying low over the locality to berth at Cardington. On 4 October 1930, at 6.30pm, the R101 set off to India. At 2.00am, over the small town of Beauvais, it crashed, exploded and became an inferno. Only six of the fifty-four on board came out alive. The R101 disaster put an instant end to British efforts with rigid airships and the successful R100 was sold for scrap.

In those pioneering days New Bradwell was chosen by Sir Alan Cobham as a likely site for an aerodrome during his campaign to make Britain air-minded in 1929. His plan was to persuade a number of towns, cities and urban districts to establish their own aerodromes. Sir Charles Wakefield paid for some ten thousand schoolchildren to have free trips, and the tour lasted twenty one weeks, between May and October, covering 110 towns and cities. The aircraft was a DH61 christened *Youth of Britain*, a large machine for the day, a single-engined biplane with the pilot's cockpit behind a spacious cabin.

During June 1929, New Bradwell were hosts. The location was the large meadow on the other side of the river opposite the Newport Road Recreation Ground. Access was gained by building a temporary footbridge over the river from the old bathing place.

At around eleven, Cobham and his team flew in and were greeted by the chairman of the Wolverton Urban District and council members, who were given a free trip and afterwards briefed about the possibilities of aviation and the importance of establishing an airport locally. Then it was the turn of the children. Evelyn Godfrey, Margery Kightley and Jim Cook were selected by popular school vote, and were given a seven minute circular flight over Stanton Low and Haversham.

After this, the general public paid sixpence for a programme and access to the field, and five shillings for a flight. The flights continued until dusk. The three children from Bradwell each wrote an essay explaining how they felt on the flight and expressing their views on aviation and its potential. Each was rewarded with a photograph of the aircraft autographed by both Sir Charles and Sir Alan.

Yet the Wolverton Urban District Council turned down the chance to have an airport at Bradwell. Colonel L.C. Hawkins wryly commented that the aerodrome would only be used for forced landings.

At the time, local women preferred factory, shop or office jobs with fixed hours and free evenings. But such jobs were scarce. Domestic service was far and away the biggest source of female employment. Many a young girl went into big houses in the area with a starting wage as little as four shillings a week. To earn this, one young lady went into service at Wakefield Lodge to work seven days a week. She got up at five o'clock in the morning to start work at six o'clock prompt. The first job was to clean five or six large grates with black lead and burnish the fire irons. After a quick change into her day uniform of blue dress and white apron, she continued her daily tasks and after a hurried and often frugal meal, she changed again in the afternoon to a black dress and white apron for the remainder of her day. The working day continued until seven, later if there were guests.

Time off was one half day per week and one Sunday a month. For the former, all her tasks had to be completed before she was allowed out so it was sometimes four o'clock before she could get away and then she had to be back by ten o'clock. On her Sunday off, she had first to attend morning service and again be in by ten. When working around the house, the maids had to hide in cupboards or behind curtains when any member of the family happened by or entered a room. On no account were they to be seen.

Some young girls took daily help jobs in households of local tradesmen. One such young lady recalled being severely admonished for letting a couple of peas go down the sink while she was shelling them. Her first duty of the day was to sift the ashes from the fires, saving the cinders to burn again. The ash was used on the garden. The rest of the day was spent getting meals, doing the housework and washing. For a ten hour, six day week and Sunday morning eight until ten, she received the princely sum of four shillings and she added 'The rest of the week was mine'.

Stony Stratford unemployed were more fortunate than their fellows at Wolverton and New Bradwell in as much as Colonel Hawkins made available part of his premises at 18 London Road as a workshop. There he provided a wood-turning lathe, benches and various tools for the manufacture of toys and small articles and for the repair of boots and shoes. The raw materials for these activities were given by sympathetic people and firms, leather by Woollards the leather dressers, and scrap wood from Wolverton Works and local shops.

On one occasion, three men took a commission to build a hen coop. They set about it with gusto and completed it quickly, erecting it in the workshop because of the weather, with a view to putting it on wheels to deliver. But it would not go through the doors, so it had to be taken to pieces and re-erected on site. The story was told many times for over fifty years after the event. Wooden toys were made for children of the unemployed for birthday and Christmas presents, like the author's railway engine made for a Christmas present. The boiler was a small tree trunk turned on the lathe and all three brothers played in it over the years; it stood in the back yard defying the elements, and it was too heavy and strong to be moved until they reached their teens.

At Wolverton, the Church Institute was open all day, giving Wolverton men a place to meet, talk and play billiards. Bradwell unemployed had no facility at all.

To supplement the dole, cut in 1931, men took to living from the land, from whatever was in season. Blackberrying, mushrooming and nutting were popular as these were easy to harvest and there was little fear of provoking the law. Shops would buy for a small price, which would get lower as the market was flooded, so house-to-house sales or collecting to order were preferred.

Some poached rabbits. One Stratford man was caught in the act and the Buckingham magistrates confiscated his ferrets and nets and fined him five pounds. He pleaded he had no money and had been out of work for two years. He promised not to poach again, stating he had found someone to buy his ferrets and nets if they would release them, and he asked for time to pay. The magistrates were sympathetic so the police reluctantly returned his property. Walking home, he spied a likely spot, dropped his ferrets down a warren and had an exceptionally good day's hunting. Next day, returning to Buckingham, he paid his fine, had some change and walked home again. A few men went rabbiting legally, gaining permission from farmers, sometimes paying a fee and sometimes sharing the catch with the farmer.

After eight weeks the dole ceased and relief had to be found through transitional benefit *via* the local public assistance committee.

One Stratford man, Fred Barley, decided to challenge the system. He was single at the time and was summoned before the Public Assistance Committee for a means test. Fred, after much questioning, was informed that his father must keep him. Fred replied 'He's thrown me out' (but he hadn't). 'Then your sister who is working at the Printing Works must assist you', retorted the Chairman. 'She does not want anything to do with me' said Fred. The Chairman replied, 'I'm afraid there is no money granted, Barley, all I can offer you is Newport Workhouse', not believing any of Fred's story. 'I'll take it', snapped Fred, he was given eightpence to get to Newport by train, and walked.

Fred entered the workhouse and spent the night there. After breakfasting on a bowl of porridge, he was sent to work in the gardens. Around twelve o'clock he was summoned by the master to go before the board again and given another eightpence for his fare (again he walked). Once more he related his tale and at the end was grudgingly granted two and sixpence a week for a further ten weeks.

Another young man from Stony Stratford, after some years on the dole, became so depressed he took his own life. His mother had twice found him with his head in the gas oven but managed to resuscitate him. Each man out of work had to 'sign on' at the Labour Exchange, daily or weekly depending on where he lived.

The Wolverton Office of the Ministry of Labour was then a temporary building at the side of the Empire Cinema in Church Street, on the site of the present Post Office. The manager from 1926 until 1951 was Mr Thomas Backlog, a giant of a man weighing 23 stones and over 6ft 6ins tall. He sat behind a table in the centre of the room flanked by two clerks. His opening shot was 'Have you been unemployed Monday, Tuesday, Wednesday, Thursday, Friday and Saturday?'. If the answer was 'yes' he would bawl 'Pay him' and then delve into his pocket for his snuff box. he did not take a pinch, but a mustard-spoonfull. The spoon was kept in the snuff box, which was about the size of a two ounce tobacco tin.

He lived in Haversham and was a frequent visitor to the Greyhound Inn where he told tales of his world-wide experiences. Even in his athletic days, Mr Backlog never weighed less than 17 stones and he quickly earned the nickname 'Tiny'. He came to Wolverton not long after he had completed twenty-two years of travel and he always wore a topee and white tropical suit during the warmest days of summer.

He served in two wars. His travels in a world which then seemed a much larger place commenced in 1900 when he joined the Cape Colonial Defence Force to serve in the South African War. Later he was gold mining on the Rand and it was there he became part-owner of a racehorse which won him sufficient money to visit the Far East. In Shanghai he joined the Defence Force when the overthrow of the Manchu Dynasty loomed. His next move was to see Japan, then on to British Columbia (where he rolled logs in the Pugit Sound) before making for the South Seas. Mr Backlog next found a billet in the Cook Islands where he worked on plantations producing bananas and citrus fruits. He was on holiday in Sydney, Australia, in August 1914 and there joined the Australian Army. Such was his size that the only equipment they could provide him with was a chin strap. In the Gallipoli campaign he lost the sight of an eye, but even after demobilisation he chose to remain overseas and ended his foreign service in Zanzibar. While in Haversham, he was actively connected with the British Legion. On his retirement he moved to Little Crawley.

On the brighter side, football matches and various other games were arranged and played between the Wolverton, Bradwell and Stony Stratford men. Rev Payne of Stony Stratford supported this scheme, buying a football and allowing the use of St Mary's parish room as a meeting place.

The ladies suffered perhaps more than the men if they were unfortunate enough to be widowed, the wife of a man out of work, or one who was ill. Mrs Shirley of Wolverton Road, Stony Stratford, like many others, was forced to take in washing to support the family because her husband was ill and unable to work. Her house was full of washing from one week's end to another. The price list was threepence for a sheet and shirt, twopence for a pair of pillowslips, one shilling for a blanket and a farthing for gents' handkerchiefs. This included collection and delivery after ironing.

One of her customers was Rev E. Steer. The Reverend gentleman's sister was in the habit of paying Mrs Shirley on Saturday afternoons. On one such occasion, she called on Mrs Shirley to settle a bill of nine shillings and elevenpence three farthings. She proffered Mrs Shirley a ten shilling note and said 'You can knock the farthing off next week's bill if you will Mrs Shirley'.

One of Mrs Shirley's customers was a refined gentleman from Bradwell who had some ten shirts laundered each week. He also used the local 'bus parcel service for collection and delivery. One week a note was pinned to the cuff of a shirt: 'too much starch on the cuffs!' Mrs Shirley was quite indignant about this and exclaimed 'bloody cheek!' as she read it. When the gentleman's washing was completed she pinned an equally short note to the tail of a shirt: 'too much ---- on the tails!'

Mrs Emerton of Bradwell also took in washing for a local shopkeeper and his wife, for a regular fee of two and sixpence per week. To earn this, her son Bill collected the dirty linen on Sunday evenings, his mother washed and ironed it on Monday and Tuesday and on Wednesday morning she delivered it, spending the rest of the day doing all the housework in the living quarters. In the late afternoon, the proprietor gave her the money and asked 'Aren't you going to buy anything while you are here?'. After buying perhaps a piece of cheese and various oddments she was lucky to emerge from the shop with sixpence, the reward for three days' work.

Although there was great hardship in the area, there was also suffering in the cities, and Miss Hawkins, sister of Colonel Hawkins of Stony Stratford, organised summer holidays for poor children from the East End. They were placed with various families in the town.

In line with the national trend, the early 1930s was a peak period for the speculative builder. Acts to subsidise the building of houses by local authorities to be let at a less than economic rent were passed in 1919, 1923 and 1924. Slum clearance acts were passed in 1930 and 1933 but private enterprise predominated in the thirties. By 1931, wages, raw materials and buildings costs had, due to the world-wide trade slump, fallen below 1914 levels. The stage was set for the greatest boom ever seen in house building for owner-occupation.

In 1927 the Radcliffe Trustees sold private building plots at Stacey Hill. A start was also made on Council house building at New Bradwell in 1929. Some twenty-four houses were complete by the end of 1930. These were along the Bradwell Road, opposite the vicarage. The first tenant was a Mr Sapwell of Bridge Street, New Bradwell, who moved in during April 1930. Simultaneously one hundred houses were started by private development in Clarence Road, Stony Stratford.

The clearance of old properties began in 1930 at Stony Stratford with the demolition of houses in Parkers Yard, Bulls Yard and in the High Street (Barley Mow end and by St Giles' Church), down the White Horse and White Swan Yards, Russell Street, Church Street and the Market Square. They were all cleared by 1935. At Old Wolverton, all the remaining cottages of the old settlement were pulled down.

By the mid-1930s, the Council had built some one hundred houses in the Bradwell estate and more in King George's Crescent (1935) at Stony Stratford. A further one hundred and sixteen were erected in Windsor Street, Wolverton (1936) and in Ancell Road, Stony Stratford (1937).

Throughout this time, private building by local firms was going apace on the Egmont Estate, Frankstone Avenue and along the Calverton Road at Stony Stratford. At Wolverton the construction of Stacey Avenue, Marina Drive (named after Princess Marina, Duchess of Kent) and Gloucester Road went ahead, plus two hundred and fifty houses on the Haversham Road.

The Egmont Estate was built by Messrs Betts and Faulkner, Stony Stratford builders who took on many men from the local labour exchange, to dig footings, trenches for services, clear the soil and make the roads and paths with pick and shovel and hand carts — all for a shilling an hour.

Ernie Stones of Stony Stratford was employed on this project and remembered Mr Jimmy Betts was touring the site one hot July morning to view progress. 'Good morning Mr Betts' says Ernie 'Good morning Stones, is everything alright?' asked Betts. 'Yes Mr Betts, but just one thing. It's really hard going pushing these trucks full of soil over the rough ground to the dump. Do you think we could have the horse and cart to move it for us?'. The heavy carthorse belonging to the firm was grazing in the field next to the site. 'No you can't, Stones' was the reply; 'You know as well as I do you can't work a horse in this heat' and off he went.

Alongside this house-building was the alteration to the Wolverton Road, the removal of the tram lines and the re-alignment of the Beachampton Road, both County Council projects.

Local water supplies left much to be desired. At Stony Stratford only a trickle of water could be got from taps in the houses at the top of London Road. The pressure was so low, many houses relied on and still used wells. Householders were advised that if they were unfortunate enough to have a fire, they had not only got to raise the fire brigade, but also to inform the police station so that they could arrange to have the water turned off from the rest of the town to allow enough pressure for the hoses.

The water supply for Stony Stratford came from three artesian wells along the Calverton Road, alongside which was a pumping house. This pumped the water to a tower on the corner of Augustus Road at the Calverton Road end, whence it was gravity-fed. The system and works were installed in 1884.

In 1931, Scott and Co Ltd of Luton started work on a new system. This involved building a reservoir on top of the hill at the southern end of Stony Stratford, at a point where the old Southern Ridgeway Road, then a footpath, crossed the Watling Street. A double trench was dug, capable of holding two six inch pipes to and from the reservoir across the fields from the pump house. Chloride was added at the pump house. The down pipe then gravity-fed the water back to the base of the old water tower where it was coupled up to the existing pipe system and the tower no longer used. This solved the pressure problem up the London Road.

On this project all the labour was again local except for the supervisors. When the mechanical shovel broke down because it could not penetrate the limestone seam the ganger handed the men picks and shovels and exhorted 'this job has got a tight time limit on it. If I catch anyone straightening his back, it's instant dismissal'. Charlie Lovatt from Bradwell started to sing *Rule Brittania*. He never got as far as 'Britons never shall be slaves' before he got the sack. When it rained, if anyone put a coat on, this same ganger, while he stood in the shelter, shouted 'You can't work with a coat on'. They were paid a shilling an hour.

At New Bradwell, town water was not laid on to houses along the Newport Road, west of the church, or to St Mary's Street, most of the houses in the St Giles, Queen Anne, Wallace and Wood Streets or Caledonian Road. As a result flushing cisterns hardly existed. All flushing had to be done with buckets of water pumped from shallow wells. These wells were rarely more than twenty feet deep and, in the 1921 drought, they had to be lowered. Many people had to go to a spring in Bounty Street to collect water for drinking. In 1932, the LM & SR Company laid down new mains to all these properties, complete with fire hydrants.

To supply the new estates over the hill at Bradwell, a pump was installed beneath the railway bridge at Bradwell Station. There was only one problem: the pump was so piped that it filled the tank which fed the water crane in Bradwell Station first, so that when the Newport engine filled up with water and, in doing so, lowered the crane tank level, the pump then automatically cut off the supply to the houses until the tank was full again. The engine men were aware of this and sometimes drained the crane tank on purpose. This upset householders, especially on wash-day Monday, so the engine men were eventually ordered not to use the Bradwell crane, but to fill up at Wolverton.

Wolverton's water supply was, like Bradwell, supplied by the Railway Company. The water came from wells sunk south of the Blue Bridge and east of the main line close to Old Bradwell. It was pumped to two tanks at the top of Wolverton, one at Green Lane, built c1887 and the other in Osbourne Street, built 1902-04. From here it was gravity-fed to both Wolverton and Bradwell.

With Stratford and Bradwell both built on low ground alongside the river, both communities had areas subject to flooding. At Stony Stratford until after the Second World War, the Barley Mow end had to live with this threat every time there was a heavy downfall. There was no warning: the water just rose, flooding all properties at times as far as York Road. At 48 High Street, one could watch the cellar filling up after heavy rain and lowering just as quickly after the rain stopped. Even in dry weather, one could hear the sound of running water beneath the cellar floor.

Bradwell suffered like Stony Stratford but had an added hazard in the form of Bradwell Brook. The combination of brook and river made the Corner Pin area extremely vulnerable. At Wolverton, the Stratford Road was the blackspot. This was alleviated when the Railway Company put a large storm drain across the carriage works, with its outfall into the canal.

After heavy rain and storms on Wednesday 18 October 1939 the river rose to around eleven feet above its normal summer level and the floods were the worst for many years. The bridge over the Ouse along the Wolverton-Haversham Road was completely washed away. Originally built between 1837 and 1840, it had been raised and widened in 1938 at a cost of £13,000. A temporary footbridge, three feet wide, was placed across the river but it was some ten weeks before a steel bridge was thrown across. It had recently been used for a temporary road conversion at Weedon.

One of the highlights of the week between the wars was Wolverton's Friday Market. The Market Hall attracted tradesmen from the locality, Northampton, London and many other places, and Wolverton was packed from early morning until late evening. Most came from surrounding villages and towns by 'bus. The market was open from 6.00am until 6.00pm. Perishable goods were sold cheaply from 5.30pm to 6.00pm, which ensured a crowd until the end.

During those hard times, if an ordinary working man had a reasonable job as a tradesman in Wolverton Works or in a motor works, he could have a good life. In the 1930s motoring came within the range of a working man: a Morris or an Austin, on the road for £100 cash or instalments. Archie Sayell of Bradwell was one of the first working men locally to own such a car.

By 1934 the economic crisis had peaked and unemployment began to ease. Locally the Railway Works began setting on and the motor industry began to boom, these in turn having a knock-on effect, creating other jobs.

1937 saw another road works improvement, of the A422 in Bradwell. The main road there still runs past the houses in Newport Road from No 127 to No 207 from opposite the site of the Morning Star public house, past Queen Anne Street, the County Arms and Corner Pin, turning right to the foot of Wolverton Station Hill.

The County Arms Hotel had a large assembly room then used by auctioneers, itinerant salesmen, concert parties and for dances. Stabling was also available, and it also had a covered bowling alley. This was still there in the 1920s though not used. It was sometimes called Pin Alley and, being on the corner, could be the reason for this spot being known as Corner Pin.

From the steps of the County Arms in 1936 the land where the Clock Tower now stands was a field enclosed by the Morning Star and its garden on the right, and by the brook on the left. The field's boundary to the north was the river. Separating it from the road, a short blue brick wall (still there) running parallel to the road from the brook, continued by a spiked iron fence up to the Morning Star public house. Access was through a gate opposite Queen Anne Street. Each side of this gate were poplar trees, seven in number, nicknamed the seven sisters. This was the field where fairs and circuses were held.

3 September 1939 saw the end of many of these things, some good, some bad. It was the least unexpected war in history.

28

OPPOSITE LEFT: A view of Cosgrove lock looking toward Stoke Bruerne, showing the lock keeper's cottage (right) and swing bridge (left). The latter was used to transfer the tow horses from the main canal towpath to the Buckingham Arm towpath. BELOW: Outside the Barge Inn, Cosgrove (L-R) 'Sooty Nichols' (of growling dog performance and the Bury Field walk race challenge with 'Rubarb Kingston'), Jack Ecclesfield, Harry Ratcliffe, Sid Ecclesfield. RIGHT: Taking the Sunday dinner down to the Cosgrove bakehouse for cooking — A. Andrews, Sid Ecclesfield, Sandy Key, Ted Ecclesfield and two young ladies. LEFT: Len Adams taking home the pudding at Hanslope (1950s). RIGHT: A row of cottages at Haversham, c1912. BELOW: The Greyhound Inn, Haversham, c1920.

ABOVE: The picturesque Manor cottages at Calverton. CENTRE: Passenham Mill, in winter garb.
BELOW: The plank across the Ouse at Stratford, connecting the Shoulder of Mutton field to the Windmill field; Miss Audrey Waine en route to Passenham.

ABOVE: The Mill race and wheel, Rodgers Mill, Stony Stratford (latterly known as Catts Mill). BELOW: British Legion parade at Wolverton; Stony Stratford Boy Scouts Bugle Band at far end of parade, outside the Palace cinema.

ABOVE: The Wolverton Station Hill as it was until the Bradwell by-pass was built in 1938. CENTRE: Looking down the Canal Hill, Bradwell, on the left the Baptist Chapel (built 1936), Bridge Street, Spencer Street and High Street. BELOW: Stratford High Street looking north c1928. The houses and shops alongside the LMS lorry were demolished in 1930.

32

ABOVE: The top end of Stratford High Street c1930 looking north: (left) the India and China Tea Co and George Barley, tailors; (right) 'Coddy' Jones, greengrocer and fishmonger, LCM Butchers, W. Green (Porky) butchers, Hassel glass and china dealer and W. Wilyman at No 14, chemist. CENTRE: Wolverton Front c1930 looking towards Stratford: (right) the Fire Station and Works main entrance; (left) Muscutt, W. J. Hyde, confectioner, LCM Butchers, Muscutts, newsagents and the Post Office. BELOW: The top of the town looking toward Wolverton c1935, the Council drain cleaner and his cart (also used as the night cart) at the top of Russell Street. The cycles parked outside the Forsters show the trust and honesty of the day and that the photo was taken during licensing hours (11.00-2.30).

ABOVE: Haversham Bridge from the Wolverton side, after the 1939 floods and destruction of the bridge.
LEFT: Fred Chambers, the Co-op milkman, coming through the floods along the Newport Road, New Bradwell in 1939. RIGHT: 'Darby Nichols' pushing a customer through the floods at the bottom end of Stratford, the Rising Sun public house in the background. The white-fronted building was one of the houses that made up Parkers Yard, the remainder behind. They were all demolished in 1935; the gap became the Rising Sun car park.

ABOVE: Floods at the bottom end of Stratford in the mid-1930s, Phelps the bakers, No 119 High Street, left. BELOW: In the early '30s, floods at Stony Stratford, Barley Mow End, looking north: the first building on the right at the end of the orphanage wall is Eales' general shop-cum-dairy. At the far end of the houses are the Gas Works, on the left the Rising Sun.

LEFT: Stony Stratford Water Tower was the southern side of Augustus Road at its junction with the Calverton Road, built in 1884, along with the pumping station, by John Franklin, builder of Stony Stratford, for the Stony Stratford Parish Council. Demolished c1950, on its site in 1952 were built two bungalows for retired people. The tower supplied the town until 1931, when the reservoir was built atop the hill up the London Road. From this time until it was demolished, the area around and beneath the tower served as a council garage and storeroom. During the war it acted as a home guard post and strongpoint. RIGHT: Mrs Nash at the front door of No 1 Council Villas, New Bradwell, in June 1930. BELOW: The WUD's first council houses were completed in April 1930 at New Bradwell, the first tenants being Mr and Mrs Sapwell (No 2).

ABOVE: Winsor and Glaves building team at Marina Drive 1936 — Back row L to R: Ken Ebbs, Ron Glave, Arthur Dowdy, Joe Ratcliffe, Eli Ratcliffe, Bill Lake, George Glenn, ?, Walter Mynard, ?; 2nd Row: Arthur Spiers, Jeffcoat, T. Winsor, Rocky, Jack Onan, Billy Goss, Tom King; 3rd row: Arthur Stanton, James Dunbar, Charlie Mead, Sid Harris, Reg Brockman, Percy Ogden, Bill Ratcliffe, Frank Fountain, Fred Gardiner; 4th row: Harry Wilkins, Sid Howe, Arthur Elliott, J. B. Glave, J. E. S. Winsor, W. J. Winsor, Bill King, Charlie Fountain, Tom Savage, George Fountain; 5th row: Harry Winsor, Harold Winsor. LEFT: Bulls Yard, Stony Stratford — all the houses except two that occupied this site were demolished in the early 1930s. RIGHT: The last four cottages in Stratford High Street built next to the Gas Works yard and demolished in 1937 along with four more that stood next to the Barley Mow public house on the other side of the street, now the car park. After the war, a house for the Gas Works Manager and a Gas Showroom were built here.

ABOVE: The gas showroom and gasometer in later years; the Gas Works have been demolished. BELOW: The eastern end of Church Street and the Market Square, with the sheep pens ready for market day. The cottages behind were demolished in 1935.

ABOVE: The R100 returns from Canada in August 1930, passing over Stony Stratford en route for Cardington. The photo was taken by Mrs Waine of Clarence Road. CENTRE: Part of Cobham's team at New Bradwell in June 1929. BELOW: The advertising material lining the Haversham Road during Cobham's visit.

ABOVE: The Wolverton Co-op Butcher's display (15-19 Church Street) Xmas 1930, on extreme right Alf Crisp (slaughterman), next to him Dick Richardson. The shop closed in 1958 and moved to premises on the Square. BELOW: George Tarry, butcher of 27 St Mary's Street, New Bradwell, showing his Christmas display.

ABOVE: Donkey Hall of Stony Stratford is hawking his produce around Wolverton at the corner of Bedford Street and Aylesbury Street. Button's butcher's shop is in the background. Note the dry measures for potatoes (pottle). BELOW: Green and Sons, pork butchers of 10 High Street, Stony Stratford, with their 1936 Christmas display; in the doorway are Mrs Green and son, Ken, with the other son, Dennis, to the right.

ABOVE: The Wolverton Road pre-1934, the Mill drive entrance just past the first oak tree on the left.
BELOW: The Wolverton Road in 1934: clearing the trees to realign the road. When finished, this left a large grass verge on the right by the railings, as it still is today.

ABOVE: A reaper and binding machine in action, cutting the wheat and binding it into sheaves ready to be placed in shocks for drying. (JS) CENTRE: Trying to outdo the horse, a converted BEAN car tows a mowing machine at Wicken, c1930. BELOW: Threshing in the locality about 1930; in action here is John Starsmore senior, Aveling and Porter engine and Humphrey thresher, both bought new in 1880 at the Royal Show at Doncaster, the former for £300, the latter for £130. The engine was used by John Starsmore for over 50 years before being sold in working order. (JS)

ABOVE: Stratford's last carrier, Teddy Ratcliffe of Potterspury, is here with his well-known donkey and cart. BELOW: A peaceful scene on the Wolverton section of the canal c1933, looking toward Cosgrove, Hickman's wood-yard on the left and a horse-drawn pair of barges en route to London; a single horse could only pull two barges on wide and well-maintained canals.

ABOVE: A view of Wells and Sons of Loughton, boot makers and outfitters of yesteryear, still going strong today. LEFT: Arthur Cowley, baker of 16 Market Square, Stony Stratford, the third generation of Cowley's to bake bread at this bakehouse. They have lived in the town for centuries and the founder of the business, Mr Daniel Cowley, a former licensee of the Bull Hotel, took over this bakery in the 1870s. He was followed by his son, Hugh Cowley. Arthur has the distinction of being the last trader in the town to use a horse-drawn vehicle. The bakery closed down during 1990. RIGHT: Sayell's fish and chip shop in Spencer Street, New Bradwell, with Mr and Mrs Sayell and son Sid.

LEFT: Getting a float ready at Bradwell for the 1935 George V Jubilee; on the left is Fred Chambers. RIGHT: Waiting to join the Wolverton Coronation Parade of 1937, Bert Petts to the fore, dressed as 'Old Mother Riley'. BELOW: Spencer Street, New Bradwell, decorated for the 1935 Jubilee.

ABOVE: Silver Jubilee street party (High Street, Gas Works end) in the Barley Mow Yard, seated on right Mont Parker, ?, Glad Owen, Frank Atkins; left: Ron Owen, ?; ladies standing on left: Mrs Brown, Mrs Robinson (with tea jug), Mrs Jenkins; standing on right: Jean Foddy and Mr Hughes, the Styles family standing at the gate. BELOW: The Stony Stratford WVS Float 'A Market Stall' in Jimmy Knight's Co-op Bakery Yard, ready to join the Town's Parade during the 1937 Coronation — front left: Mrs Lake; front right: ?; centre left: Mrs Coates, centre right: Mrs Barden, ?; at rear: Mrs Knight.

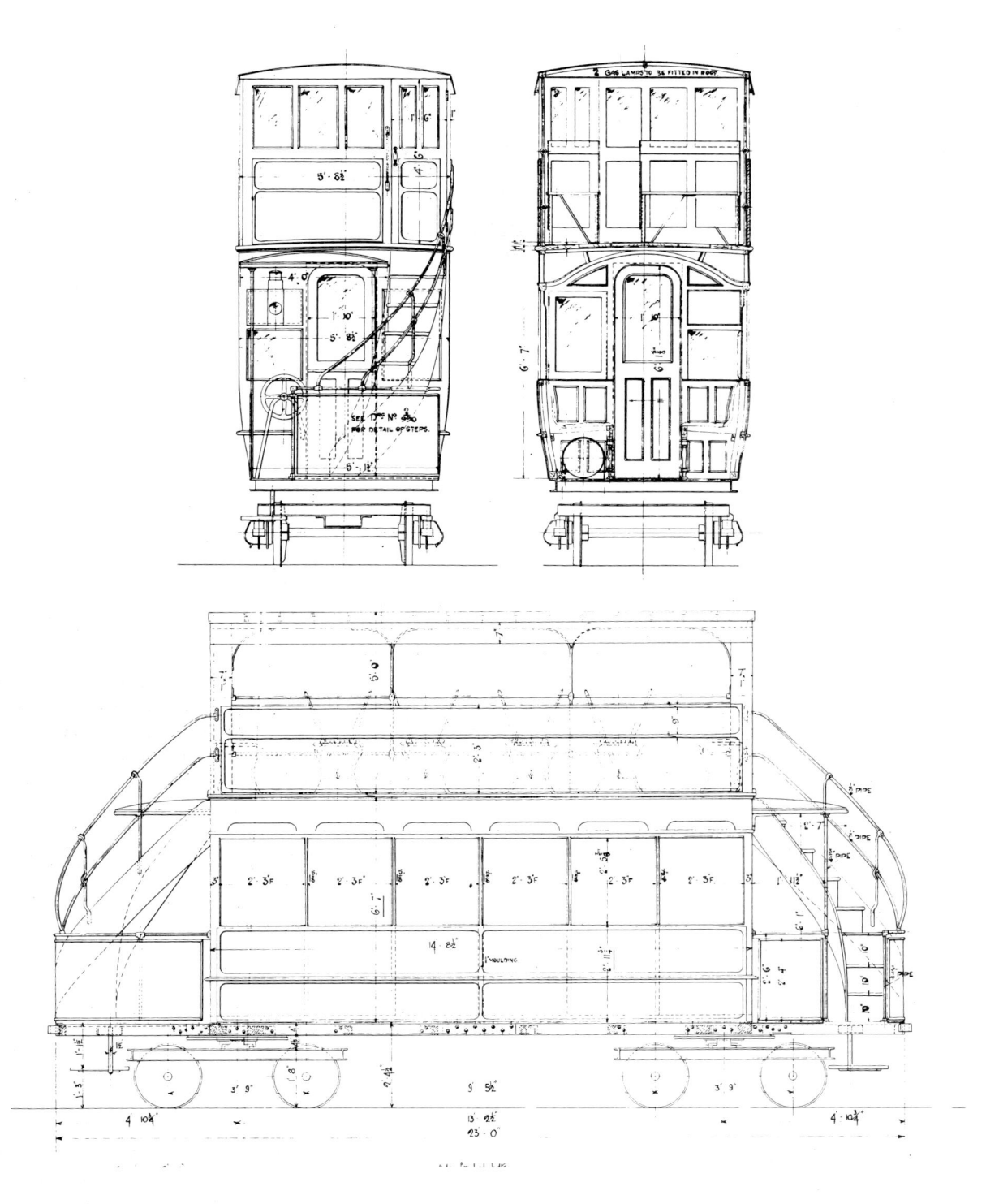

Drawings of No 4 & No 5 tram cars of the Wolverton and Stony Stratford steam tram.

Getting About

Before 1919, local public transport, other than the railway, was supplied by the oft-recorded Wolverton and Stony Stratford steam tram that plied between Stony Stratford and Wolverton railway station.

Motor 'buses were first introduced in 1913 when the London and General Omnibus Company, which had just acquired the Bedford Depôt of the New Central Omnibus Company and had been running a service from Bedford to Newport Pagnell, extended this to Stony Stratford. The 'bus company soon recognised the prospect at Stony Stratford of traffic to Wolverton Works and market. It quickly added a service between Stony Stratford, Wolverton and Stantonbury. These 'buses had been running only a few months when the War Office requisitioned the fleet and the whole of the Bedford Omnibus operation was closed down on 22 November 1914. The Tram Co, following the departure of the 'buses, suffered escalating costs of maintenance to track and rolling stock, so they purchased a 'bus. This new Seldon motor-bus, registered number BD 3451, ran the tram schedule on off-peak periods. A notice was inserted beneath the timetable which read — 'The Motor Bus now takes the place of the Tram as occasion demands'.

In 1919, the General sold its Bedford operation to the National Steam Car Co, which was renamed the National Omnibus and Transport Co Ltd in February 1920. The Bedford garage was re-opened in August 1919 and the Bedford, Newport Pagnell and Stony Stratford route was re-introduced in the spring of 1920, along with a half-hourly local service between Stony Stratford and Stantonbury. These National 'buses were stabled overnight in the yard of Hayes Watling Works. In 1923, United Counties arrived, running a Northampton to Stony Stratford (the Cock Hotel) service *via* Wootton, Yardley Gobion, Potterspury and Old Stratford, using a building at the rear of the Bull as a garage.

The National Co quickly introduced some fourteen routes to the surrounding villages, and in 1926-27 rented the old Tram Depôt as a garage. This continued until December 1933, when Eastern National (part of the Thomas Tilling group) transferred to United Counties (also Tilling) all its local services, with the exception of the Stony Stratford–Stantonbury and Stony Stratford–Bedford services. The United Counties also took over the Tram Depôt lease and purchased it outright in December 1934. The now small Eastern National fleet took over the garage at the rear of the Bull.

Private 'bus operators came on the scene too. In the 1920s it was fairly easy to obtain small passenger vehicles on HP and so fierce competition arose, culminating in a free-for-all which lasted until the 1930 Road Traffic Act was introduced.

One of the first on the road was Frank Johnson of Park Road, Stony Stratford with a model T van fitted with loose forms placed down each side. His first job was taking eight workmen morning and evening to and from Wolverton Works, on a contract with the men concerned. For the remainder of the day and evening, he traded as a carrier, touring the villages selling paraffin and travelling to and from Stony Stratford and Stantonbury carrying passengers. This van carried a board with the legend 'Step in, I'm lonely'. The business prospered so he bought a 'bus and plied between Stony Stratford and Stantonbury, also running excursions and taking on private hire work.

Another operator was Malcolm Jelley of Cosgrove. Commencing in the early '20s, he also operated between Stony Stratford and Stantonbury and ran workmen's 'buses to and from Wolverton Works. Prospering, he expanded to four vehicles, an AJS Pilot, a Crossley Alpha, a Reo Pullman and another Reo. He ran an express service to London on Thursdays and Sundays from Cosgrove *via* Stony Stratford, Stewkley, Leighton Buzzard, Northall, Dagnall, Hemel Hempstead, Kings Langley and Watford, thence to London. The terminus was in Duke Street behind Selfridge's. Jelley also conducted excursions and tours. He was taken over by United Counties on 26 February 1934, and later became tenant of the Bridge Hotel, Leighton Buzzard.

Another operator was R.J.E. Humphrey of Old Stratford who, with his two sons, started up in the early '20s with a Model T Ford, providing a passenger service between Collingtree and Northampton on Wednesdays and Saturdays as well as the Stony Stratford–Stantonbury service, otherwise using his vehicle for goods. In 1928 he sold the haulage side to Percy Westley of Stony Stratford. The passenger side prospered and he added services to Woburn *via* Old Bradwell and Fenny Stratford, Stony Stratford to Shenley *via* Old Bradwell and Loughton, Stony Stratford to Great Linford, Stantonbury to Wicken *via* Stony Stratford and Old Stratford, plus excursions and tours. There were three vehicles: a Leyland Lioness, Leyland Cub and a fourteen-seater Chevrolet. The firm was taken over by United Counties in October 1934.

J.H. Bates of 32, Jersey Road, Wolverton was yet another operator, who opened up in 1923 on the Stony Stratford–Stantonbury route. He also ran an express workmen's service from Stantonbury to Cowley, Oxford, taking the young men of the locality to Pressed Steel late on Sunday evenings and collecting them the following Saturday lunchtime. He also held an excursion and tour licence. His three vehicles were a Star Flyer, a Chevrolet and a Reo Pullman. He sold out to Eastern National on 26 February 1934, who immediately resold the business to United Counties.

As a small boy in the infants class 'Chirp' Eglesfield was always talking. One day the teacher exclaimed 'Eglesfield, you do nothing but chirp, chirp, chirp, now be quiet!' The name stuck. He was a late-comer to the arena, starting on 5 November 1930 under Cream Line Coach Service. 'Chirp' operated a local service from Stony Stratford *via* Wolverton to Stantonbury jointly with Messrs Bates, Brown, Humphrey, Jelley and another from Cosgrove to Wolverton, plus a workmen's service from Stantonbury, Wolverton and Stony Stratford to Vauxhall Motors at Luton on Sunday evenings, collecting the men Saturday lunchtime. The fleet consisted of two Bedfords, a Star Flyer and a Chevrolet. 'Chirp's' garage was the ex-furniture store of Stafford Holland, the furniture-remover of Stony Stratford, at the bottom of the town alongside some cottages beside the Barley Mow Public House (now demolished and used as its car park). The business was acquired by United Counties in May 1938.

The last independent operator between Stony Stratford and Stantonbury to survive was Brown's Super Coachways of Wolverton. Brown operated this service, along with excursions and tours from the early '20s. His business was bought by United Counties and taken over on Sunday 24 June 1945.

Gammonds (formerly W. Heaman) of Bedford's Blue Coaches ran a Bedford–Oxford service twice daily, one on Sunday calling at New Bradwell (Stantonbury), Wolverton and Stony Stratford. The daily services ran through the area around 8.30 in the morning and 4 o'clock in the afternoon to Oxford, 12.30 lunchtime and 6.30pm to Bedford. Extra journeys were operated from Stony Stratford to Buckingham, this 'bus being stationed at Stony Stratford on a permanent basis and also used as a duplicate on the Oxford run as required. Arch Pettifer of Stony Stratford was the driver.

The Bedford–Oxford service connected with Associated Motorways (Red and White Services and Black and White Motorways Ltd) routes to the south and west of England. Gammond's business was acquired jointly by the City of Oxford Motor Services and Eastern National on 1 January 1942 and operated, firstly by the City of Oxford until August 1942, then by Eastern National.

These pioneer operators gave many locals an opportunity to visit places hitherto out of their reach. A great many had perhaps only travelled as far as Northampton or Bedford, unless they or the head of the family worked on the railway and were entitled to privilege travel — one free pass per annum and quarter fare on other journeys.

These coach operators, from the early 1920s, emulated the railway companies of the day, running Sunday day-trips to the sea-side and evening mystery trips around the local countryside. They were not without incident. On one occasion a 'bus load of rustics boarded the vehicle early when one lady, taking her first trip to the sea, was so overcome she wet her drawers and the 'bus waited while she went home to change. At the coast the driver pulled up to allow his passengers to view the sea for the first time. When all had descended they looked with awe at the endless strip of water. Then one countryman broke the silence: 'Cor, it's bigger than Old Neddy's Pond!'.

Although the railways for many years had run cheap day and evening trips during the summer, it was not always possible for a family man to transport his family to the nearest railway station. Now pubs, clubs, churches, and many other organisations ran annual trips to race meetings, football matches, picnics, exhibitions etc, on a door-to-door basis.

For the most part these organised trips ran smoothly. Generally each individual paid a weekly sum of say two shillings to the organiser. This would cover the fare, one meal and some spending money. After the venue and date had been decided, he arranged terms with a local 'bus owner. Sometimes the organiser spent the money; no money, no 'bus, no outing. Such occasions were resolved by the individual going to ground, riding it out, or possibly receiving two black eyes.

Just after the 1939-45 war, an outing to a race meeting was organised by a Northampton man working in Wolverton Works, involving in excess of two hundred men (seven 'busloads). They had paid their weekly sums and, as the day drew nigh, the organiser told them 'No need to worry about food [meat was still tightly rationed]; my colleague at Northampton is a butcher and he will supply cooked meats, pies and pastries so just bring a loaf of bread'. The day arrived and, all over North Bucks, groups of men stood at pre-arranged pick-up points all with the *Sporting Life* protruding from their pockets and clasping loaves of bread under their arms. After some two hours they began to realize that there would be no trip to the races that day. This story has been told and retold.

On the early 'buses, mechanical problems often upset the schedule. The annual choir outing of St Giles was to visit Portsmouth in Navy Week. The 'bus broke down on the way back, so the choirmen decamped to a public house while the repair was completed. Vicar Steer was so worried about the choirboys being late home, he sought out the local police to get in touch with Sergeant Rollings at Stony Stratford to go round to all parents and wives.

Sunday school outings, maybe to Wicksteed Park or Woburn Woods for a picnic, also held small hazards. On one occasion the children had to take their own mugs. Many excited children left the 'bus to walk to the picnic area, all swinging their arms, banging their cups or mugs against tree trunks. There were a lot of handles in fingers, tears and thirsty youngsters.

Until the introduction of the 1930 Traffic Act, timetables were non-existent. Many a time if, say travelling to Bradwell, the driver saw a crowd waiting outside the Palace Cinema, he would quickly turn around, ask his Bradwell passengers to get off, pick up the bigger load, return to Stony Stratford, then return to collect his stranded passengers at Wolverton. Or, if four buses were on the stand at Bradwell or Stratford, one driver would quickly run along the line and say 'I'm away next' (this was normally just before a timetabled National 'bus was due to go); passengers on the other three would tumble out and he would be away with all the fares. Loading capacity was mainly ignored; the drivers would cram as many on as possible. This mainly occurred at pub closing times, at the beginning and end of cinema performances, fair days or similar events. Sometimes a constable stood at the Palace Cinema waiting for the 'bus. The driver who spotted him would quickly turn up Jersey Road, go along Church Street, down Ratcliffe Street and so back on to Stratford Road and thence to New Bradwell. Anyone unfortunate enough to want setting down at the Palace or between these two points had to walk back.

When the new system of licensing came in 1930, five proprietors besides Eastern National applied. It was decreed that the number of 'buses on the road was excessive; a basic frequency of fifteen minutes until mid-day and every seven to eight minutes after that was laid down. Movement of workmen's and school 'buses were exempt.

The Traffic Commissioners made no attempt to divide this workload between applicants but dismissed them to work it out between themselves. This complex situation was solved by Frank Bryan, Eastern National Traffic Manager and his assistants after months of negotiations. The solution came into effect in April 1933, and that timetable continued more or less in its original form for around thirty years.

The last United Counties 'bus ran through the three townships on Saturday 25 October 1986 and the Milton Keynes Shuttle was introduced next day.

ABOVE: A montage of the Wolverton and Stony Stratford steam tram featuring Billy Newton of Stony Stratford, its conductor for many years. OPPOSITE: Two views of the tram, hauled by a Krauss engine. BELOW: The tram 'bus: put into service on 28 October 1916, this Seldon motor 'bus BD 3451 ran the Stony Stratford-Wolverton service in place of the tram during low-loading periods. Here it is in the Tram Depôt, in LNWR livery, after a complete overhaul in Wolverton Works in 1920. After the closure of the tramway in 1926, this 'bus continued, after a further overhaul and modifications at Wolverton Works, at Berkhamsted Railway Station.

W. SACH
WOLVERTON
SELECT YOUR FURNITURE FROM THE LARGEST STOCK IN THE MIDLANDS
JEFFERY & CO. NORTHAMPTON
HODGES & SEARS.
23. THE DRAPERY. NORTHAMPTON.
THE BEST PLACE TO BUY DRAPERY OF EVERY DESCRIPTION IS
ADNITT'S. NORTHAMPTON

WOLVERTON & STONY STRATFORD
990

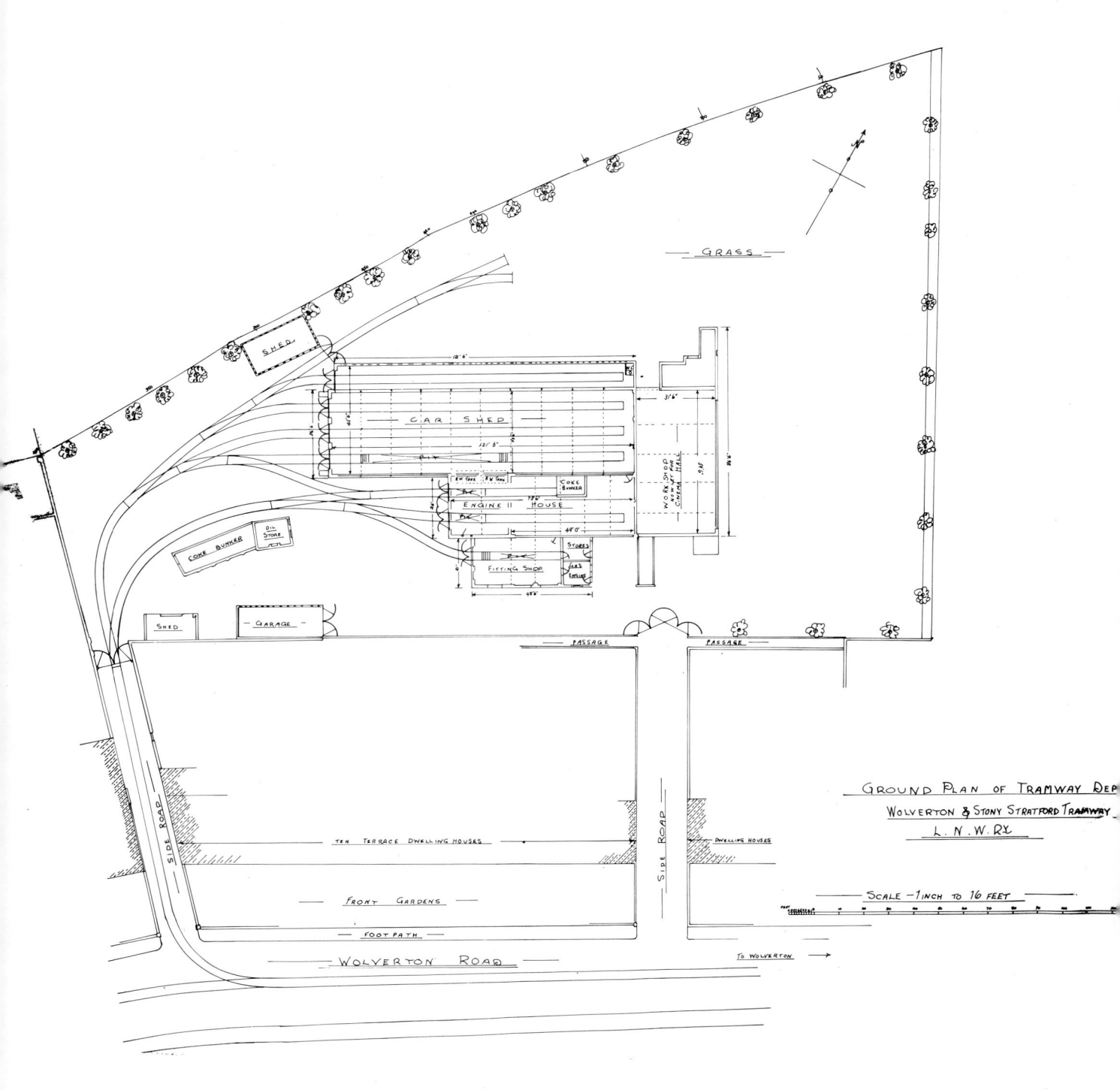

Plan of Tram Depôt showing location of Stony Stratford's Empire Cinema.

Wolverton & Stony Stratford TRAMWAY SERVICE.

Week-Days.		Saturdays.		Sundays.	
Stratford Depart	Wolv'rton Depart	Stratford Depart	Wolv'rton Depart	Stratford Depart	Wolv'rton Depart
a.m.	a.m.	a.m.	a.m.	p.m.	p.m.
8 30	8 0	8 30	8 0	7 0	7 25
9 20	9 15	9 20	9 15	8 0	8 25
10 25	9 55	10 25	9 55	8 50	9 10
p.m.	11 5	11 30	11 5		
12 0	p.m.	p.m.	p.m.		
1 15	12 30	1 10	12 0		
2 45	1 45	1 55	1 35		
3 55	3 30	2 45	2 15		
5 0	4 20	3 55	3 35		
6 20	7 10	5 0	4 20		
8 0	8 15	5 45	5 30		
8 45	9 45	6 55	6 5		
		8 0	7 30		
		8 45	8 15		
			9 45		

The Company's Motor 'Bus takes the place of some of the Trams as occasion demands

POST OFFICE DESPATCHES.

London & South   8.40 a.m.
Birmingham & North   9.25 a.m.
London & all Parts

10.30 a.m. | 2.50 p.m.
                8 0 p.m.
                8.45 p.m.

Sundays   8.0 p.m.

The Post Office is open on
   Weekdays, 8.0 a.m. to 7.0 p.m.;
   Sundays, 8.30 a.m. to 10.0 a.m.

The National Steam Car Co., Ltd.

St. John Street,
        BEDFORD.
Telephone: 772.

BEDFORD & NEWPORT

Leave Bedford	Leave Newport
9 30 a m	11 10 a m
2 30 p m	4 10 p m
6 30 p m	8 10 p m
Sundays	
2 30 p m	4 10 p m
6 30 p m	8 10 p m

This service runs in connection with the 'Bus for Stantonbury, Wolverton & Stony Stratford

Bedford & S. Stratford

Leave Bedford	Leave S. S.
Week-days	
10 30 a m	8 40 a m
Saturdays	
9 0 a m	8 40 p m
Sundays	
12 15 p m	8 40 p m

This 'Bus works between Stony Stratford and Stantonbury during the day. Also runs to meet the Newport to Bedford 'Bus at Newport, leaving Stony Stratford at 3.20 p m and 7.20 p m.

Tram and Steam Timetables.

THE NORTHAMPTON MOTOR OMNIBUS Co., Ltd.

Northampton and Stony Stratford.

WEDNESDAY AND SATURDAY ONLY.

Passengers will be taken up and set down at Guildhall Road, Northampton.

	LEAVE	a.m.	p.m.	p.m.
—	Northampton	8 0	2 0	6 0
5d.	Wootton	8 15	2 15	6 15
6d.	Collingtree Turn	8 20	2 20	6 20
8d.	Courteenhall	8 25	2 25	6 25
10d.	Roade	8 30	2 30	6 30
11d.	Stoke Bruerne Turn	8 35	2 35	6 35
1/1	Alderton Turn	8 40	2 40	6 40
1/2	Grafton Regis	8 45	2 45	6 45
1/4	Yardley Gobion	8 55	2 55	6 55
1/6	Potterspury	9 0	3 0	7 0
1/9	Old Stratford	9 10	3 10	7 10
1/11	Stony Stratford (arr.)	9 15	3 15	7 15
	LEAVE	a.m.	p.m.	p.m.
—	Stony Stratford	9 30	3 30	7 30
2d.	Old Stratford	9 35	3 35	7 35
5d.	Potterspury	9 45	3 45	7 45
7d.	Yardley Gobion	9 50	3 50	7 50
9d.	Grafton Regis	10 0	4 0	8 0
10d.	Alderton Turn	10 5	4 5	8 5
1/-	Stoke Bruerne Turn	10 10	4 10	8 10
1/1	Roade	10 15	4 15	8 15
1/3	Courteenhall	10 20	4 20	8 20
1/5	Collingtree	10 25	4 25	8 25
1/6	Wootton	10 30	4 30	8 30
1/11	Northampton (arr.)	10 45	4 45	8 45

LEFT: A timetable of the first Stony Stratford-Northampton 'bus service in 1919. These buses continued until c1948, departing and arriving at the Market Square (Horse Trough), Stony Stratford. BELOW: Charlie Curtis, driver, and Bill Lamb, conductor, of this open-top, double-decker, solid-tyred National 'Bus 2061 c1923 — an AEC YC, seating 44. The photograph was taken at Winslow. TOP RIGHT: Ron Page, partner of Ron Gardener, posing alongside their Parlour Coach. CENTRE: Frank Johnson with his father-in-law, Mr Fry, in front of his then new Lancia motor coach, at Park Road, Stony Stratford. OPPOSITE ABOVE: Ron Gardener stands alongside his Reo c1930. CENTRE: R. J. E. Humphrey's Leyland Lioness, PP9925, (RW) RIGHT: his Leyland Cub on the 'bus stand at the top of the town, Stony Stratford (RW) and BELOW: his fourteen seater Chevrolet LO KX2221 with Northampton-built Grose bodywork, at Wolverton Cemetery Gates. (RW)

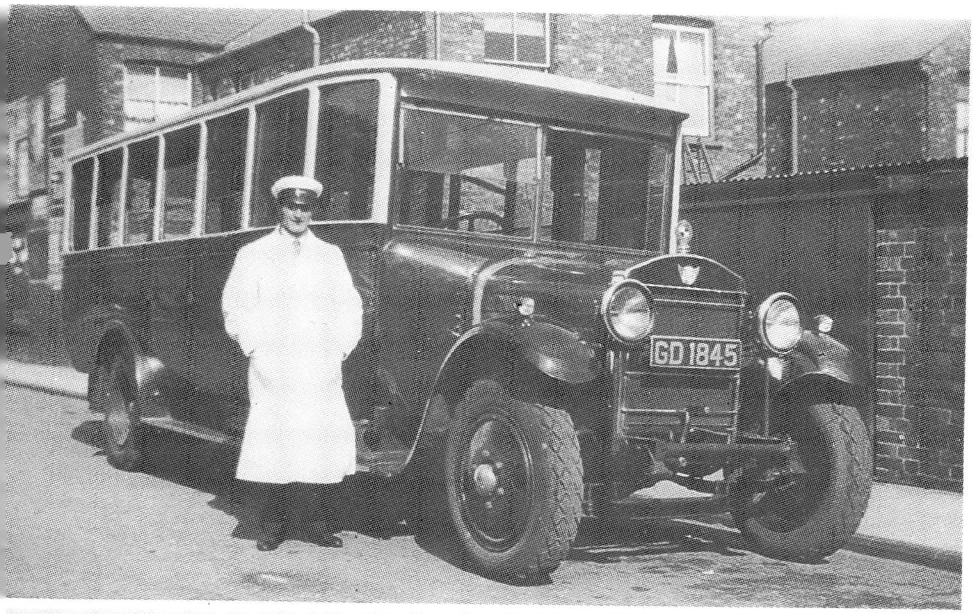
GD 1845

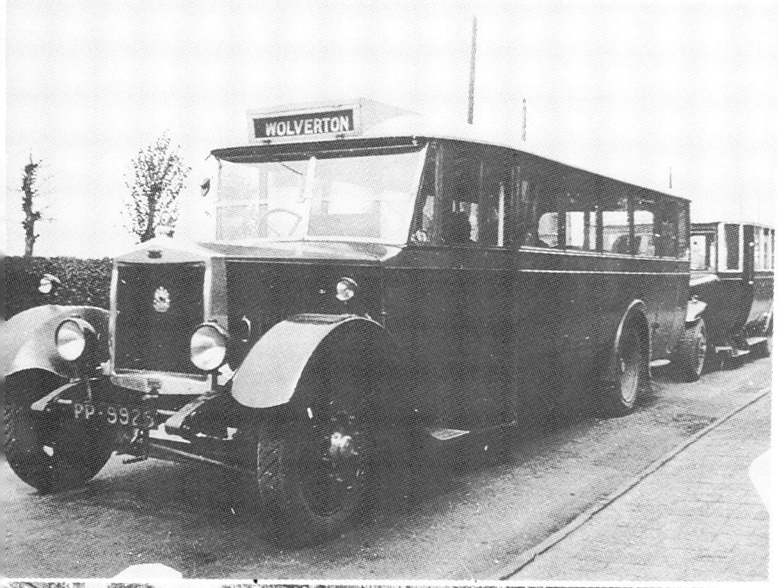
WOLVERTON

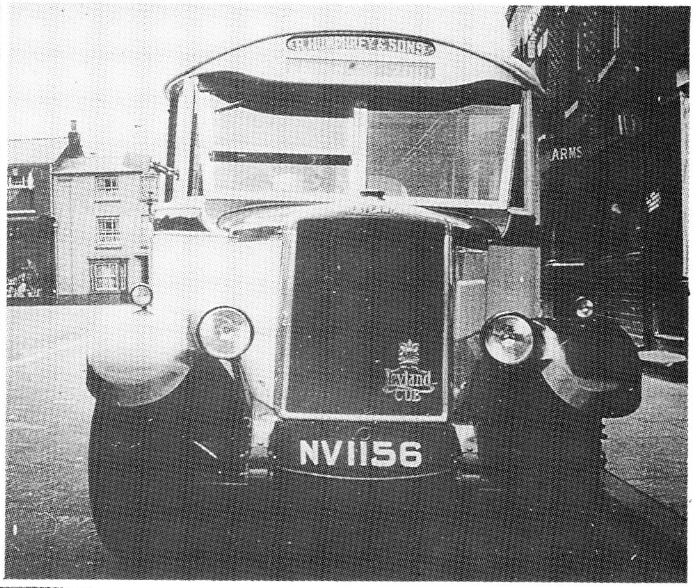
B. HUMPHREY & SONS
ARMS
Leyland
CUB
NV1156

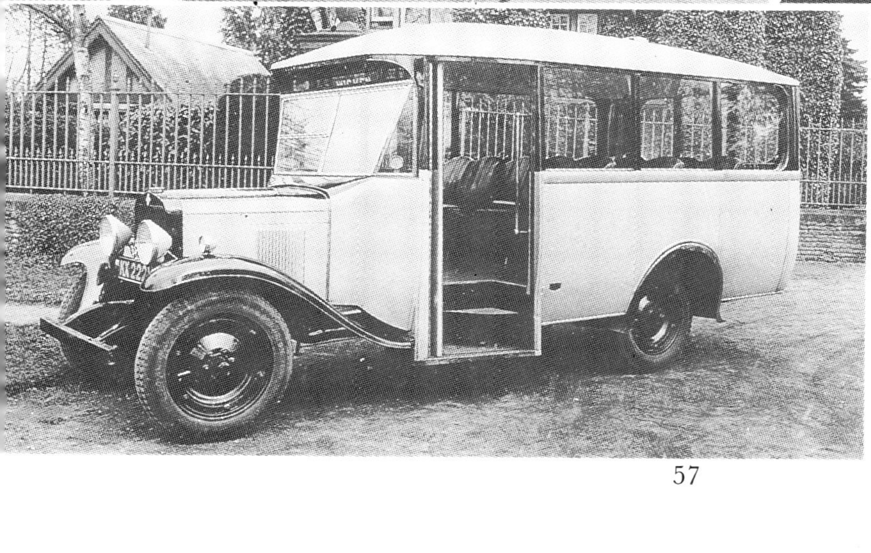

ABOVE: Bates' Star Flyer, NH 9892, at the top of the town, Stony Stratford, 1933. CENTRE: Malc Jelley's Grose-bodied Crossley Alpha 368, NV728, used on his Cosgrove London service. (RW) BELOW: Tragedy along the Wolverton Road (fifty yards past the Lodge, Wolverton side) at 10 o'clock one Sunday night in March 1936. Driver Cheerie Daniels of Stony Stratford swerved to avoid an oncoming car and overturned. Mr Thomas of St Giles Street, New Bradwell was killed and among the passengers injured was Dora Jones (later Mrs Fensome) of New Bradwell. Cheerie himself was badly burned by acid from the battery. The 'bus was a 20-seater Commer Invader, RP 9868.

ABOVE: The National 'busmen of Stony Stratford Depôt in 1930, taken in front of the old Tram Shed doorway: back row L to R: Geoff Warren, Vic Barley, Fred Smith, George Goodger, Ralph Taylor, Dick Blair, Reg Bonham, George Rollings, Bert Smithers, Charlie Curt, Walt Payne; second row: George Autin, George Ratcliffe, Harry Smith, Frank Harrup, Doug Dicken, Charlie Spiers, Archie Sargent, Alf Watt, Happy Brown, Bill Prior, Bill Cox; kneeling (fourth row): A. Clarke, Harry Carpenter, R. Cooper (Inspectors), Mr Kishere (Area Supt), Harry Sexton (Stony Stratford Depôt Manager), ? Ireland (Clerk), Bill Beeton, Ron Page; sitting (fifth row): Walt Stevens, Jack Gould, Percy Drinkwater, Doug Pickering and Bob Hudson.
BELOW: Busman's supper at the Cock Hotel, Stony Stratford, c1950.

ABOVE: An outing from Stantonbury Social Workmens' Club, St Giles Street, New Bradwell: the 'bus is National No 2043, BM8320 and an AEC YC type 28-seater, c1920. The gentleman on the running board wearing a buttonhole is Mr Nash, the steward.   LEFT: J. H. Bates' 'bus *The BlueBelle* is employed here for a photographic club outing. BELOW: Fred Derricutt of New Bradwell and his solid-tyred charabanc on a day trip: Mr and Mrs Fred Derricutt, Mr and Mrs Dick Capel, Mr and Mrs Ted Gray and son, Mr and Mrs Fred Townsend, Mr and Mrs Vic Gray and family.

ABOVE: Two of Brown's 'buses take the inhabitants of Old Bradwell on their annual outing to play cricket against the Metropolitan Police in London in June 1939. The large gentleman with the dog is James Smith, landlord of the Victoria Inn. On his right is Alan Chapman who was called up two weeks later for the Militia, then in 1940 taken as a prisoner of war. On his left Doug Garner. The two 'bus drivers are (left) Ron Page and (right) Fred Smith. CENTRE: A mini-bus of yesteryear is off to Towcester Races — an outing from the Red House, Newport Pagnell: second from left Ted Cowley of New Bradwell; the man in the bowler checking his change is Harry Burt of Haversham, next to him B. Stretton and next to him H. Cowley. BELOW: The front of the White House at Stony Stratford after conversion into offices and 'bus station, opened 28 August 1955 and the new United Counties 'bus garage built in the grounds of the White House, and opened on 3 July 1955, with a capacity to hold twenty-four buses; parked in the doorway is 366 FRP 827, a Bristol LL 5G. (RW)

ABOVE: Hayes-built tug, *Douro*. BELOW: At Hayes Wharf, Old Stratford, preparing for side launching into the basin — the road steam tractor has just towed a boat on bogies from the Watling Works at Stratford; the hull will now be jacked up, the bogies removed and the slipway built beneath it.

Making it Work

When Wolverton Urban District was formed in 1919, local residents were woken every day by three steam whistles summoning men to work at the Roberts Foundry at Deanshanger, E. Hayes of Stony Stratford and the Railway Works at Wolverton.

From 1927, the Railway Works whistle was the only one left. It blew first at 7am, then at 7.30am, 7.45am, 7.50am and finally at 7.55am. At 12.25pm it blew for dinner break and again at 1.15pm, 1.20pm and 1.25pm to recall the men. The end of the working day was blown at 5.30pm.

During the Second World War, the whistle ceased to summon men to work, but was used as an air-raid warning. After the war the whistle once more called the men to work, but only sounded at start and finish times. Around 1965, it was replaced by an electric siren. The Railway Works were the main employers.

E. & H. Roberts Foundry at Deanshanger was founded by John Roberts of Deanshanger in 1820 next to the Buckingham arm of the Grand Junction Canal; the firm developed over the years to become E. & H. Roberts Ltd, Agricultural and Hydraulic Engineers and Iron Founders, whose main product was wind engines and pumps.

By 1874, the foundry had become an agricultural engineering firm of some repute. This was due mainly to the efforts of Edwin Roberts who, in partnership with his brother Henry, concentrated on designing new farming implements: harvesters, ploughs, carts, wagons and water carts. They also manufactured binders, drills, hoes, rakes and corn grinding mills for agriculture, kitchen ranges and bakers' ovens, and manhole and drain covers for local councils.

In 1885, seventy-five were employed and by 1910 this had doubled, necessitating more buildings. The original Fox and Hounds was converted into offices and a new public house of the same name built eighty yards away. All the raw materials (pig iron, coal, coke and timber) were transported by canal, the firm having its own wharf behind the factory.

A substantial export trade was established throughout the Empire, and to such countries as South America, France and Algeria.

Edwin Roberts died in 1907 and Tom, one of his sons, became Managing Director. There was a serious fire in September 1912, which gutted all the factory buildings. It began alongside the canal where the wheelwrights' and carpenters' shops were. They were all rebuilt incorporating the most modern machinery of the time.

The foundry also had seven heavy cart horses, a familiar sight in Stony Stratford and Wolverton, hauling various farm implements *en route* to the Wolverton Goods Yard for despatch. They brought back various stores such as bolts, rivets, screws and kegs of paint etc, making two trips a day other than Saturday.

In 1927, the decline in agriculture and the economy forced the Company into liquidation. A swift closure was followed by the sale by auction of all the assets in 1929.

Messrs Godwins of Quinington, Gloucestershire, bought the patent rights of the Roberts windmill and pump and continued to manufacture them at their workshops, taking with them four former employees — Jack Burrows, Daniel Barrett, Tom Bailey and Len Smith — who were all experts in the manufacture and construction of this machinery, thereby perpetuating the Roberts tradition.

In September 1935, the factory was re-opened by Wreschner, a refugee from Hitler's regime, as a chemical plant trading under the name of Morris Ashby Smelting Co. Later this company formed Deanshanger Oxide Works Ltd, product name Deanox. In 1982, Deanshanger Oxide Works Ltd was sold to Harrison and Crosfield PLC. Deanshanger Works became Harcross Chemical Groups, Deanox Division; today approximately 140 are employed.

The Wolverton Co-operative Society, which amalgamated with the Stony Stratford Society, became the second highest employer of male labour in the district, with branches at Bradwell (two), Loughton and Hanslope. It owned its own Abbey Farm at Old Bradwell and ran its own dairy and bottling plant at Wolverton. The confectionery was also made at Wolverton while bread was produced at its Stony Stratford bakery. Each morning horse-drawn milk floats and carts would emerge from the backway of the dairy into Buckingham Street to deliver milk to Bradwell and Stony Stratford, while men with hand trucks would deliver the product around Wolverton. Motor vans delivered to the surrounding villages. Horse-drawn bread vans plied from the Stony Stratford bakehouse to Wolverton and Bradwell and motor vans delivered to the villages. There were also mobile butchery and grocery vans, giving door-to-door service. All the customers had to do was hand in their requirements for the week. This would be made up in boxes and delivered free of charge. Other traders, grocers, butchers, fruiterers, fishmongers delivered by means of errand boys mounted on three-wheeled tricycles or two-wheeled trade 'cycles, the former having a large box in front supported and steered by two wheels and the latter an iron framework into which fitted a wicker basket.

In 1878, McCorquodale's came to Wolverton, because the then chairman of the L & NWR Co, Sir Richard Moon, wanted a printing works to employ the daughters of his workmen. G. McCorquodale readily agreed and opened a branch in 1878 with approximately twenty employees, on land purchased from the Radcliffe Trustees. When the factory first opened, it manufactured official registered envelopes for the GPO.

The first building consisted of one floor, running north to south, in use until 1897. A six hp gas engine at the north end provided power. The office was in part of this building and in later years became a paper warehouse; the engine house was the first men's dining room. The first three-floor building was erected in 1884. At the time, general envelope-making started on the ground floor and a little later, general printing, ruling and binding. By 1886 there were 120 females and 20 males employed. In 1889, a further three-floor building was added, part of it running parallel with the Stratford Road, the ground floor used for a packing department. A 12hp Crossley gas engine was installed. Some cottages were built for employees, and a house for the then manager, John Appleton. Around 1890, a dining room was built in the well between the two three-floor buildings, opened by Mr G. McCorquodale, founder of the company.

In 1894 another three-floor building went up. The ground floor was used as a paper warehouse, the first floor as a miscellaneous department and the top floor for folding and sewing.

In 1897, the cottages were pulled down and another three-floor building went up. The ground floor was used as a large machine and printing department, the first floor as the ruling department and the top floor for binding. Gas engines were installed on each floor. In 1904, a works Fire Brigade was formed.

In 1905, an envelope works was built on the northern side of and parallel with the Stratford Road. This building was 300ft long by 100ft wide, and the whole works was re-organised and re-arranged. A power house was also built and two 85hp suction gas engines with dynamos were installed. All other gas engines were scrapped and, where practicable, direct drive was introduced on new machines. In 1911 it became necessary to increase the power units with a 300hp suction gas engine with generators and dynamos. This was in use until 1924, when all the plant was scrapped, and arrangements made with the Northampton Electric Light and Power Company to supply power through the LMS Railway Works.

A government contract was secured in 1910 for postal stamped stationery and another ground floor building erected on the south-west end of the envelope works. This was known as the Inland Revenue Works. A government staff of around fifteen was appointed to supervise. Soon after, four acres were acquired on the south of the Stratford Road and another building built in 1912 and extended in 1914.

Immediately after the Armistice of 1918, a large army hut was bought as a dining, reading and recreation room. Three table-tennis tables and two full-sized billiard tables were installed.

Towards the end of 1920 and early 1921, a new case room, standing forme and stereo department was built behind the three-floor building erected in 1897. In 1923 contracts were secured for the production of postal orders and old age pension forms. Special machinery was designed and constructed and all stamped stationery transferred to the factory on the south side of the Stratford Road. A further contract brought production of widows' and orphans' pension forms. The additional workload culminated in a further large extension on the south side of the Stratford Road. By 1938 some four hundred million postal orders were produced annually.

In 1926, another floor was built over the warehouse to bring the offices into a more central position. Also in 1926 an automatic fire protection system was installed and the Fire Brigade disbanded. During 1935-6, a new small machine printing room was built in the yard on the north side of the General Works measuring 386ft long by 29ft wide. The yard at the east end was roofed for storage of reel paper in 1937.

This was the Works in its final form. The total frontage of the various buildings on the north side of the Stratford Road was 986ft. The whole factory covered approximately 4¾ acres with the addition of about 2½ acres of land let as allotments to the Bucks County Council.

After the 1939-45 war, the Bucks County Council built a new Fire and Police Station and police houses on the land previously let to them pre-war on the south side of the Stratford Road.

Within the Works, a great celebration took place on the evening of 5 October 1946, the centenary of McCorquodale and Co Ltd. Six Directors joined employees, with their wives including Mrs Hugh McCorquodale, better known as Barbara Cartland, the novelist. She was a frequent visitor to Wolverton in support of charitable and national efforts during the war.

Over 1,000 guests attended the celebrations, including pensioners, in part of the 1910 building cleared and suitably decorated. Among them were two former employees who had commenced at the Wolverton Works when it first opened in 1878.

A non-stop programme from 6.30 to midnight included dancing to the ten-piece Rhythm Aces Band under Doug Dytham with C. Cunniffe as MC, and the Rt Hon Malcolm McCorquodale announced an extra weeks' wages to all employees and cash tokens 'to old pensioner friends'; each man got £5 and each woman £3.

It was a happy workforce, relatively free from dispute. There was a strike in 1911 concerning ladies' pay and conditions and two national strikes in 1926 and 1959.

To encourage women to remain as long as possible, the Directors in the early 1890s decided to give a grant of £10 on their wedding day to those with ten years' service, £15 to those who had completed fifteen years, and £20 to those completing 20.

A Good Samaritan Society was started in 1912 and continued as a voluntary movement until 1926 when about half the employees were members. This movement was then re-organised and all employees agreed to a deduction from wages of 1½d per week for juniors and 2d per week for seniors. From time to time the Company gave substantial donations. The Reading Room was used for dances, whist drives etc in aid of this fund.

At their peak, the Works employed more than 800 people, producing between 110-125 tons of goods per week. In 1986, Norton Opax took over McCorquodale and the Wolverton factory was divided into two distinct sections — McCorquodale Envelopes and McCorquodale Confidential Print. Norton Opax were in turn in October 1989 taken over by Bowater Industries PLC.

The old factory, which had been on the northern side of the Stratford Road, was vacated and totally demolished by September 1989. The envelope section was transferred to new buildings on the southern side of the Stratford Road, along with the new office block. The Confidential Print section took over the completely refurbished 1912 Post Office building.

The following are the names of Managers since the factory opened: Porteus; Simpson; J. Culross; J. Archer; G. H. Yuill (1886-1888); J. Appleton (1888-1902); T. Barrett (1902-1905); Col L.C. Hawkins (1905-1914); H.E. Meacham (1914-1951); K.D. Carter (1951-1968); R. Waterfield (1968-1985). Confidential Print: E. Pankhurst (1984-1985); D. Holland (1985-1988); Jackson (1988-1989); Salmon (1989-) and McCorquodale Envelope: R. Thomas (1984-1989); R. Harris (1989-).

Grocer Tailby commenced production of horseradish sauce commercially c1933. Before that he traded in the same premises in Wolverton Road, Stony Stratford. Tailby was a regular worshipper at the Baptist Chapel on The Green. Here he met a Mr Hancock, a London businessman who was also a lay-preacher and visited Stony Stratford regularly as such. Tailby became host to Hancock, and they became friendly. Tailby was in possession of an old country recipe for horseradish sauce which he sold in small quantities in his shop. Hancock sampled this relish and, being a businessman, recognised its potential.

Along with Tailby, Hancock formed Hancock and Tailby. They converted the grocery shop into a small factory and installed grinding machines and a bottling plant. The raw horseradish came by the ton from all over England and was supplemented by that collected by locals.

In the early 1930s, when unemployment was rife, two young men of Stony Stratford, one a native of Akeley, hearing that Tailby required horseradish, set off on 'cycles armed with spades and sacks one Monday morning. At Akeley the horseradish was prolific. 'Are you sure it's O.K. to get this?', asked one. 'Yes' replied his Akeley friend, 'the farmer said he didn't mind.' Quickly filling two sacks each they went to see his mother, who supplied them with a bread and cheese lunch and gave them 6d each for a drink at the local. Parking their 'cycles and sacks of horseradish in the yard behind, they entered the bar. After buying their drinks an irate farmer came in, ordered a drink, nodded and said, 'Been to see your mum, Jack?' Turning to the landlord, the angry farmer declared, 'Some B.... has dug up half my field of horseradish and left holes all over the place. If I could lay my hands on him . . .' The guilty pair quickly consumed their beer, beat a hasty retreat and 'cycled back to Stratford undetected. They sold their two sacks each for two shillings each.

Sometimes horseradish was scarce; then it was imported from Sweden. The cream came from London's United Dairies and was delivered for a time by Reynolds Motor Transport Company of Stony Stratford, but in the main, daily by rail. The horseradish was sent out in 50lb bags round the town for people to scrape by hand at home, for which they received seven shillings per bag.

The product was bottled in four sizes, the largest a quart kilner for the catering trade, and was despatched around the country by rail transport. Although it was bottled by machine, the capping and labelling were done by hand.

Miss Dorothy Shirley (later Mrs Smith) was manageress in charge of some ten part-timers and responsible for the preparation and measuring of ingredients. The establishment was sold and closed down in 1955. The buyer asked Dorothy to transfer to London as manageress in a new factory but she declined and had to swear she would not reveal the recipe.

The oldest established industry in the District was without doubt that of Sharp and Woollard, leather dressers, of Church Street, Stony Stratford.

It goes back to the Penn family of Stony Stratford, who founded a tanyard in the town c1600. Around 1790, the tanyard, at the bottom of Horn Lane, (the Tan House was at the end of Mill Lane, Western side at its junction with the Market Square), was in the possession of Mr Warren.

In 1819, the business was bought by Samuel Sharp of Towcester and continued in his name by his son, William. The firm acquired a factory in Newcastle Street, London when Mr F.W. Woollard Snr joined.

The Stony Stratford factory was, for a time, owned by Mr Thomas Manning, but under his guidance it failed, and returned to William Sharp around 1850, who appointed F.W. Woollard as manager, making it Sharp and Woollard, leather dressers.

During 1919-1974 the company dressed leather in a variety of forms — for surgical appliances, harness, saddlery and casemaking, including work for Davis, the Royal casemaker. Twelve people were employed; the firm ceased trading at Stony Stratford in 1989.

E. Hayes started as an agricultural engineer in the early 1850s. This developed into the construction of portable steam engines for threshing and ploughing. In 1857, Hayes designed a windlass for use with his portable engines. This overcame the problem of stopping to reverse an engine's motion at every turn of the plough, drags, cultivators or other appliances. One of the earliest demonstrations of steam ploughing in England took place at Stony Stratford in 1861 before a distinguished gathering, using the Hayes double drum windlass.

The windlass was equipped with two drums supported by a strong, four-wheeled frame. The ploughing could be done by cable, applying either the round-about or to-and-fro methods. The ingenuity of the invention lay in the drive from the engine to the windlass, which consisted of three flat pulleys. The centre one was loose and the outer two drivers. The latter was so devised through gearing that, according to which of these pulleys the belt from the engine was driving, it turned the winding drums one way or the other. Selection was by means of a lever with a selector, through which the driving belt passed. An additional feature was the provision of a pin through the drive selection lever which, when pulled out, allowed the lever to drop into the central position, actuated by a weight, thus disengaging the drive.

Around 1860, Hayes began experimenting with marine propulsion and appears to have been involved with J.E. McConnell of Wolverton Loco Works, and Rickett (both Rickett and Hayes at one time were pupil engineers under Mr McConnell at Wolverton) of Buckingham Foundry in road steam cars. On an 1859 excursion in one of Ricketts' steam cars, which had undergone some alterations at Hayes Works, a contemporary says 'With a party consisting of The Marquis of Stafford, Lord Alfred Paget, Mr. J.E. McConnell and two Hungarian noblemen, they proceeded to the residence of Mr. McConnell. From there through the town of Stony Stratford at a rapid pace to Cosgrove Hall, the residence of J.C. Mansell Esq. where they embarked on his steam pleasure boat'. Perhaps the seed of boat-building at Stony Stratford was born that day.

It appears that Hayes at first provided engines for barges on the nearby Grand Junction Canal. From this small beginning developed the building of vessels which found their way all over the world on lakes, rivers, canals and oceans, from a boatyard landlocked and some 90 miles from the sea. These tugs and launches were drawn either by horses or steam engines on a large chassis along a mile of the Watling Street for side launching at Hayes Wharf at Old Stratford, in the basin of the Buckingham Arm of the Grand Junction Canal, thence to London or Bristol. These craft were up to 70ft long (the locks were only 72ft long). Depending on their draught, the engine and all the fitting-out was done here. If the draught was over 4ft, the fitting-out and engine were installed when it reached the Thames at Brentford. Larger craft over 70ft long or more than 14ft wide (the locks were 14ft 6ins wide), were built in sections (pre-empting H. Kaiser of the USA and his construction of Liberty Ships using this technique by some 50 years) and assembled in a basin at Brentford on the Thames, travelling there by rail or road.

These larger boats, fitted out at Brentford, went by sea. One sailed to Hull and then across country by canal to Liverpool. Others hugged the English coast to other ports while a few ventured quite safely on the high seas. In 1902, the *Curlew*, 70ft long, steamed battened-down all the way to South Africa.

As its fame grew, the firm received orders from governments, companies and private individuals from all over the world. The types built were many and various as were their destinations. There were six tugs for the London County Council Fire Brigade, housed for years under Waterloo Bridge, stern-wheelers for traffic on the Nile, tugs for the Admiralty and the Russian Government, launches for Central Africa to carry loads of nuts for margarine making, shallow-draught boats for Middle East oil companies, private launches for Indian princes and the beautiful *Suzette* with its two saloons and special furniture for the Sultan of Morocco.

Probably the most remarkable shipment the firm made was a large boat sent in sections for re-assembly in the Middle East. It was used for years on the Dead Sea to carry pilgrims on their way to Mecca.

Edward Hayes, grandson of the founder, died in 1920. Two boats were built with diesel propulsion, under the supervision of E.H. Littledale. A Thames tug, name *Sparteolus*, was launched in 1925. The last boat built was named *Barra*, and went to the West Indies, taking three weeks to arrive under its own steam. Around 80 were employed at its peak, with a production of some three boats per year. The firm went into voluntary liquidation during 1925, mainly through the large amount of ex-Government vessels put up for sale during the post-war period, coupled with the trade depression of the time.

It was taken over and run as a heavy duty garage under the partnership of Messrs E.H. Littledale, a former pupil of Hayes and ex-road racing driver who, as works manager, had been running the firm since 1920, R. Eridge an ex-Hayes apprentice, and A.D. Bates the works foreman. Some time later, the latter withdrew from the partnership and the London Road Garage, as it became known, continued under the ownership of E.H. Littledale until his death; it was then taken over by Blue Boar Garages.

The Illustrated London News of 20 January 1877 gives some indication of the class of workmanship carried out by Hayes' men: 'Steam Barge for the Corporation of Manchester. In a limited competition for design, Messrs. Mestayer and Gunson, civil engineers of Manchester, were successful; and they, as agents of Mr. Edward Hayes engineer of Stony Stratford, have supplied the barge to the Corporation.

Specification: Flat-bottomed; 68 feet long; 14ft 10ins wide; 5ft 6ins deep.
Displacement: 3ft 6ins to carry a hundred boxes (of manure) each containing half a ton.

The barge is fitted up in the most substantial manner possible and does great credit to Mr. Hayes, the engineer. It is the first of its kind that has ever been constructed'.

Founded in 1949 at Shepherds Bush, London, Richard Daleman Limited was the first new industry in the WUD. In November 1960, Mr Bushell, a director of R. Daleman Ltd, purchased 2.8 acres of land to build a comparatively small factory for the extruding of plastics. In mid-1962, the factory opened, starting in a small way, employing only three people, the work mainly being tubing and fittings for fluorescent lighting.

The firm quickly expanded and has grown into one of Europe's leading plastics manufacturers. Its workshop area now covers 7,500m^2 (1.85 acres) and it employs some 120 people. Modern equipment and machinery have been installed which provide clear, coloured, plain and patterned sheet from standard acrylic polystyrene and high-impact acrylic materials. In addition, the Company produces extruded rod, tube, profile sections from a variety of materials. In March 1990, it ceased to produce moulded products due to the closure of the injection moulding department. A substantial proportion of its production is exported, mostly to continental Europe.

In 1990, the Company was bought by a Southern Ireland group of companies, namely IRG International and merged with another of the Group's recent acquisitions, KSH (Belgium). The combined organisation is now trading under the name IRG Plastics Limited.

In recent months, the production of plastic sheeting has been split from the tube, rod and diffuser production and the latter has become a company in its own right (still operating from the same site in Old Wolverton and under the same IRG banner); known as Richard Daleman (Profiles) Limited, it employs some 32 people.

The first major industry to come to Wolverton, Myson-Qualitair arrived during the last decade of the WUD's existence. The Company had its origins in 1933, when the British Unit Heater Company was founded by S.J. Holmes and R.J. Barrett. Basil Tanner, who later became Managing Director of Copperad, joined in 1933.

In 1939, a lease was acquired in St Pancras Way, London, where manufacture of unit heaters was commenced and the name 'Copperad' first appeared. In 1947 the company changed its name to Copperad and moved from NW1 to a nine-acre site at Colnbrook, which was extended over a fifteen year period to 250,000 sq ft by 1962 when the company went public. Two years later, in 1964, Copperad obtained a 35 acre site at Old Wolverton, Bucks, where a second factory comprising 130,000 sq ft was built.

In 1969 Copperad was acquired by the Ideal Standard Group and the following year an 85,000 sq ft extension was built on to the Wolverton factory, which enabled the Copperad factory at Colnbrook to be closed in 1971.

In October 1974 Copperad was bought by the Myson Group; it remains a subsidiary of this group. Myson absorbed the Qualitair Air Conditioning company based in Sittingbourne in April 1988. At the end of 1988, the Sittingbourne activity was transferred to Wolverton. In November 1989 the factory name was changed from Myson Copperad to Myson-Qualitair. Myson, a highly respected name in the heating and ventilating industry, manufacture a complete range of heating and air conditioning products for buildings services.

A Hayes tug fitted out and awaiting dispatch.

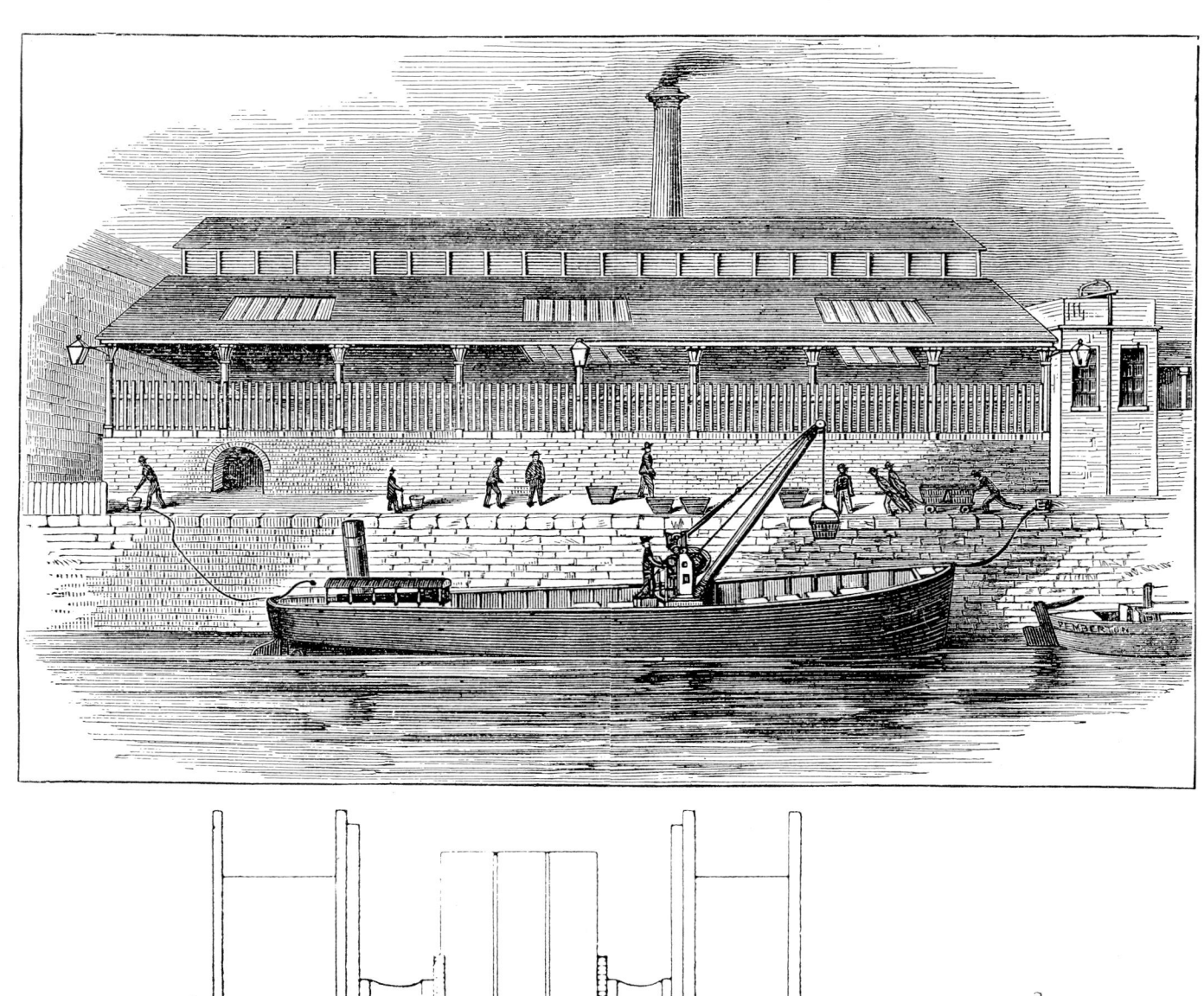

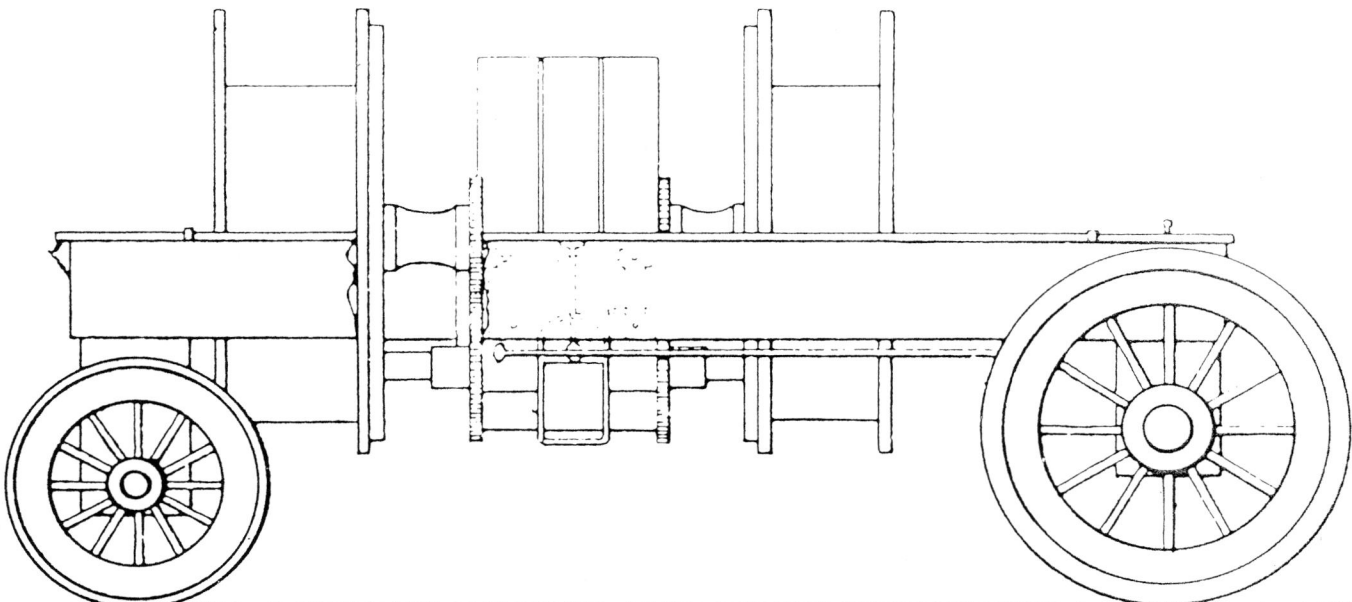

ABOVE: The steam barge built by Hayes of Stony Stratford for the Corporation of Manchester, seen here at work. (ILN) BELOW: This piece of machinery, the Hayes Double Drum Windlass, controlled the direction of drive of a rope or hawser, thereby obviating the need to reverse the engine either when using the to and fro or roundabout system when ploughing, harrowing or like work.

ABOVE: The E. and H. Roberts First Prize Medal Deanshanger Cart and First Prize Medal Northamptonshire Cart. CENTRE: Roberts' Improved Lorry. BELOW: Roberts of Deanshanger's Cambridge Roller and Clod Crusher.

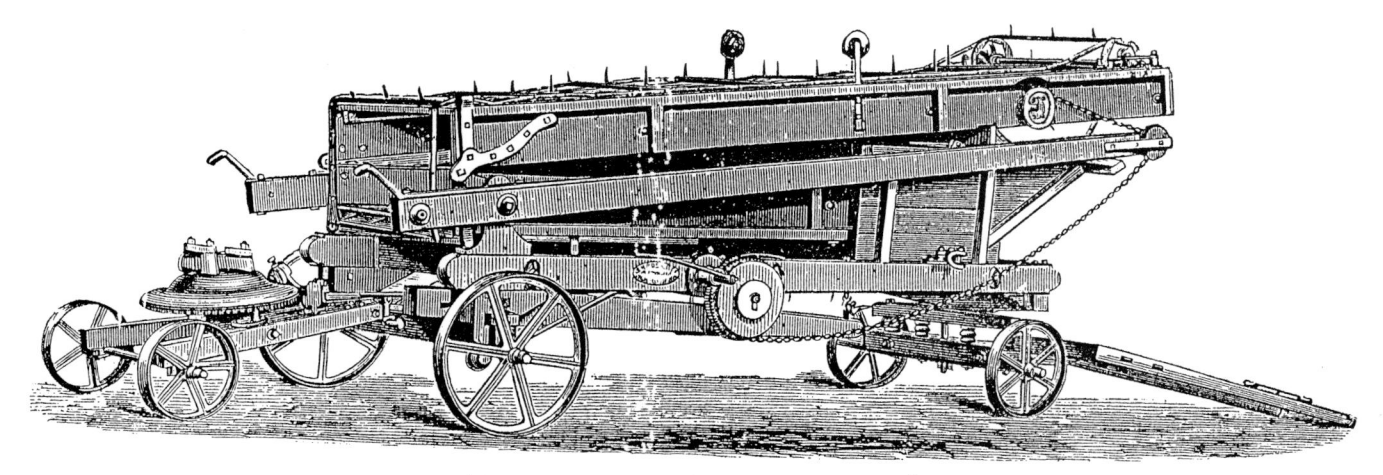

ABOVE: The Roberts Elevator. CENTRE: A view of Roberts' Deanshanger iron foundry in the 1920s, and BELOW: Deanshanger's men of iron: the workforce photographed along the Works wall, c1900.

LEFT: After the fire at Deanshanger Iron Works on 11 September 1912. RIGHT: Perhaps E. & H. Roberts' most notable product, its wind engines, were erected all over the world. The one illustrated was one of three constructed at Wicken to supply the village with piped water. BELOW: McCorquodale's first three-floor building, built in 1884, and the 1894 and 1897 buildings, all of three floors.

ABOVE: McCorquodale's large machine room, decorated for Christmas.
BELOW: McCorquodale and Co Ltd, main offices, built 1926.

The Home Front

Local preparations for war had been going on throughout 1938, with the recruitment of ARP personnel, the issue of gas masks, and an exercise simulating a bombing and gas attack. School children were willing participants, acting as casualties, tagged to indicate their 'injuries' and driven to various First Aid Posts in (mainly Co-op) vans converted to temporary ambulances. The call-up of the first militia men was in July 1939.

On 1 September 1939 the blackout began with what was to become a familiar cry: 'Put that light out'. In the three towns, electric street lighting had only been completed two weeks before this six year switch-off. Local Territorials were called that same day (the advance guard on 24 August). They had been mobilised a year earlier in 1938 during the Munich crisis and stood to at the Wolverton Drill Hall for one week.

When the first evacuees arrived, tea was waiting for them at the Labour Hall at Bradwell, the Council School at Stratford and at Wolverton, before they were taken to their new billets.

Local schools were reorganised and the newcomers absorbed into the local systems. Of course, there were fights in the playgrounds between local lads and Londoners, but this soon settled down.

Yet by Christmas, most of the children had gone home, as the winter had been severe and the promised air raids had not developed. Some families remained, especially those who had found houses.

On the outbreak of war, public meetings were called to form committees to supply comforts for local men and women in the Services. There was instant support for the 'Comforts Fund'.

When the London blitz started in September 1940, the government operated a 'trickle' scheme, under which small parties, mainly of mothers and small children, left London each week. The Regents Hall at Stratford was a transit point, but by now the early goodwill had evaporated so compulsory billeting powers were invoked. Some evacuees were undesirable, while householders justifiably resented having their property damaged.

On Monday 8 January 1940, food rationing started. Two Stratford butcher's errand boys went to start work early one morning when they heard the sound of hammering from above the shop. Creeping upstairs, they saw the manager, with the floor boards up, placing tins of corned beef between the joists. The boys crept downstairs and, after a few minutes, made themselves known by shouting 'Where are you?' They kept their knowledge to themselves, but on occasion they helped themselves.

To supplement the rations, rabbit and poultry keeping became the norm and pig clubs were formed. One day Jim Blunt, the chimney sweep at Bradwell, was heading towards the Progressive Club at 11 o'clock for his morning refreshment, when he met four chaps coming in the opposite direction. 'It's no use going to the club Jim, they have run out of beer' they shouted. 'That means I'll have to try the Foresters' retorted Jim. There Vince West, the landlord, greeted them with 'Looks like the club's ran out of beer! Two pints each, that's all'. Jim sat down with his first pint and started a conversation with Vince, claiming he had been busy all morning killing and dressing a pig. They both extolled the virtues of home-cured bacon and the combination of dishes it would provide. By this time Jim had consumed his allocated two pints: 'I suppose I'll have to go now, Vince', Vince whispered 'You can have another if you like'. 'Thanks' said Jim and from behind his hand, mouthed 'How would you like a piece of bacon?' Vince nodded his head briskly. Jim consumed the proverbial gallon, and at two-thirty, the then closing time, prepared to go home. With Vince framed in the doorway of the pub, Jim stood on the path. Vince declared 'That's it, I shan't be opening tonight'. 'Why is that?' murmured Jim, 'I haven't got any more beer now; that's why' exclaimed Vince, 'And I ain't got no b----y bacon either' voiced Jim, as he went off chuckling.

All rationed and scarce items could be obtained from the Black Market, if one knew the contacts, and at a price, usually exorbitant. To illustrate this, an incident occurred round the Old Road, during the blackout.

A courting couple was standing against one of the buttresses of the main line railway bridge one evening, quietly doing what courting couples do, when a large covered lorry pulled up beneath the bridge.

Out got two men, standing furtively alongside the vehicle, one clutching a sack. 'Here's one coming, come on,' cried the shorter of the two. Down came the back of the truck and within was a bullock, tied up. Meanwhile, over the bridge rumbled a slow goods train, loose-coupled and making a tremendous noise. While the train slowly passed overhead, the bullock was despatched, the noise from the train masking the sounds from the temporary abattoir, and the lorry was away. The courting couple, after witnessing this act, decided to be like dad and keep mum.

The local Territorials, after mobilising, remained at Wolverton Drill Hall until 17 September 1939. After this the Battalion was formed at Newbury Racecourse, its billets in the racecourse buildings. The men slept ten to a box, on stone floors; all companies were allotted loose boxes. Training was carried out on Greenham Common, an hour's march away.

At Christmas all the Battalion was granted ten days' leave, and this turned out to be embarkation leave. On 18 January 1940, the 1st Bucks landed at Le Havre, snow everywhere. They moved up to a place called Wahagnies.

The enemy invaded Holland and Belgium on Friday 10 May. After several postponements the Battalion moved into Belgium on the 14th as part of the 48th South Midland Division. After being in action for three days, during which French colonial troops retreated through the Battalion lines, the Battalion was ordered to withdraw on the 17th. They took up position at a place called Lesdain. On 20 May, the enemy crossed the river near Bleharies; C Company under Captain Parry counter-attacked with the bayonet and the enemy withdrew hastily over the river. After two more moves in as many days, they were given another destination, Hazenbrouck, a town in the S-W corner of the semi-circle round Dunkirk where the 1st Bucks were to make their last stand.

They withstood and held back the Germans on 25, 26 and 27 May; on the 28th they were surrounded by tanks and under heavy artillery and mortar fire, and down to their last ammunition, when orders were given to stand fast until dark, then make a break.

Of those who fought at Hazenbrouck, ten officers and around two hundred ORs succeeded in getting back to England, out of the Battalion strength of eight hundred.

The names of Cassel and Hazenbrouck are, I believe, mentioned in no official record of the war and yet their defence must surely have contributed as much, perhaps even more than the defence of Calais, to the successful evacuation of the BEF from Dunkirk.

To the men who fought there, the last and only tribute came from their enemies. In a German broadcast on 3 June 1940 describing the capture of Cassel and Hazenbrouck, the announcer said 'We must recognise that the British fighters were magnificent. We must assume that these were their crack regiments. Each soldier was of marvellous physique and full of fighting spirit. In Hazenbrouck our soldiers had to storm each house separately. The castle [convent] took an extra day to capture. Our men found nothing in it but a heap of ruins.'

Cassel was defended by the 4th Oxfordshires, (also a Territorial Battalion), and the 2nd Gloucesters who, along with the 1st Bucks, formed the 145th Brigade. This news was a great shock for the local community, losing so many men, killed, wounded, missing and as PoWs, in such a short time. Nothing was heard of the survivors for some weeks; those that did survive were destined to spend the rest of the war in captivity, thus deprived of freedom and family.

It was on 14 May that Mr Eden broadcast an appeal to the country for Local Defence Volunteers. This, ironically, was the day that the local Territorials moved into Belgium. At home signposts were being removed and place names obliterated on roads and railway stations. In the meadows along the Ouse from Stony Stratford to Bradwell and all the big fields, large posts were driven into the ground to prevent enemy planes and gliders from landing.

All over the country, in two months, over 1,000,000 men had volunteered. Wolverton (Works platoons and Town platoons), Bradwell and Stony Stratford formed 'B' Company, which was part of the 2nd Bucks Battalion Home Guard. Their HQ was Wolverton Works, under the command of Major P. Dewick. This HQ had a twenty-four hour manned wireless room in the Works. From it orders were issued to the Police and ARP as well as the Wolverton Town, Bradwell, Stony Stratford and Newport Pagnell platoons of the Home Guard, the Battalion being under the command of Colonel Hagley who also had his HQ in the Works.

The Wolverton Works platoons were responsible for guarding all railway property, including all the bridges from the Blue Bridge to the Viaduct. For a time McCorquodale's had its own platoon, but this was later incorporated in the Railway Works platoons. The remainder of Wolverton members and those from Bradwell had their HQ at the Wolverton Drill Hall under Major Ansell. At Stony Stratford the HQ were the Council Schools in Russell Street under the command of Major Campbell, later Lt Col Campbell; he handed over to Major J. Knight.

These men built pill-boxes, firing points and erected road blocks. This was done on Sunday mornings and two or three evenings a week and initially two all-night duties on road blocks were achieved — this was after they had already done a hard day's work of twelve hours.

A typical road block comprised a large tree trunk the width of the road, pivoting at one end, which was fixed by a large pin or bolt to a wooden bollard. At the other end was a large cartwheel, which could be rolled across the road; a sandbagged redoubt with a 360° fire arc commanded the obstacle, one of which was positioned at Debbs Barn along the Wolverton Road, and another at the junction of the Beachampton and Calverton Roads.

During that post-Dunkirk period, everyone was parachute and fifth-column conscious. Along the Old Bradwell–Loughton Road, Archie Chapman and Fred Smith were on duty at the road block. After checking a few early evening travellers, a car was signalled to stop; it accelerated and sped through the block. Archie did not hesitate and shot at the fleeing car, aiming at its red tail light. The bullet passed through the back of the car, literally parting the driver's hair, cutting a groove in his scalp and carrying on to smash the windscreen. The driver then stopped. Major Ansell was summoned and the wounded man (a local) was taken to the doctor's surgery at Bradwell where his wound was dressed and he was sent on his way.

As the evenings darkened in October 1940, two CSMs from regular units were attached to B Company at Wolverton Drill Hall, lectures and training classes were introduced and these two lectured on dress and equipment of German parachute troops, street fighting, maps and map-reading, despatch-writing, collection of intelligence; on musketry, first aid, bombing, the Lewis gun and the spigot mortar. Musketry was practised on the miniature range at the Drill Hall and in Jimmy Knight's paddock at Stony Stratford, using .22 rifles. The .300 rifle practice was carried out in the sandpit in Fountains field, next to the reservoir, along the London Road at Stratford. Grenade throwing was carried out on a range at Towcester.

Incidents occurred. The bridge and road block detail at the Drill Hall had mounted guard with the proverbial forty rounds. On the order 'ten rounds load', one man failed to depress the last bullet with his thumb so the bolt passed over it, and pushed it into the chamber. On pulling the trigger before applying the safety catch he put a bullet through the Drill Hall roof; everyone hit the deck amid a great deal of banter.

With the issue of American Lewis guns the Stony Stratford platoon decided to try them out in Jimmy Knight's paddock. The author worked for Jimmy at the time and helped him build a firing point; the stone wall that ran along the Vicarage Road was reinforced with sandbags to act as a butt. Saturday afternoon the Lewis gun team arrived; all were ex-Great War men with Lewis gun experience. They brought with them the men who were to make up the LMG sections and proceeded to strip and assemble the weapon and explain its working. They were also watched with some interest by Jimmy's horse. Come the time to fire and, before they had loosed off one drum (97 rounds), the chickens (about 300) were flying all over the place. The horse bolted, knocking down the gate and went galloping down the High Street towards Old Stratford. Jimmy rushed into the shop and said 'The horse has bolted' and ordered me to 'cycle after it. He was peacefully grazing along the road at Bears Watering. After this, machine gun practice was only carried out after the horse had been taken down to the Vicar's field.

The issue of spigot mortars gave the force a piece of sub-artillery capable of knocking out a tank. Each platoon received one. Gun teams were selected and sent on one week courses. The firing range was in a field at Hanslope. Within this field was an old cattle hovel. It was explained that this hovel was to be used for line ranging only, on no account as a target. The Drill Hall detachment fired first and, with their opening shot, hit the building square on and demolished it. A new firing range had to be found in the south of the county. It was said that the Hanslope Home Guard spent the rest of the war's Sunday mornings rebuilding the hovel.

Easter of 1942 a member of the Stony Stratford HG, Frank Morton, was to be wed. Seven fellow members of his platoon were invited to be Guard of Honour, including Arthur and Gerald Pittam and Ted Styles.

After the ceremony at Old Wolverton Church, the Guard of Honour attended the reception but beer was in short supply so they went to the Galleon Inn. As they ordered the first round, a small boy came in the bar and pulled Arthur Pittam's trousers, saying 'Billy's in there', pointing to the canal. Down on the bank the boy Davis said 'He's in there'. CSM Styles took charge: 'Spread along the bank and look for bubbles, first one to spot any get straight in and fetch him out', he ordered. Arthur Pittam spotted such a disturbance, dived straight in, felt a body with his foot and got him out. Styles administered artificial respiration, sent for Doctor Lawrence and resuscitated young Billy Bull.

Exercises and training continued. During one night exercise a section of the Stony Stratford Home Guard was crawling along a ditch in the early hours of one Sunday morning, when the sergeant leading the patrol stopped and hissed 'Sh sh, listen, it's a cuckoo'. Cyril Gleadhill replied 'Yes, there's six more b------ creeping along this ditch'.

Although the area was never bombed as a target, perhaps the Railway Works was searched for and maybe saved by its rural location. According to police records, some six hundred bombs dropped within a six mile radius of Wolverton.

The first bombs were on Beachampton in 1940, where two cottages were demolished and two elderly persons killed. At Calverton incendiaries were dropped at Middle and Upper Weald, along with oil bombs, the fields pitted with small white craters. Luckily no people or buildings were hit.

A stick of seven bombs fell across the meadow from Stanton Low straight towards the Black Horse, the last one falling in the field between the Newport line and the road; Bill Wood from Bradwell was passing at the time and he thought they were chasing him. At the same time a land mine landed in Linford Wood, but did not explode, hanging in a tree by its parachute; it was detonated by the military. A short distance away seven bombs were dropped at the Red House in Newport Pagnell. On Sunday 20 October 1940, at 8pm at New Bradwell a basket of flares was dropped at the western end of Bridge street, falling on the allotments (now the school playing field).

Two bombs were dropped (since the war, a further two unexploded bombs have been discovered), and fell at the western end of the High Street, one in the road outside the doctor's house, creating a thirty foot crater, the second demolishing numbers 71, 73 and 75 High Street. Five were killed — Mr G. Bardell at number 73, Mrs O'Rourke and her three children who were down from London and staying for the week-end at number 75.

Not only men were recruited on the Home Front. Women were directed into war work, including wives and mothers. In the Railway Works part-time labour was used on aircraft and in the shell forge, along with pensioners. To use the participants efficiently they were paired off, one working in the morning and the partner carrying on in the afternoon. By 1943, ninety per cent of women between 18 and 40 were in industry or the services.

Many local young ladies were directed to work in industry. Printing works employees were sent to Pressed Steel at Oxford. Young shop assistants were sent to Allens of Bedford and to arms factories in Slough. Some were more fortunate and worked at Wolverton Works. All were trained in new skills, such as turning, milling and coil-winding and the speed with which women took to industrial work far surpassed the most optimistic predictions.

The main industry in the area was of course Wolverton Works, whose war effort is well recorded in the three books on the Works. McCorquodale's printing works took on government wartime contracts, such as army paybooks and air letters but this was less than the peacetime workload, so some of the girls were directed to other factories.

Seeking refuge from the London blitz was Skipper and East, a well known City printer who specialized in cheque and other high-class printing for banks and commercial houses, and part of the McCorquodale Group. They took over the Regents Hall at Stony Stratford and ripped up the dance floor to secure their machines.

Also from London, the small engineering firm of Holmes took over premises behind the Bull Hotel, previously the changing rooms and clubhouse of Stony Stratford Rugby Club, which they quickly converted into a small machine shop to produce gun components and the sten gun.

Also down what was known as the 'Old Back Way' (Vicarage Road) Gowland and Sons, a small family firm of precision engineers, set up in a large loft behind 92 High Street. They manufactured jewel screws, watch parts, iridium pivots, compasses and instruments for aircraft, remaining until 1957 when the business was taken over by a Mr Rous and moved to London.

Two PoW camps were built in the district, one at Haversham, between the New Estate (at the top of Brookfield Road) and Field Farm. The other was at Wakefield, Potterspury. At first the Haversham camp held Germans but later Italians were interned here; the Wakefield Camp held Italians all the time. The prisoners were taken round the district to work on farms by Vic Davis and Percy Westley's furniture vans. Around forty inmates of the Wakefield Camp were employed in Wolverton Works doing labouring jobs.

During the London blitz the Wolverton Works Fire Brigade was called out and put on standby at Reading and, when Coventry was bombed, they stood in reserve at Solihull. As an additional support for the Stony Stratford and Wolverton Works Fire Brigades, fire-watching duties were introduced.

At Old Stratford in the Black Horse field was the local Observer Corps post, with its radio room and living quarters. These posts were positioned at five mile intervals to track raiders, passing on details of the position and estimated height of incoming aircraft, together with numbers and type.

There was a large military presence in the area from the beginning of the war. With airfields at Cranfield, Wing, Finmere and Horwood and later on Americans from Bedfordshire and Northamptonshire airfields, the surrounding towns were the airmen's playground.

In the Windmill Field at Passenham, parallel with and along its northern side, there was a searchlight unit of some one hundred men. This consisted of sound locators that worked in conjunction with searchlights to find and illuminate the target, like the Observer Corps, joined in a chain across the country. Concrete gun emplacements were also laid here and along the London Road opposite the reservoir, but guns were never installed.

At the Crown Inn, Stony Stratford, some forty Military Police were billeted and a similar number in the commandeered premises of 18 London Road, Colonel Hawkins' former house (this building had already been purchased by the Stony Stratford Workmen's Club).

Some Free French Naval officers were billeted at the Bull for a time. One was taken away by the authorities in mysterious circumstances, rumoured to have a short-wave wireless transmitter. The Victoria Hotel at Wolverton housed forty Royal Engineers attending courses in the Railway Works on maintenance of ambulance trains and bridge assembly. For a time troops of the USA Transportation Corps also attended these courses but they lived on the premises, in a dining car and a sleeper.

In 1939, Whaddon Hall was commandeered by the army, the Hall itself and adjacent buildings becoming an Officers' Mess and quarters. Within its grounds was erected a wireless station and a camp of spider huts to house Corps of Royal Signals personnel. Hanslope Park was commandeered too and became an army wireless station also manned by Royal Signals. After the war it was taken over by the diplomatic wireless service.

The WVS at Stony Stratford, under the leadership of the wives of Doctors Habgood and Lawrence, set up a Forces Canteen in the Public Hall. This was manned all day every day by unpaid volunteers.

Activities at Bletchley Park during the war had their impact inasmuch as noone really knew what was happening there, only that it was some government department. It was in fact the Government Code and Cypher School. Literally hundreds of young persons, mainly women, of university education, mostly mathematicians, were billeted in each township.

These we now know worked on 'ULTRA', the cypher-breaking operation, seven days a week. Due to the long hours and lack of public transport they had their own 'bus service.

Savings weeks punctuated the war. There was War Weapons week of 1941, followed by Warship Week in 1942, in which the locality raised enough money to purchase a corvette, named *Whaddon Chase*, Wings for Victory week in 1943 and Salute the Soldier campaign in 1944. All these were launched with troops and airmen in procession through the streets, along with the Home Guard, ARP services, Fire Brigades and many other organisations, headed by the Wolverton Home Guard Band. Afterwards there were fêtes, whist drives, dances and the like.

A giant £ thermometer stood outside Wolverton Works Canteen, the height of the building (50ft) and some two feet wide, painted white, with red numerals and graduated in hundreds, thousands and tens of thousands, with a large adjustable black marker. After the fighting had finished in Europe and the Far East there was a final 'Thanksgiving Week' with a target of £60,000 being exceeded by £14,000.

8 May 1945 was proclaimed V-E Day by Winston Churchill. Street parties were arranged to celebrate the event, but the atmosphere was somewhat tense, for all thoughts were with the men still in conflict in the Far East.

On Saturday 9 June 1945 a Welcome Home Dinner was arranged for all the Bradwell men taken prisoner five years earlier at Hazenbrouck. It was held at the Progressive Club. All the ingredients were contributed by the township population from their own meagre rations. Entertainment was provided by a concert party, supported by Harold Hood's Futurist Dance Band.

There was a burning local patriotism in the Wolverton District; the area had lost many men in the retreat to Dunkirk. Later, at the fall of Singapore, another large contingent of local men were taken prisoner. Most of these were serving in the 5th Beds and Herts Regiment. No power could break the spirit of these people, neither the horror of war nor the legacy of hard times.

LEFT: The Wings for Victory parade at Wolverton Park in 1942: A Bradwell entry 'The Richest Jewel in the British Empire' (India) — front: Neville Clamp, Jill Clamp, second pair John Welch, Colin Clamp. RIGHT: New Bradwell's ARP Rescue Squad — back row: Eric Cafe, Reg Brockman, Jeff Wilson, Walt Bull, ?; front row: Clem Lister, Bill Meacham, Bill Turvey, Norman Lockwood. BELOW: A Works Section of the Home Guard — back row: Jack Brown, ?, Wilf Griffiths, Jack Blunt, Jim Griffiths, Fred Beals, George Gear, ?; centre: Bill Swindells, Maurice Brock, Cyril Warr, Bill Sykes, Bill Carroll, ?, Les Brown; front: Gordon Etherington, Miss Shelton, Mrs Davis, Sgt Buttram, Lloyd Gee, Horace Hill, Win Lamb, Maisie Walker and Henry Welford.

ABOVE: The CO, 2I C, Officers and NCOs of No 1 Platoon, C Coy, 2nd Bucks HG outside Wolverton Drill Hall, their HQ — standing: Bill Gammon CSM, Doug Hendricks, Sid Sayell, Eric Riley, Bignell, Ted Glenn, Arthur Stones, Don Dockerell, Oscar Callow, Bill Withers CSM; sitting: Lieut George Sharp, Capt Charlie Green Adj, Major Ansell OC, Major E. S. D. Moore 2nd IC, 2nd Lieut Frank Allen, Bill May, Frank Lucas.
BELOW: Stony Stratford's NFS men outside the Silver Street Fire Station — back row: Bernard Berry, Bill Onan, Dick Tucker, Jack Slaymaker, Tommy Inglish, Ro Ibell, Fred McMillan, Reg Giles; middle row: Bert Holland, Harry Wells, Len Barby, Reg Smith, Allen Richardson, Den White, Stan Cockerill, L. Watson; front row: Bert Driver, Bill Young, Fred Whitehead (WO), Arthur Yates (SO), Dennis Chipperfield (LF), Ro Kightley and Owen Holman.

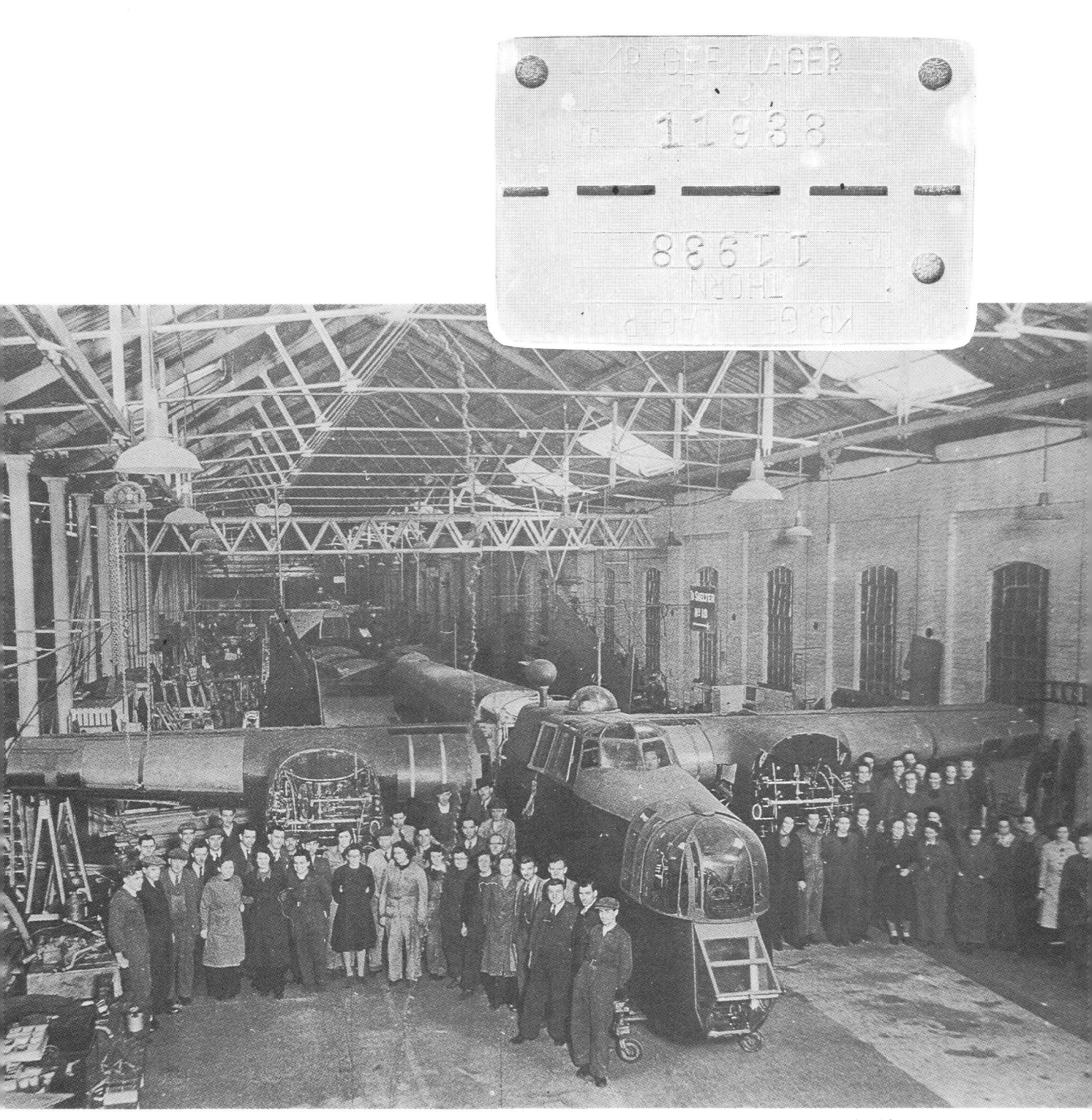

The last Whitley Bomber to be repaired at Wolverton. Most of the workers on these bombers had been transferred to other aircraft work in the factory when this photograph was taken. INSET: Norman Bunce of New Bradwell's PoW identification tag; Norman, a member of the Wolverton Company of the 1st Bucks Battalion of the Oxon/Bucks Light Infantry Territorials, was taken prisoner at the Battalion's last stand at Hazenbrouck in 1940.

WELCOME HOME DINNER TO
BRADWELL
RETURNED P.O.W.

Progressive Club Concert Room
New Bradwell
SATURDAY, JUNE 9th, 1945

THE GREAT WAR 1939--1945

The Committee of the Stony Stratford Comforts Fund would like to express to you their grateful thanks and sincere appreciation for the part you played in the service of your King and Country

The balance of the Fund has been distributed to :—
1. British Legion.
2. Soldiers', Sailors' and Airmen's Family Help Society.
3. Soldiers', Sailors' and Airmen's Incorporated Help Society.
4. Local Good Samaritan Society.

This is given as a gift to those who badly need help, and we feel sure you will approve of such action.

Name _R. G. Westley_

LEFT: The Welcome Home Dinner menu for Bradwell's returned PoWs. RIGHT: A Wolverton V-E street party. BELOW: A card sent to all Stony Stratford ex-servicemen on the winding-up of the Stony Stratford Comforts Fund.

Say it with Music

The district has been well served by musicians with all kinds of bands, modern and old time, brass and by orchestras. There were five brass bands in the Urban District: Bradwell Salvation Army (bandmaster L. Healy); Bradwell (Mr Johnson); Stony Stratford (Mr Wilmin); Wolverton Town (Mr Sharp) and 2nd Bucks Battalion HG 1940-45 (D. Dytham). Added to these were the two Boy Scout bands of Wolverton and Stony Stratford.

Bradwell Silver Band was formed on 15 January 1901, and is still going strong, with a record of continuous existence the envy of many other bands in the area. It carried on through two world wars, due undoubtedly to strong family connections that are still prominent today. Bradwell also had a Drum and Fife Band, for they participated in the parade that opened Wolverton Park in 1885.

The band's first title was Bradwell Excelsior, then Stantonbury St James, Bradwell Town, Bradwell Recreation Brass Band and finally Bradwell United Brass Band, its name until 1955. The band has always been self-supporting, as well as supporting local charities, including fine work done in connection with the Stantonbury Hospital Fund. Many remember when they raised £147 at Kenilworth Road, the ground of Luton Football Club, when Manchester United were playing their first match after the Munich air disaster.

A tradition unique to Bradwell band is that of its Christmas morning tour of the town playing carols. This begins at 6.00am, when the inhabitants of New Bradwell are awakened to the shattering strains of *Christians Awake*. This time-honoured custom began (before the demolition of the railway-owned houses) with the first blow at the corner of Bridge Street and Church Street as the author can verify, for the first time I heard it (without warning) I nearly shot out of bed, wondering what on earth had happened.

Later in the morning the band collectors called on houses with boxes for the band fund. One collector was once calling door-to-door and not doing too well. Walking up a long garden path, he reached the front door and knocked. After much muttering from within, the front door opened slightly and an old lady peered through 'Yes. What do you want?'

'We're collecting for the Bradwell Silver Band'.

'What's that you say?'

'We're collecting for the Bradwell Silver Band,'.

'You what?' screeched the old lady.

'We're collect, Oh never mind' and he turned on his heel and walked back down the path.

'Mind you shut the gate' she bawled.

'Oh, bugger the gate,' mumbled the collector;

'Yes, and bugger the Bradwell Silver Band an' all' cackled the jubilant old lady.

As well as being a popular concert band, the band has always entered contests, latterly competing against other bands from all over the country. A strong emphasis has always been and still is put on the junior band, with lessons free of charge twice a week. Today Mr Clive Keech, cornet player and senior band musical director, is responsible for the learner classes.

Stony Stratford Band was formed in the 1860s, and before 1914 was prominent at carnivals and fêtes. Yet, by 1919, they were struggling for musicians, no doubt due to the loss of men to the war and perhaps the reluctance of survivors to don uniform again.

The Bandmaster at the time was Mr Wilmin and their HQ was the Crown, landlord Mr Randle. The Chairman was Mr McLean of Cox and Robinson and the Secretary, Mr Fred Southam. Every week on practice night at the Crown band members paid one shilling subscription. This in itself was not conducive to membership during such lean times but, at the dedication of the War Memorial on the Green, Bill Gallop played *The End of a Perfect Day* on his cornet. Sunday night open-air concerts held on the Market Square were a regular feature from late spring at seven o'clock, after evensong at the church.

Mr Wilmin died and the baton was taken up by Den Meakins. After many efforts to rekindle interest, the band finally wound up in 1929. Mr McLean sold the instruments to the NUR Band at Northampton along with half the uniforms, the remaining uniforms going to the Potterspury Band. Just a few weeks before the end four new instruments were bought for £80. Surviving players tried to purchase their instruments with a view to reforming the band at a later date, but for some reason this was refused by Mr McLean. So ended the Stony Stratford Brass Band.

Wolverton Town Band was formed in the early locomotive era of Wolverton Works. It played at the opening of the Science and Art Institute in 1864, and its bandmaster was Mr Tattersall. The Bandmaster from 1914 to 1919 was Mr Frank Sharpe, one of the old stalwarts of the North Bucks brass band movement. Mr Sharpe handed over to Mr Frank Brooks in 1919, who gathered around him numerous first-class players, many of whom had just returned from the forces. They entered their first competition in 1919 in the Church Institute, a quartet contest for local bands. Wolverton won and this was the beginning of the band's most successful period. In 1920, the band entered the National Brass Band Festival at Crystal Palace, (4th section). The test piece was *Il Trovatore* by Verdi; 25 bands competed and Wolverton came third.

In 1921, it was agreed to engage Mr Fred Mortimer, then conductor of Luton Red Cross Band. Up to the Second World War the band gained many successes both nationally and locally. At the Crystal Palace in 1922, competing in the second section, they again came third. The community was so proud of this achievement it collected enough money to present each member of the band with a medal.

The band stood down during the war. In 1948 it changed its name to the Wolverton Town and BR Band, and continues under the able direction of Mr Colin Stephens.

The Wolverton Home Guard Military Band was formed in 1940, Doug Dytham bandmaster. It comprised bandsmen from Wolverton, Bradwell and the ex-Stony Stratford band, with one or two from Newport Pagnell. At full strength it consisted of around forty bandsmen, the band sergeant being Sid Dytham.

This band was unique. It was the only HG band in the country and its bandmaster, Doug Dytham, was an 'honorary' member of the HG as he was already a wartime Special Constable. HQ was the old Ambulance Room in the Railway Works where they paraded for practice one night a week and on Sunday mornings. They also led the Battalion on Sunday morning route marches.

The band not only performed for local parades and displays such as Warship Week, but also turned out to lead members of the armed forces for similar events, giving concerts all over the county. Rehearsing the mid-section of *The Light Cavalry* in preparation for an event in the south of the county the bass section, which included basses, trombones and euphoniums, had only to play one note for two bars, then miss a bar, and so on through the piece. One bandsman repeatedly fluffed it, putting one note in on the bar he should have missed. Doug, bearing in mind some of the Stratford men had not blown an instrument for ten years or more, said 'Come on! look at your music, if we get it right this time, I'll buy you all a pint'. They got through it right down to the last bar when Bill Blackburn (an accomplished musician and later to become Bandmaster of

Wolverton Town Band) put one in. 'What did you do that for Bill?' sighed Doug. 'I thought I would save you a bob or two' laughed Bill.

On another occasion at a parade at Hanslope, where the band was leading a contingent of troops, Doug was detained at work and sent a message that he would meet the band at Hanslope. Arriving at the venue with some fifteen minutes to spare, he parked his car and sought out band orderly Jack Boswell. He looked him up and down (Jack was wearing brown shoes instead of the regulation boots and gaiters) and upbraided him 'What the h . . . are you doing with brown shoes on and where are your boots?' 'The boots hurt my feet' replied Jack. Worse was to come. 'Come on then, where's the music?' questioned Doug. 'I've forgotten that an' all' mumbled Jack. 'B . . . . . me' sighed Doug and had to hold up the parade while he returned to Wolverton to collect the music.

After leading the stand-down parade through Wolverton at the head of the Battalion in December 1944, the band passed into history.

The Stony Stratford Boy Scouts Band was formed in 1922, and in the first instance was a drum and fife band. Mr George Webb taught the boys both music and the instrument. He had been Deputy Bandmaster of the RE Band during the war.

On practice nights during the summer, George would march them to Oakhill Lane, then march them up and down the lane. Returning to Stratford, they would strike up a stirring tune like *Marching through Georgia*, to let the residents know they were about. In the winter months practice took place in the Scouts HQ, which at that time was at the bottom of the White Horse Yard and, after the troop moved to a loft in the Cock Yard, became a stonemason's workshop.

Around 1930 the band exchanged its fifes for bugles and the tutoring duties were undertaken by Arthur Jones. Arthur lived at Wolverton and was a prominent member of the British Legion and also blew the *Last Post* and *Reveille* at the Wolverton War Memorial on Armistice Day, for he had been Bugle Major in the Oxon and Bucks Light Infantry.

The band was well-known around the district, working in association with the Scout gymnastic team for charity organisations, playing at scout camps, giving marching demonstrations at fêtes and leading parades. On the large British Legion and Armistice Day parades it played a complementary role to the Stony Stratford Band and, on the latter's demise, it accompanied the Wolverton Town Band.

The band broke up on the outbreak of war in 1939, mainly because most of the instrumentalists joined up and the remainder had other war-time commitments, so the band just faded away.

The Wolverton Light Orchestra was founded in 1927 as the Frank Brooks Orchestra. After the war it reformed under the leadership of H. Nutt as the Wolverton Orchestral Society. In 1977, under Arnold Jones, it again changed its name to the Wolverton Light Orchestra.

After a modest beginning with some eighteen players, the Orchestra supported concerts arranged by the Wolverton Hospital Committee and the British Legion. On 26 January 1930, it gave a Grand Concert at the Scala cinema, Stony Stratford. Throughout 1932, a calendar of concerts was performed at the Church Institute, Science and Art Institute and at the Scala.

In 1933, regular Sunday evening concerts were started in the New Empire Cinema at Wolverton, interspersed with performances at Newport Electra Cinema, Wolverton Scout Hall and McCorquodale's Reading Room. These commenced at 7.45, which allowed the faithful to go straight from church, and provided a programme of popular light orchestral music with a soloist. Admission was free, programmes cost twopence and there was a silver collection, the proceeds to a local charity. This programme of Sunday night concerts continued until the beginning of the war, by which time there were some thirty players. In 1938, a musical fantasy in four acts was produced — *Lionel Dennier Steps Out*. Brooks wrote the libretto and H. Nutt the music. The principal roles were sung by local amateurs, including Connie Elliott and Eileen Dormer, who was a dancing instructress and choreographer.

During the first year of the war, concerts were devoted to the Wolverton Forces Comforts and Christmas Fund. By the autumn of 1940, the loss of players to the Forces and the wartime working hours of the remainder had seriously affected the Orchestra's capability. It still managed a few performances each year, relying on a core of local players backed by guest musicians. In November 1945, Harold Nutt became conductor, on the resignation due to ill-health of Frank Brooks.

Harold Nutt had spent his war service in the Beds and Herts Regiment as a bandsman, during which time he played for the BBC Symphony Orchestra under Sir Adrian Boult, and the Bedford Symphony Orchestra, and had conducted the latter in works which he himself had composed. He was music master at Wolverton Grammar School. Under his influence the Orchestra extended its repertoire to include overtures and suites.

One concert which he conducted on 10 November 1946 in the Works Canteen exemplifies the high standards attained. This concert, with the Musical Society Choir, concluded with a performance of *Hiawatha's Wedding Feast* by Coleridge-Taylor, for chorus, orchestra and solo tenor, soloist Arnold Jones.

From the mid-1940s until the mid-1950s concerts were given at Buckingham Town Hall and Thornton Convent School and for some years the Orchestra accompanied the Wolverton Choral Society in concert performances such as *Carmen* in 1948 and *The Messiah* in 1953. From the mid-1950s, interest waned and the Orchestra ceased to function for nearly six years.

At a meeting in 1961, a wave of new enthusiasm revived it with only twelve players, soon increasing to over twenty; Arnold Jones was appointed the new conductor.

Its first appearance as a reformed group was at a flower show in the Works Canteen in September 1962. The first actual concert was given in Moon Street School in December 1962 and another a week later in St Giles Church, Stony Stratford, followed by concerts in Northampton and surrounding towns and villages. It also performs with the Wolverton Gilbert and Sullivan Society, and gives regular concerts in Bletchley and other parts of Milton Keynes.

In January 1990 Arnold Jones resigned as conductor after 28 years and his son Robert took over. He is a local music teacher and the Orchestra continues to thrive under his direction.

With the advent of syncopated music in the early 1920s and the introduction of wireless, many local bands were formed to play this popular music for ballroom dancers.

Some bands diversified and played both modern and old time dance music, and became known as 50-50 bands but, as the numbers of old time dancers increased, old time bands were formed to cater for them.

Here are just a few of the bands that appeared during the period. Modern bands: Blue Bird Mouth Organ Band; Harry Ward and His Rhythm Boys; Bill Axby and His Night Owls; the Ambassadors; the Embassy Trio; Synco Orchestra (Walt Hellenburg); the Lyric Orchestra; the Rhythm Aces; the Collegian Swingers; Les Nichols Carlton Players; Cecil Stones Accordion Band; Tom Clarridge's Orchestra and Tom Clarridge's Amazons; old time bands: Joe Lovesey's Orchestra; Bright Knights and Gay Nineties (Geo. Davis); 50-50 bands: Jack Pool Band; Jack Durdin's Band; Harold Hood's Futurist Band and Harold Batterson's Band; other bands: Doug Blunt's Band; Jock Jamieson's Band and The Marina Trio.

The district had suitable buildings for this popular pastime. At Wolverton there were the Science and Art Institute, Church Institute, Drill Hall and Works Canteen all capable of accepting in excess of two hundred dancing couples. Smaller dances were held at McCorquodale's Reading Room, the Craufurd Arms, the Victoria Hotel and later the Scout Hall. Bradwell had the County Arms, the Bowyer Hall and Labour Hall. In the beginning Stony Stratford had small dance venues at the Public Hall, St Giles Parish Room and the Cock Hotel. In 1933 the Regents Hall was built, which allowed the town to compete with Wolverton in staging larger functions in what was originally the engine shed for the Stony Stratford–Wolverton tram.

Badminton Clubs were formed all over the district and used the premises five nights a week. An afternoon Badminton Club run by Miss Salmons of Newport Pagnell also used the Regents Hall most afternoons. Mrs Winterbottom of Cosgrove Hall used it for her parties, balls and concerts, the music always provided by the Rhythm Aces Band. On the outbreak of war it was commandeered by the government as a billet for evacuee families. Then Skipper and East, a London printing firm, took it over for the remainder of the war, and pulled up the dance floor. After the war no licence for wood could be obtained to restore the flooring, so it became a factory. J.H. Vaverusare, manufacturer of bakelite, set up his operation there. It was produced from coconut shells, using a minimum of resin, like many things at the time in short supply. On Ceylon's independence, export of coconut shells ceased so the factory closed, and today (1990) it is used as a store for exhibition stands.

The Lyric Orchestra was one of the first dance bands, formed in the 1920s by George Webb Snr of Stony Stratford, with three brothers (a fourth played in the Bedford Salvation Army Band) whose father was the organist at Deanshanger Methodist Church. The first players were George Webb (flute), Cyril Webb (string Bass), Jack Webb (violin), Fred Nichols (piano). After a while Fred Nichols was replaced by Harry Ward. They played at the Science and Art Institute for the Students' Ball, at Buckingham and Newport Town Halls and at many private parties in the large houses of the district. In 1930, George Webb was appointed choirmaster at St Giles Church, Stony Stratford, and decided to call it a day.

Harry Ward formed the Rhythm Boys, later leaving to join Jack Wilson's band at the Coventry Hippodrome. The Orchestra then took on a new look. Jack Webb became leader, playing violin and saxophone, Bert Bent was the pianist and Charlie Hardwick clarinet and saxophone; Paddy Lucas was on the guitar and drummer and vocalist was Henry Hood, who used a megaphone to throw his voice. The New Inn at New Bradwell became their HQ. They remained the leading band in the district until the formation of the Rhythm Aces.

The Rhythm Aces emerged from a rhythm club formed at Wolverton in 1932. The club held sessions every Friday night in the dining room of the Crauford Arms, dancing to records of the big bands of the day. There were many budding musicians among its members, but the piano at the Crauford Arms was unplayable.

The proprietor of Eva Herbert's music shop (13 Stratford Road) came to the rescue and agreed to lend a piano every Friday night. So Monty Henson, Charlie Hardwick and Doug Frost every Friday pushed a piano on a small set of wheels to the Crauford after work and returned it Saturday morning.

Within a few months they formed their own band; in 1934 Doug Frost was manager and Charlie Hardwick leader; the band members were Bill Axby, Ron Glave, George Aggutter, Roy Brittain, Cliff Applin and Monty Henson.

They were all young and mostly apprentices in the railway works on low wages without the cash to buy orchestrations. However, Doug Frost was a friend of Oliver Thornycroft (stage-name Olly Aston), son of Thornycroft the photographer of Stony Stratford, and Musical Director of Kingston Hippodrome. At Olly's flat, Doug Frost and Monty Henson were shown stacks of scores with the instruction 'help yourself'.

Doug Frost arranged their first dance at the then newly opened Regents Hall at Stony Stratford. Doug Dytham took over as leader in 1935 and ran it for fifty years until the band wound up in 1984.

Over the years they entertained over a radius of forty miles for Sir Jocelyn Lucas, Prince and Princess Nicholas Galitzine, Mrs Hugh McCorquodale, Northamptonshire Regimental Ball, Bedfordshire Regimental Ball, government departments, officers' messes, Huntingdonshire Police Ball and Bedford 41 Club.

Mrs Winterbottom of Cosgrove Hall was a regular patron, engaging them to play at her house parties and for charity concerts across the county. The rehearsals were held at her home, she herself being a singer of some quality. It was at one of these functions that Mrs Hugh McCorquodale (Barbara Cartland) heard the band and hired it to play at her daughter, Renée's, (now Marchioness of Northampton) coming-out party, at their Park Lane residence.

The band performed at Mrs Winterbottom's Christmas Eve house party, and Boxing Day Ball in the Regent Hall at Stony Stratford, to which she invited her house guests, tradesmen and friends around the district. She liked to be presented with bouquets by children on these occasions (which she bought herself) afterwards throwing them to the crowd as a goodwill gesture.

During the war, the band played at Saturday night dances held at the Science and Art Institute for the local Forces Fund.

Doug once received a phone call from the Mayor of Towcester enquiring whether he had a specific date free in his band diary for a charity function at Towcester Town Hall.

Doug replied that the date was free, but his petrol ration for that month had gone and the only hire car large enough to transport the band was in the same position. The Mayor told him to book it, assemble the band at his address and he would supply the transport.

The day arrived and so did the transport! It was Towcester fire engine — the old-fashioned type where you had to stand on a running-board each side of the escape, which ran along and atop the centre of the engine, hanging onto a rail. They travelled to and from the dance with their instruments lashed to the escape.

The Rhythm Aces were the resident band for the BBC broadcast of 'Works Wonders' in the Works Canteen in March 1948, Brian Johnson compère, and Doug Dytham arranging all the music and they performed at Lord Hill's golden wedding at St Albans. Lord Hill was on the board of the BBC and could have obtained the services of any BBC band, but he chose the Rhythm Aces because he had heard them play at the South Beds Golf Club, and liked what he heard. Not once did the band ever advertise.

Tommy Clarridge, a Bradwell man and a musical virtuoso, formed the Amazons in 1934, its original members Billy Wise, Stan Baldwin, Stan Nichols, Bill Tunningley and Tom himself. In 1938 Tom and Billy Wise entered the Carol Levis discoveries competition on BBC radio with an act called 'The Wise Bros', Billy playing the drums. They won their programme and all the series. Tom entered the Berks, Bucks and Oxon Accordion Championships in 1939 and won it, repeating this feat in 1950 and 1951.

On the outbreak of war, Tom volunteered and joined the Royal Engineers, taking his accordion. He was in France by the end of 1939, and was among the last to be evacuated on 17 June from St Nazaire on the *Lancastria*. The ship sunk, there were around 5,000 troops on board and more than 2,000 lost. Tom was saved but his accordion lies on the sea-bed in the Bay of Biscay. Back in England he ran a regimental dance-band, playing saxophone and clarinet.

After the war he formed and managed a trio. The trio eventually developed into a seven-piece band, later reformed with eleven players as the Tommy Clarridge Orchestra. It performed on a regular basis at Oxford and Cambridge colleges, Oundle College, Watford Town Hall and Westcott Atomic Research Centre. The band eventually broke up and Tom joined Doug Dytham and his Rhythm Aces.

Joe Lovesey formed his Old Tyme Dance Orchestra just after the war in 1946. Joe had joined the Wolverton Town Band as a boy and in the services became a member of a military band. After the war he rejoined the Town Band.

At the beginning of the war he had formed a 50/50 band of some seven players, occasionally calling on the services of his daughter, Marjorie, as vocalist, and this band developed into the Old Tyme Dance Orchestra.

The Orchestra ranged over four counties, Bucks, Beds, Northants, and Oxon, with an occasional longer trip which included Manchester, Swindon and a BBC audition in Birmingham, and thrived until 1958 when Joe retired through ill-health.

In the late twenties and early thirties a unique band could be heard at New Bradwell — the Blue Bird Mouth Organ Band. It played every Saturday night at the County Arms Hotel, and later reformed as an accordion band.

'A night out for a tanner' was the slogan used at the Labour Hall at Bradwell for its League of Youth dances on a Friday night. For sixpence (2½p), one not only gained entrance to a dance with music by Cecil Stone and his Accordion Band, but also to a fish and chip supper, delivered to the Labour Hall during the interval by Sayell's fish and chip shop in Spencer Street. When there was no supper, the entrance fee was fourpence.

Bim Morris' Collegian Swingers was formed in 1937 by Bim from ex-Wolverton Technical College students. It broke up on the outbreak of war and after the war Bim played solo on the piano, touring local clubs and playing at weddings. Today (1990), he still entertains on piano and organ, often accompanied by his wife, Madge.

Jack Durdin and his band were ideal for weddings and the Bright Knights old time dance band was founded by Bert Walker at the end of the 1939-45 war, staging a benefit dance in Wolverton Scout Hall for a Town Band player who had been ill. After the dance, some of the twelve volunteers decided to form a regular band. The six original members were Bert Walker, Reg Grace, George Webb, Ted Butler, Harry Andrews and Dan Roberts, and they played at Oxford, Witney, Bedford and Luton. They were regular performers at Vauxhall Motors, SKF Works and Dunstable Town Hall. Bedford Police Ball was an annual event and they were frequent visitors to Bedford Corn Exchange. At Oxford the Randolph Hotel was perhaps their big night of the year, when the band teamed up with the Rhythm Aces to make a twelve piece orchestra, for the Ladies' Night of the Oxford Freemasons. In 1970, the band called it a day, because of its members' other commitments.

Dancing classes supplied the young dancers to fill the halls and the best known instructor was Wolverton's Bill Fielding, who ran classes both at the Church Institute and the Victoria Hotel, sixpence per session. Bill and his band also ran dances on Friday nights at the Victoria Hotel for the same price.

On a Saturday for between one shilling (5p), and half a crown (12½p), one could have an enchanting evening. No alcohol was served but tea and soft drinks were obtained in the interval, or half-hour pass-outs to a handy public house. There were hardly ever any scenes of fighting at local dances. Any sign of bad behaviour and the ushers would quickly move them out.

The Wolverton Orchestra produced two outstanding musicians: John Gray and John Exton. John Gray is now Head of Double Bass Studies at the New South Wales State Conservatoire of Music in Sydney, Australia, and Professor of Music at the University of Perth.

Among the most popular entertainers in the district were Charlie Scott and his wife, Tina, formerly Miss Lavinia Hollingsworth. Charlie was a Bradwell man and a fine musician; a pupil of Mr C.K. Garrett of Newport Pagnell, his first appointment was as organist at the Church of St Peter's, Tyringham. After Tyringham he took over at St James' at Bradwell.

Charlie left to play at Old Bradwell and for seven years was organist at Emberton. He returned to New Bradwell and at his retirement had completed twenty-five of his fifty years at St James. For forty-three years he was both organist and choirmaster.

He also taught piano and at one time had forty pupils. He played for professional artists at concerts at both New Bradwell Clubs and was relief pianist at the Scala and Palace cinemas in the days of silent films. His wife, Tina, was a polished elocutionist and together they produced over 20 pantomimes, Charlie responsible for both music and lyrics over 25 years.

In the early 1920s, Charlie formed a concert group called the Stantonians, which began with a pierrot show, followed by variety acts consisting of sketches and monologues, ballads, duets and comic songs, plus a comedian. Charlie composed all the songs and accompanied all the artistes on the piano. This concert party travelled the district giving performances at village and town halls, all for charity, right up to 1930.

In 1926, he produced his first pantomime, *Cinderella*, involving nearly all the community. The Progressive Club hosted the St James' Church Amateur Dramatic Society, all the rehearsals free of charge.

Tina Scott's elocution lessons produced most of the young actresses and Charlie retained the name Stantonian 8 for the chorus girls. Mrs Leather and Mr W.P. Pidgen arranged the chorus dances and other dances were devised by Eileen Dormer and performed by pupils of her School of Dancing. Tina and the village ladies produced the costumes, John Ellis, stage and effects, John Ellis and T. Tapp being stage managers.

During January the show opened with seven performances at the Progressive Club. After six nights at the Top Club, Wolverton, it returned to Bradwell for three nights at the Side Club, and then went on tour right through to Easter, visiting most of the towns and villages in North Bucks and South Northants, terminating at Renny Lodge where the troupe gave the patients, (then called inmates) a slap-up tea before the entertainment began.

In later years, the Bradwell British Legion Ladies Section put on *The Jolly Minstrel Show*, which was broadcast on TV. This minstrel troupe was formed to amuse fellow-members of the New Bradwell branch of the British Legion and, when the BBC women's programme *Your Turn Now* visited Northampton, the troupe formed part of a live programme held in the YMCA in Cheyne Walk, Northampton.

The Coopedians were a concert party formed by Wolverton Co-op employees to raise money for charities; Bert Appleton was the organiser. Rehearsals were held in the Co-op Rooms at Wolverton. The opening performance was always at the Scala cinema, Stony Stratford on a Sunday night, then the show went on the road through the winter months.

At a performance at Buckingham Town Hall, a sketch was being performed that entailed the hall being plunged into darkness and the lights switched on again at a given phrase. The stage manager was not available so one of the cast named Fred offered.

As an actor called Green gave Fred his cue, Fred duly put out all the lights. On hearing 'There are only the two of us here', Fred had to switch the lights on (when Green would be pulling up his trousers). But between cues, Fred had dropped his hand from the switch panel and could not find it again. Green repeated 'There are only the two of us here' twice more, then 'There's only one bugger now', as he marched off stage, getting the biggest laugh of the night.

Most churches had strong choirs. At the Wesley Methodist Church, Wolverton in 1951 Arnold Jones was choirmaster. Today, 40 years on, he is still organist/choirmaster. In 1954 he staged a performance of *The Messiah* with an augmented choir and orchestra, and this became an annual event with 22 performances until 1976. He also put on concert versions of *Merrie England*, *Tom Jones*, *Carmen* and the Savoy operas, out of which grew the Wolverton Gilbert and Sullivan Society. *HMS Pinafore* was staged at the Wolverton College of Further Education in 1975 and 1990 saw *The Sorcerer* at the Stantonbury Theatre. Arnold has been the musical director for the whole of this period.

Other operatic groups include the New City Players, who have produced musicals at the Wolverton College under the energetic direction of Mrs Joan Walker, and more recently, the Music Makers have been producing musicals at the Radcliffe School, their Musical Director Ralph Mazzone, another pupil of the late Ken Garratt.

The Wolverton Choral Society functioned from 1921-1940 under the baton of C.K. Garratt of Newport Pagnell. Rehearsals were on Mondays in the Science and Art Institute and concerts mostly in the Congregational Church. At Wolverton a new Wolverton Choral Society was formed in 1945 with Harold Nutt as conductor. This was not a large group but from 1948-1954 choral works were performed with the WLO (or Wolverton Orchestral Society).

The Wolverton Drama Society was formed in 1947, its first production *The Importance of being Ernest*, in the Church Institute. This group of high-class amateur actors rehearsed and also performed in the Congregational Church building. On the opening of the College of Further Education in 1955, this became the group's stage with *Dear Octopus*. From 1950 until 1970, Mrs Louis Smart was the leader. The group fully supported the Wolverton Carnival Commitee.

In the late 1940s, Ron Faulkner conducted two choirs: a ladies' choir which met and rehearsed in the Memorial Hall at Old Stratford and a male voice choir which rehearsed in the schoolroom of the Methodist Church in New Bradwell. Around 1950 he merged them to form a mixed choir called Orphean Singers. It met weekly in a back room of the Hanslope Working Men's Club. Many fine amateur singers have graced the Orpheans' ranks including the late Bob Fielding, David Marshall (an outstanding tenor voice), Jacqueline Hardie and Psyche Pyne. At one stage the choir had a membership of around fifty voices, but a breakaway faction left to form another group.

When ill-health forced Ron Faulkner to give up the conductorship his place was taken by John Hardcastle, a member of the choir then living in Northampton, who still conducts the singers (1990). Forty years on they still rehearse in Hanslope, though no longer in the Working Men's Club.

Herbert (Bert) Lunn, a Yorkshireman by birth, came to Wolverton in 1927 when he transferred his headmastership from Lane End Bucks to Wolverton Boys' School. An urban councillor for eighteen years representing Calverton and later the combined ward of that village and his town of Stony Stratford, Ratepayers' president, Freemason, sportsman, bowler captain of the town team and a Bucks County player, choirmaster and schoolmaster, he was choirmaster of Lane End, Wolverton St George's, Wolverton and St Mary's, Stony Stratford. He formed the boys' choir of the Council School in 1927 and this achieved high distinction in the competitive field with successes in London's Westminster Hall, Bedford, Buckingham, Northampton, Kettering and Berkhampstead. It was his choir that won the LMS Challenge Cup at the Temperance Union Festival on eight occasions out of ten; for this the cup was *given* to the school.

Armstrong Gibbs, one of the greatest judges of children's choirs, gave Bert's Wolverton Boys' School Choir the highest marks (98 out of 100) that he had ever given. He wrote 'He possesses that elusive and vital quality that is able to inspire his singers with the real enthusiasm and sense of poetry which alone can raise the standard of singing from merely good to something arresting and electric. He is one of the very few really first-rate choir trainers that this country possesses'. Bert himself was the possessor of a fine tenor voice, a gold medallist and in 1935 winner of the challenge rose bowl at the Northampton Musical Festival.

The Wolverton and District Gilbert and Sullivan Society was formed in 1974, its first performance in 1975 *HMS Pinafore*; formed at the Methodist Church, Wolverton it has rehearsed at this Church, West End Methodist Church and the Madcap Theatre, and performaces were first at the Wolverton College of Further Education then Stantonbury Theatre, with some 50 society members singing in each show, yet one more evidence of the extraordinary musical talent in the three towns.

Wolverton Town Band c1955 photographed in the Works Canteen — back row: Basil Hayfield, Doug Horton, Brian Clarke, Sid Dytham, John Adams, Stan Essam, Bill Jones; middle row: Nick Dytham, John Wilson, Tom Axtell (Treasurer), Mike Tebbet, Sam Horton, Harry Andrews, George Clarke, Pete Hollyoak, Ray Savage, Ron Andrews; front row: Reg Barden, Bill Axtell, Norman Bates, Maurice Falk, Bill Blackburn (Bandmaster), Mr Moore (President), Doug Dytham, Doug Pickering, Bill Anderson and Jim Malone (Secretary).

ABOVE: Bradwell Band in the early 1920s, behind the St Giles Street Club — back row: W. Kightley, J. Sheering, C. Bissell, S. Dytham, B. Breedon, A. Haseldine, R. Thompson; middle row: A. Campbell, M. Pepper, F. Alderson, S. Saunders, C. Carrol, H. Jones, H. Walters, B. Jones; front row: F. Adams, T. Kightley, B. Walters, E. Johnson, Dr Miles, P. Hardwick, J. Amos, A. Packer and B. Mallard. BELOW: Stony Stratford Band playing down the High Street, the Cross Keys on the left.

ABOVE: Wolverton Scouts Bugle and Drum Band at a camp at Gayhurst, Whitsun 1919. BELOW: The 2nd Bucks Battalion Home Guard Band, at the northern end of Wolverton Park — outer semi-circle: Walt Kightley, Brian Clarke, Cross, Frank Cross, ?, Bill Mallard, ?, Horn, Fred Fielding, Bill Jones, Maurice Falk, Jack Boswell, Reg Bardin, Bill Anderson, ?, Jim Malone; inner semi-circle: Sid Dytham, George Lambert, Bert Breedon, Tommy Chater, Abbott, Harry Andrews, George Clark, Fred Southam, Tom Wilmin, Martin Pepper, Bill Blackburn; front four: Doug Dytham, Major Percy Dewick (Coy Commander), Col Hagley (CO 2nd Bucks) and Saggars.

ABOVE: The 1932 Rythm Club at their HQ, the Crauford Arms, in 1932 — sitting: Doug Frost, Thelma Henson, Fred Miles, Flossy Mayo, Jim Garrington, Evelyn Hawkins, Beryl Taylor, Charlie Hardwick; middle row: Frank Rice, Dolly Dickens, ?, George Webb, ?, ?, Dora Hince, ?, ?, ?, ?, Poole, Elsie Hull, Elma Turvey, Reg Brown, ?, Paddy Lucas, Lloyd Bennett (accordion); back row: 3rd along Fred Scott, 7th along Eric Sykes, Roy Brittain (cymbal on head); 2nd from right Jack Drinkwater (landlord), 3rd from right Bill Wyatt. BELOW: The Rythm Aces Dance Band c1937 — back: Mont Henson (bass), Bill Jones (drums); front: Sid Dytham, Basil Stantone, Doug Dytham, Ron Glave, Eddie Hart and Sid Glave.

ABOVE: At Mrs Winterbottom's 1937 Boxing Day Ball in the Regents Hall, Stony Stratford, the Rythm Aces Band are onstage, and Mr and Mrs Winterbottom centre front. BELOW: The Lyric Band at the Science and Art Students' Ball, New Year's Eve, 1933 — at back onstage: Fred Nichols; standing third from left, Fred Adams, next George Webb and Doreen Hince, seventh Bill Arnold, tenth Cyril Stayley; front: Bert Bent, Jack Webb, Henry Hood, Paddy Lucas (guitar), Charlie Hardwick, Bill Axby (trumpet), ?.

ABOVE: Tommy Clarridge's Amazon Band of 1934 — standing: Stan Baldwin, Bill Wise, Bill Tunningley; sitting: Stan Nicholls and Tom Clarridge. BELOW: Harold Batterson and his band 1947 — Stan Nicholls (saxophone), Bill Cochrane (trumpet), Ken Dunkley (drums), Harold Batterson (guitar) and Hubert Hyde (piano).

ABOVE: Bim Morris and his Collegian Swingers at Buckingham Town Hall, 1937: Cliff Meakins (trumpet), Harry Grace (alto sax), Ken Gray (drums), Ron Green (guitar) and 'Bim' (Jazz) Morris. BELOW: The Bright Knights Old Time Dance Band play at a British Legion Ball at Buckingham Town Hall — back: Ken Savage (drums), Fred Nichols (bass); front: Harry Andrews (french horn), Dan Roberts (guitar), Reg Grace (violin), Stan Jones (accordion) and G. Webb (piano).

ABOVE: Harold Hood's Futurist Band: Charlie Walker, Bill Campbell, Doug Pickering, Harold Hood and Gwen Ebbs. BELOW: Joe Lovesey's Old Tyme Orchestra.

ABOVE: Joe Lovesey's Old Tyme Orchestra at the Wolverton Works Canteen with a group of the dancers.
BELOW: Wolverton's Works Wonders, 12 March 1948 — men: Newbold, Doug Campbell, John Warren, Mont Henson (bass), Frank Westley, Les Ince, Bill Wise, Ben Burbidge, Doug Dytham, Ron Glave (sax), Sid Dytham, Stan Baldwin, Cyril Hardwick, Dunlevy, Frank Gable; sitting: Ron Green and Tom Chaytor Jnr; ladies: ?, Rly Queen?, ?, Eileen Brickwood, Amy Wood.

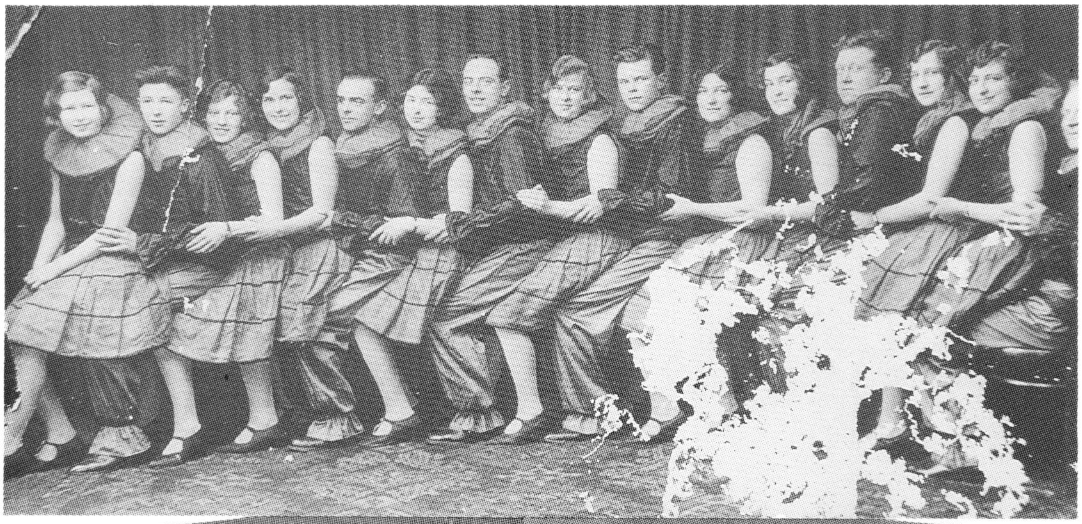

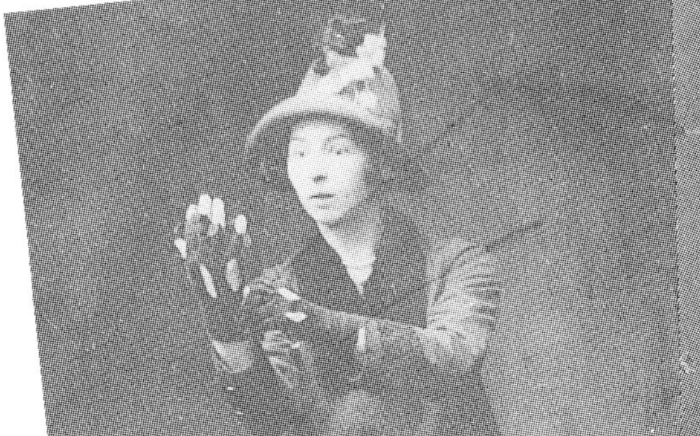

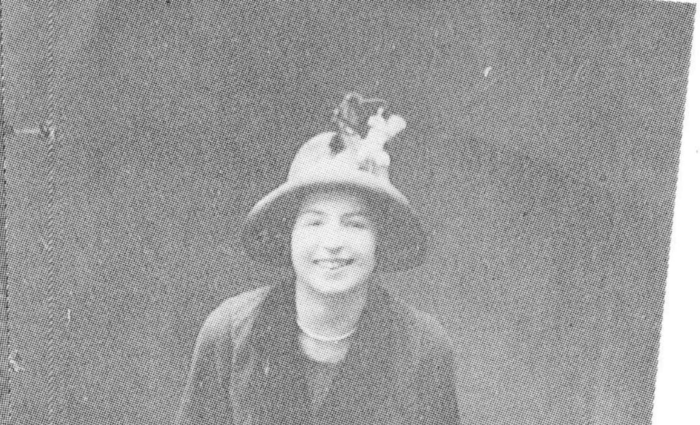

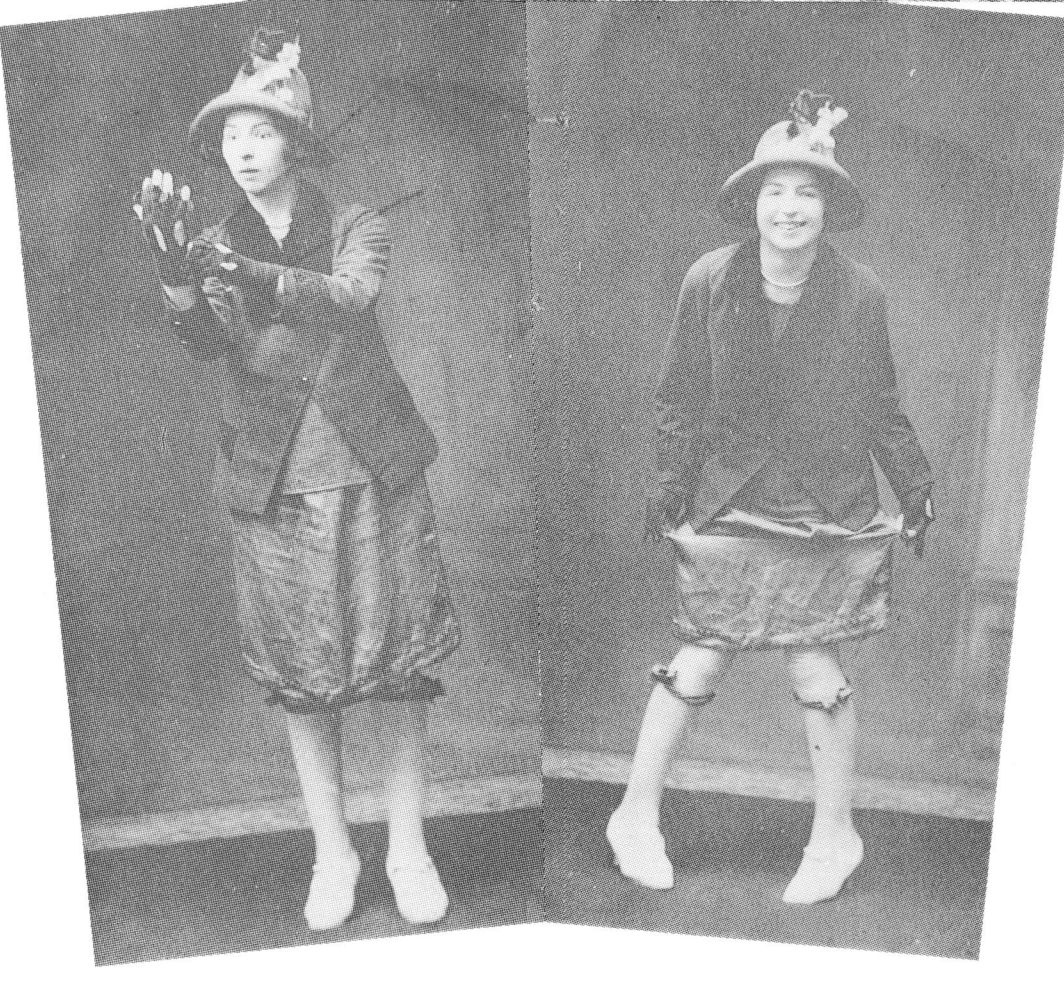

OPPOSITE ABOVE: The Co-opedians line up: Sylvia Dormer, Ron Gillrow, ?, Miss Craddock, 'Happy' Appleton, Madge Dormer, Albert Jackson, ?, ?, Cook, Doll Craddock, Bert Thomas, Phyllis Bull, ? and Percy Isted. BELOW: Comedienne Madge Dormer of the Coopedians performing and singing the *Rotton Cotton Gloves* song. ABOVE: Mr Herbert (Bert) Lunn's School Choir of 1927 — back row: R. Clarke, R. Glave, J. Kemp, A. Richardson, M. Henson, J. Goodway, W. Carvell, E. Carvell, R. Hodgson, T. Reynolds; middle row: C. Brown, F. Nichols, R. Carvell, S. Norman, W. Brocklehurst, Herbert (Bert) Lunn (Choirmaster), R. Nutt, S. Davies, J. Williams, J. Squire, front row: E. Bull, J. Morris, A. Loft, D. Briars, G. Griffiths, R. Petts, E. Kightley and T. Murphy. BELOW: Wolverton St George's Concert Party; the cast of *Cinderella* at the Church Institute in the mid-1950s.

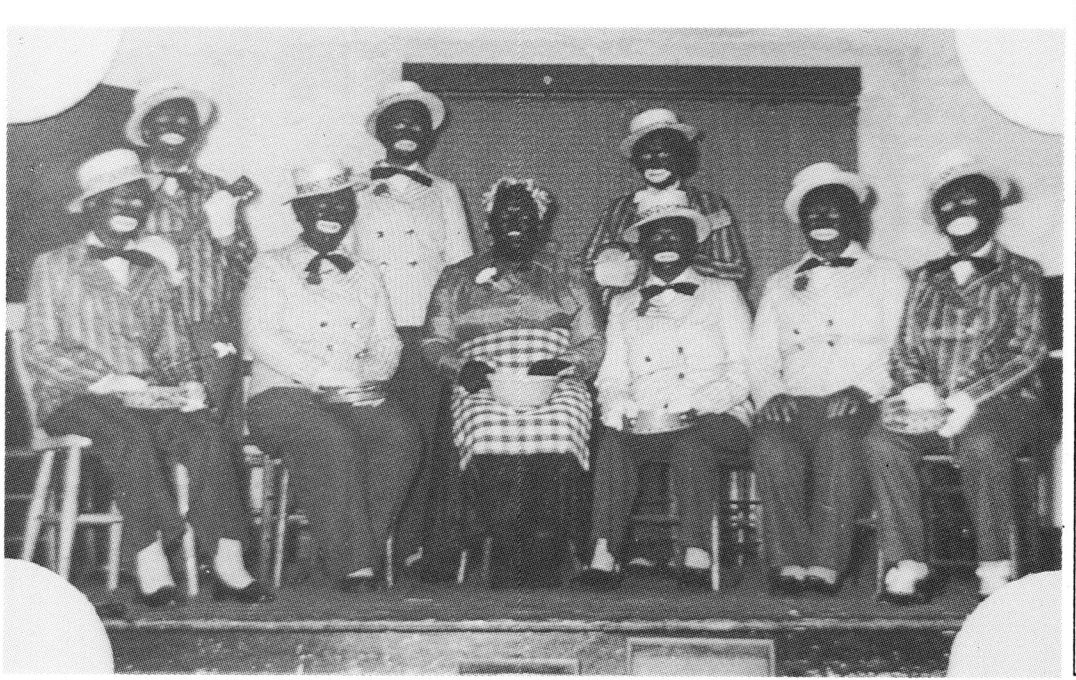

ABOVE: Some of the cast of Bradwell British Legion Minstrel Troupe — standing: Lil Stonton, Kath Dormer, Ruby Bell; sitting: Peggy Millard, Mrs Sherwell, Lily Hughes, Lily Old, Ivy Flippance and Peggy Clarke. BELOW: The Orphean singers at a performance at the Radcliffe School — men, back row: Arthur Webb, Roy Llywellyn, Dick Phillips, Jack Hawtin, Bob Fielding; 2nd row: George Webb, Frank Williams, Tom Weir, Bert Asher, Les Kingston, John Osborne; 3rd row: Derek Fielder, Len Bolton, Hugh Gregory, ?, Bob Bridge; front row: David Marshall, ?, Gordon Malthouse, ?; ladies, back row: Mrs Jones, Kath Jones, Gladys Faulkner, Gladys Hayfield, Mary Maine; second row: ?, ?, Margaret Caudle, Kath Hindley, ?, Elaine Swannell; third row: Rosie Crossman, ?, ?, Terry Rice, Joy Butcher, Jenny Threlfall, Mrs Bolton; front: Joan Crossan, Daphne Purkis, Ethel Hunt, Angela Dytham, Jennifer King, Carol Chambers, ?.

ABOVE: Dance, concert and orchestral programmes. BELOW: The Wolverton Light Orchestra at a Concert at St George's Church, Wolverton 10 June 1986.

ABOVE: The WUDC swimming pool controversy of the late 1930s attracted attention far from the locality. The above cartoon appeared in the *Northampton Chronicle & Echo* in 1937, suggesting ways of overcoming the problem. BELOW: The 'twenty foot' below the Iron Trunk, a favourite bathing spot of yesteryear, looking along the Ouse to Wolverton Mill and Stony Stratford.

That's Entertainment

Everyone looked forward to the annual visits of the travelling fair, gaff and circus.

Between the wars at Stony Stratford the fair was held on the Market Square during August and stretched the length of Silver Street and all around the Green.

Billings' big showman's engine, glittering with polished copper and brass, hauled the roundabouts and other amusements. At Stony Stratford it was always parked at the bottom of the White Horse Yard, its large fly-wheel driving a dynamo that generated electricity for the exotic lighting of the stalls and side shows. It was usually assisted by a similar engine parked behind the police station.

In the middle of the Square was Billings' Galloping Horses with a vertical steam engine in its centre and its famous steam organ, pouring out martial music. Other main attractions were Thurstons' and Abbots' bumpers, Noah's Ark and switchbacks. During the slump the boxing booths thrived; the unemployed tried to earn a few shillings by taking on the fairground bruisers, who were normally punch-drunk ex-pros, also on hard times.

All these attractions were complemented by the traditional swingboats, coconut shies, rifle range, brandy snap and spit rock stalls, the fair people producing the rock by pulling it over and over again on a hook attached to the stall. The first ride each night was free, which ensured that nearly every Stratford schoolchild was present.

Around once a year during the '20s until talkies came to the cinema, fairs were augmented by the travelling 'penny gaffs', or theatres, in Toombs Field at the bottom of the High Street; most frequently performed was *Maria Marten or the Murder in the Red Barn*.

Audience arrangements were primitive: wooden forms and coke braziers. To avoid being choked by the fumes, everyone took a water-soaked handkerchief.

At New Bradwell the travelling fair and theatre came to the fair field, (where the clock tower now stands and before the road diversion).

Towards the end of each year Sangers Circus arrived at Bradwell, erecting its big top in the fair field. Sometimes the circus processed around the streets, led by the band and with the clowns on stilts, camels, dromedary, teams of horses and caged animals. The star of Sangers Circus was Pimpo the Clown, an accomplished equestrian, trapeze artist, tight-rope walker and general comedian, all rolled into one.

With all three townships alongside the Ouse it is no wonder that the river has played a large part in leisure. It offered local anglers first-class sport, for it contained practically every type of coarse fish in the country, plus trout. The fame of the Ouse as a big fish river was founded on its bream and it literally swarmed with roach. Until the Ouse and Cam River Board took over c1930, upkeep was the responsibility of landowners.

All the river from beyond Beachampton to Haversham Mill, and the whole of the canal from Cosgrove to Fenny Stratford plus the Buckingham Arm, until just after the war was controlled by the local angling clubs of Deanshanger and Old Stratford, Stony Stratford, Wolverton and Bradwell. Then the Birmingham clubs began to take an interest in local fishing.

On either bank of the Ouse, meadow land made it perfect for swimming. There were swimming holes galore at Stratford; the Poplars at Passenham Mill, the sluice gate pool at Rogers' mill, 'rhubarb island' at Woods or Wolverton Mill, and the Barley Mow.

Other spots along the river needed a little attention but this was part of a day's swimming for youngsters. First, steps would be cut in the bank, then the reeds would be cut down and with these a raft made and, from a suitable tree, a rope suspended for swinging into the river Tarzan-fashion.

Around 1934 the swimmers who used Rogers' Mill formed a club, which erected changing sheds, provided a spring board and fenced a portion of meadow off. Diving was mainly performed off the top of the sluice gate piers. The 'official' bathing place for the town was the Barley Mow.

The Town Close or Barley Mow Field belongs to the town and is administered by the Street Charity. The bathing place was fenced off pre-1900. Floods gradually washed the bank down and the bathing area silted up. After efforts to repair the damage C.P. Woollard sought the Parish Council's help and they granted £5 toward the costs. But town benefactor Mr Ancell heard about it and instructed Woollard to 'make a good job of the bathing place and send the bill to me!' He called in John Franklin, a Stratford builder, who made and lined the bank with concrete blocks keyed six feet in, with wooden steps into the river. Dressing rooms, lavatories, springboard and a shelter for spectators were built and enclosed by a fix foot corrugated-iron fence.

Here all the schools held their swimming lessons, the County Council paying, and the private schools of the Misses Stockings, Mrs Slade and the Orphanage each contributing. Mr Pratt was caretaker until the war, at a princely wage of seven and sixpence per week (37½p).

At Wolverton the recognised bathing place was below the railway viaduct along the Haversham Road. About a mile upstream a popular place for young men was known as the '20 foot', on the Stratford side and on the Cosgrove bank, just below the aqueduct. Here the canal had originally crossed the river *via* nine locks before the present embankment and aqueduct had been built. There was also a suitable tree for diving.

Bradwell's bathing convenience was at the bottom of the Newport Road Recreation Ground, with changing sheds and springboard, though some used the stretch of the canal from the Old Bradwell road bridge to the eight arches.

In 1936 the Ouse was declared unfit for swimming and school swimming lessons ceased. This caused concern and was the beginning of what was to become a twenty-eight year battle to get a swimming pool for the district.

During May 1937, the Council announced river bathing places were to open, and the demand was so high they felt duty-bound to allow bathing that summer. Rev Claude Coltman said they had been unable to find a bathing pool for Wolverton, the river was unsuitable for bathing and they couldn't afford to test it.

The Council decided to provide new dressing sheds at Bradwell's Newport Road and Wolverton's Viaduct bathing places. At Stony Stratford they built a completely new bathing place on the river along the Calverton Road on Council land next to the pumping station. They dredged a large basin some two feet deep and concreted it for paddling. The line of the old river bank was denoted by concrete posts driven into the river bed at twenty feet intervals. Affixed to these were lifebelts and warning notices.

In July 1937, eight Urban District headmasters wrote to the Council regretting it had not been possible to provide suitable facilities. They could not accept responsibility for sending children to the bathing places. In the 1950s the Orphanage at Stony Stratford built its own pool and allowed district schools to use it.

In the early '30s interest in boating was reawakened by the collapsible canoe. These were built by their owners. In 1920, Rev C.F. Farrar travelled by canoe from the source of the Ouse at Brackley down to the Wash, taking several weeks.

Fred Beales of Stony Stratford decided to emulate this feat during the Wolverton Works holiday week in July 1937, and kept a journal. Fred and his canoe *Zephyr* began their voyage at the Iron

Trunk at Wolverton. He assembled his canoe on Friday evening for an early start the following day. On 3 July Fred began his unusual holiday. As he glided between the rushes to the Wolverton Viaduct he saw the first of the Special Holiday Trains taking Wolverton Works holiday-makers on their more orthodox trip to the seaside. With open water down to New Bradwell he encountered a few fishermen. Beyond New Bradwell to Haversham Mill, he experienced his first portage, then paddled through Linford Bridge to Newport Pagnell and a beer at the Pig and Whistle.

He made good headway to Tyringham and its picturesque barrel bridge and on to Ravenstone Mill, beyond which he passed numerous fly fishermen. He arrived at Olney at 7.30pm, pitched his tent and made his way into town to quench a terrible thirst.

Continuing his voyage the next day he stopped at the Mill Inn, Newton Blossomville for lunch, then passed Turvey in early afternoon and reached Harrold for tea at the Riverside Café. He made camp at Odell. The next day he passed Pavenham *en route* to Kempston Mill and Bedford, where he bivouacked below Cardington Bridge. An early start found Cardington Airship sheds with a solitary observation balloon. Past Willington and Tempsford Bridge to St Neots he ended another day's paddling at a site, for a shilling the night.

The following day, after leaving St Neots it began to rain and Fred was forced to stop and put spray sheets up. At Brampton he was advised he had no right to the river so he pressed on to the Mill House, a further portage, Huntingdon, and an overnight stop in a boathouse. On to Houghton Lock, St Ives and Holywell, with the Boat Inn. He met the only professional fisherman on the Ouse, Bill Metcalf, a fellow canoeist.

Next day saw him bound for Denver, Brawnhill Staunch and the start of tidal water. At Earith Bridge, Fred took a wrong turn, the left fork *via* the New Bedford river instead of the Ouse *via* Ely and Littleport to Denver Sluice, and at Mepal and the Three Pickerels he pitched camp. Whisked along the deep cutting of the New Bedford the next morning he passed the huge St Germains Sluice and, after a struggle through the mud, hauled *Zephyr* up the bank twenty feet to dry ground. Here the New Bedford river (22 miles along) joins the Ouse. Mr Beesley, the sluice gate keeper, warned him against attempting the flood tide, so he awaited the return of the Wissington Sugar Co's tug *Gilgay*, skipper Tom Edwards and mate, Horace Currie of Lynn, who took Fred and *Zephyr* on the last fourteen miles to Bentick Docks. Fred ends his saga thus:

> 'Now my journey of the Ouse is over
> and every mile has been worthwhile
> To you my friends I recommend
> a trip of similar style'.

The bank length of the Ouse from source to Wash is 380 miles.

Pubs and clubs in the Wolverton area were plentiful; rowdiness was rare, and young men could take young women to them. They offered annual outings, 'sweeps', Xmas clubs and sick and divi clubs and were the HQs of many of the Friendly Societies that flourished then.

The pastimes within these licensed premises were varied and well-patronized: crib, solo and nap, dominoes, shove-halfpenny, skittles and darts. At weekends many employed a pianist for sing-songs. Monday night was darts night. The Stony Stratford British Legion formed and ran two leagues, A and B, with a promotion and relegation system. These leagues comprised teams from Stony Stratford pubs (many fielding two) plus those from Old Stratford, Potterspury, Yardley and Cosgrove.

Throughout the winter dart season, team champions were determined by play-offs within teams. One Monday night in mid-season would be set aside to find the all-league champion, either in the Stratford Workmen's Club or the Public Hall. Likewise a team knockout would be held one Monday night for a cash prize and trophy.

The Bradwell League formed by the Bradwell British Legion began with Bradwell pubs but, within two seasons, incorporated Wolverton, Haversham and Hanslope public houses. This league held championship nights for the Chuck Barnard and Goodman Cups.

There were some eighteen pubs, inns and hotels plus two clubs in Stratford during the late 1920s and early '30s. One day, when the penny gaff was in town, one of the clowns was having a drink in the Rising Sun; he commented that there seemed to be a great many pubs for the size of the place, and so someone wrote them down for him.

At the evening performance that day he recited the following: 'The Prince of Wales, accompanied by The Duke of Edinburgh, both wearing a leaf of The Royal Oak, rode past The Foresters Arms, on The White Horse to see The Fox and Hounds meet at The Barley Mow. When they arrived, they found it was a Cock and Bull yarn and The Angel sent a message saying The Case is Altered, and advised them to return with The Crown to The Plough Inn, and dine with George on The White Swan and The Shoulder of Mutton for fear The Red Lion might come along. He had a good night's sleep and did not wake until The Rising Sun shone through the window in the morning.'

Working mens' clubs were something which the middle classes tried and failed to take over. Many were started with the idea of 'improving' the working classes, often in the direction of temperance. But the ones which succeeded were the independent ones, founded and run by working men themselves, without any uplifting motive.

Stantonbury, the first club in North Bucks, began in a small rented cottage in Queen Anne Street as the Stantonbury Social Workmen's Club, opened on 17 February 1894. The furniture and fittings were bought by the clubmen who also paid all the initial expenses. The minutes recall that a kilderkin of ale was purchased for a shilling a gallon and a bottle of whisky for three shillings (15p). A new clubhouse was opened in October 1897, the ground bought by money loaned from members and the building erected by money loaned by an anonymous lady (known as 'brave lady'). Wolverton, encouraged by Stantonbury's success, called a meeting on 11 July 1894, and not long afterwards, 93 Church Street opened its doors as a club.

In those early days many malicious rumours were touted about members of social clubs, who were also thought to be socialists — at that time only desperate people were socialists. To offset this, the management set a high standard of behaviour and the early minutes contain many entries of 'Mr. — be asked to attend the next committee meeting to explain his conduct'.

On 16 July 1898 new club buildings were opened by Mr Garside, club chairman. The secretary of the Club and Institute Union, Mr B.T. Hall, was to have opened the premises, but was late. He had to 'cycle from London to Wolverton and arrived after the opening. Stony Stratford quickly followed Wolverton's example and formed and opened their club in march 1895, at the former White Hart on the Market Square and stayed there until they moved to their present premises in London Road in 1947.

At New Bradwell the clubmen again took the lead and became the first township in North Bucks with two clubs. The Bradwell Liberal and Radical Club was formed in 1906, in the same premises as the Social Club, purchasing the land on which the present club stands some time later. At first they met in an old railway horse box, but in November 1912, new premises were opened, now renamed as the Bradwell Progressive Club. The club was unique in having fishing, bathing and boating facilities. Next came Wolverton Central Club, which moved into its own building straightaway in 1907.

All these clubs had the usual games facilities plus libraries and large concert halls. Family concerts on Saturday and Sunday evenings used mainly local talent but occasional professional shows were staged on Sunday nights, usually travelling, say between Coventry and Oxford Hippodromes.

One Boxing Day the Progressive Club had arranged a concert in the evening for the club pensioners in the upstairs concert room, but unfortunately the heating apparatus had broken down and it was bitterly cold. The pensioners sat in their overcoats. The first act was a bass singer named Fred — and he sang *'When the sands of the desert grow cold'*; he was not well received. He got little applause, and the stage manager commented 'The only appluase you got, Fred, was the O.A.P.s' teeth chattering'. Fred looked through the curtains at the audience and growled 'Bloody lot of swedes'.

At the other end of the age scale, children's treats and outings were given, the parties getting better and the outings further afield as the years went by. During the hard times of the '20s the Progressive Club gave treats which consisted of bread and jam and cake, with perhaps a magic lantern show and a scramble for a few coppers. The treat culminated with an orange and a penny to take home. On one such occasion one lady asked little Sammy Wyatt 'Do you want any more bread and jam, Sammy?' 'Not while all the others are on cake', he retorted.

Stony Stratford got their second club — a Conservative Liberal Unionist Club — in 1914, using the premises just vacated by Mrs Slade's Private School. This was purely a men's club but, around 1950, wives were admitted to one room on Sunday nights only. By 1975 women were allowed to seek membership. One unique feature was a bowls green but by 1971, the march of time had converted this to a car park. Through the '70s and '80s the club prospered, even acquiring a restaurant.

In the mid-'20s a motor-cycle racing club was formed, holding race events with printed programmes in the meadow by Haversham bridge on the Bradwell side on Sunday afternoons. Occasionally meetings were held in Luckett's field along the London Road at Stony Stratford.

Most of the competitors' names have been lost but a few are remembered: Edgar Toombs of Stratford and later landlord of the Swan, Ron Page of Wolverton, 'bus and garage proprietor, Cook from Bletchley, son of the brush manufacturer and Jack Harris from Bradwell.

Motor road racing was also organised — by R. Sellick of Bradwell — on Sunday afternoons; the course, starting at Sellick's garage, went through Loughton onto the A5 to Stony Stratford, then through Wolverton and back to Bradwell.

Another Sunday sport was whippet racing. A Whippet Club was formed at Bradwell with its HQ at the New Inn. Races were held in the Red Bridge field on Sunday mornings before large crowds.

Owners held their dogs in line; their assistants were 200 yards away, holding coloured handkerchiefs. On the words 'Ready', 'Steady', and 'Loose', the starter dropped his arm, the owners released the dogs and their assistants frantically waved their handkerchiefs. Unofficially, of course, betting took place; the club folded just before the war started.

Cinemas became popular during the '30s just after the introduction of talkies, often involving a large queue of around 500. Three cinemas catered for local needs: at Wolverton, the Empire and the Palace, and the Scala at Stony Stratford. Before the Scala, Stratford had the Empire above the old tram shed workshop, still in operation in 1923, when the L & NWR took over the tram company. It was run by a Mr Morgan assisted by a Mr Jackson and was also used for live shows.

The Scala was built by John Franklin, 1922-23, and opened by its owner, Alderman Barber. Built in its own grounds, it was well back from the road with a large area at the front, back and to one side for car parking. Also it was well away from any residential property and would have made an ideal location for a dance hall in place of the Palace in the 1960s. It was managed by T. Moss, his son John Moss managing the Palace at Wolverton. The Mosses lived in the White House next to the Scala. In 1937, the Scala was completely refurbished and the benches that had formed the cheaper seats were replaced by upholstered tip-up seats. The usherettes were issued with maroon uniforms with gold epaulettes as was the commissionaire.

The Scala had a large stage and this was put to good use by various local concert parties and musicians on Sunday evenings. There were no films on Sundays until after the war, and only then after a referendum. The post-war cinema never regained its prosperity so it closed, briefly reopening in 1955, then closing for good on Saturday 22 January 1961. The last film was *The day they gave babies away*.

Wolverton's Palace was opened on Monday 18 December 1911, as Barber's Electric Picture Palace. It worked in tandem with the Scala, closing the same day. The final film here was *The Tattered Dress*.

The Palace did not die completely, for it continued for a short time as a ballroom, bought by Mr E.W. Green of Dunstable, who completely modernised, altered and extended it. On the ground floor the main hall was fitted with strip maple flooring. A gallery was fitted for the musicians facing the larger gallery of the ex-cinema balcony, which led from the Upper Court Bar. The Low Court Bar on the ground floor led from the entrance foyer and cash box. As a dance hall it lasted but a short time and was taken over in 1969 by Zetters Social Club as a Bingo Hall, this in turn closing on November 1988.

Wolverton's other cinema, the Empire, has interesting origins for, at the turn of the century, there was a row of cottages on the site. During the 1914-18 war, their fronts were converted into shops and behind them Fred Tilley opened a toy factory. Then, the front portion was opened as a concert hall with stage facilities. In May 1923 it was refurbished and the entire premises used as a concert hall. Around 1926 the building was again gutted, completely redecorated and it became a cinema. In 1932, further alterations took place and in 1938 it was yet again modified. Like the Scala, it still served as a concert hall, including the staging of West End shows arranged annually by the Technical College's Students' Association. Of the three cinemas the Empire was the last to close. Owners London and Provincial Cinemas sold the building to the Ministry of Works for a future PO extension. In 1969, with the lease running out, it closed its doors for the last time on 17 May, showing *Carry on Screaming*, and *Carry on Cleo*.

Wolverton Amateur Athletic Club was formed in 1885, after the opening of the park in August — a recreation ground purpose-built and gifted to the town by the L & NWR Co. This seven-and-a-half-acre site embraced a 'cycle track, running track, football pitch and tennis and bowls greens. Previously all sporting activities had been held in Stacey Hill farmer Battam's big field along Green Lane.

Wolverton Whitsun Sports were a national event. On Whit Mondays it was local competitors only, but the following day all events were open. Charlie Pearce of Wolverton became world record holder on grass over four miles in 1893.

Up to 1914, the Park was host to many national and county events. In 1919, the WAAC revived the Whit Sports and George White put in his first appearance. He had been wounded at Gallipoli and had a silver plate in his ankle and foot, but on this particular afternoon he won three races. George ran until 1931, winning his last race at Colchester at the age of 42. He was regularly selected for internationals, initially for the 14-mile British Games race in 1924; George was first past the post, beating the best of Europe including the French Arab Djelba, who was third.

During the 1924 season Wolverton Sports became a one-day event and that was the year when 'cyclist Jimmy Knight was selected for the Olympic Games to ride in the 4,000 metres. On 13 March 1926, Wolverton staged the 'National' Cross Country Championships, a three-lap course at the top of Wolverton, set out around Stacey Hill Farm. Wolverton also staged the fourth women's National Cross Country Championships (first held in Luton in 1927), in 1930.

Unique to Wolverton Sports at the time was a character called 'Rhubarb Kingston' of Bradwell. Rhubarb thought he was a walk-race champion and was encouraged by a group of enthusiasts. Sunday mornings would see him in training in all weathers, bowler-hatted, wearing shorts and vest with a number on the latter, and carrying an alarm clock in one hand to time himself *en route*. His normal walking-race action was peculiar; his right arm and right leg and left arm and left leg swung forward together. On advice from one of his 'trainers' he sometimes used his arms like pistons, as he thought, to give him extra speed. His usual course was circular, from Bradwell *via* Haversham, Castlethorpe, Old Stratford, Stony and Wolverton and back to Bradwell. Sometimes he changed his itinerary and went *via* Haversham and Newport Pagnell.

On race days his 'team' would have him in the crowd with all his gear on and he would be given a good rub-down with axle grease. When the walk-race started they would push Rhubarb on the track to a welcoming roar from the crowd. As he passed the finishing post, about six laps adrift, two or three chaps would rush on to hoist him shoulder-high amid acclamation from the crowd, and present him with a trophy of some kind. They would also alter his alarm clock and point out he had nearly broken the world record.

'Sooty' (Tom) Nichols, a cattle drover of Yardley Gobion, was a familiar sight travelling the district with his wife, Aggy. Sooty's party piece was to retrieve pennies from a bathfull of water with his mouth in the local pubs.

If the landlady was in agreement and the company and atmosphere were right, Sooty would be challenged. A bath would be produced, water poured in and pennies tossed in. Tom would get down on his hands and knees, circle the bath growling like a dog, then thrust his head in and, one by one, remove the pennies, after each one giving another growling, barking and circling performance. There was usually more than enough to buy his beer for the evening. As a finale someone would produce a sixpenny piece and place this in the centre of the bath, surreptitiously sticking it to the bottom with soap. After nearly drowning himself, he would eventually get it out.

One day the supporters of 'Rhubarb' and the followers of 'Sooty' arranged a challenge walk-race between the two, to be held in Bury Field, Newport Pagnell one Saturday afternoon. On the day both contestants were in racing strip. Both had been worked up by their respective supporters and they started punching one another at the start line. As the start gun went off they turned Rhubarb around the other way so that both contestants went round Bury Field in opposite directions and, every time they passed one another, they started fighting. After about six laps and roars of applause from the 1,000-plus crowd, both contestants were given prizes and money.

Two outstanding athletics just coming into their own in the '30s were Bradwells' Seabrook and Bert Busby. Bert was a quarter- and half-miler, who went to work at Luton Vauxhall, running for the works team and Luton AC. Now living at Bury St Edmunds, he ran in the 1985 World Veteran Championships in Canada, coming third in the 200 metres 66-70 age group.

After the Second War, the Club got off to a good start with the 1947 Whit sports — 2,500 attended. The 1948 Diamond Jubilee attracted 4,500, but by the early '50s interest had waned and the Club held its last Sports day on 13 June 1953.

However, Wolverton Works continued to hold their sports day and the WAAC competed. By 1962 membership was down to 73, and this lack of interest had a knock-on effect, so that Wolverton Works held its last sports day on 11 August that year. The WAAC left the Park in 1967 and made the Radcliffe School its HQ. In 1976 the club's annual meeting changed its name to Milton Keynes Athletic Club.

None of these athletics could have reached the heights they attained without the support and effort put in by administrators such as Tom Beckett (Trainer), Fred Swain (Secretary and Chairman 1931-47), Sid Coles (Secretary 1931-48) and during the post-war period Geo. Barr (Secretary and Chairman) and Derick Griffiths (Secretary 1950-65).

Football was the major sport in the district. Stony Stratford from 1923 was given a Sports Ground by the Ancell Trust, consisting of tennis, bowls and croquet courts plus a football pitch and cricket square. For some reason Stratford never attained the same glory on the soccer field as did their neighbours, Wolverton and Bradwell. In 1919 Stony Stratford Town were playing in Canvin's field at the top of London Road. This was at the southern end of where the avenues are now built. In Hassell's field another Stratford side played: Wolverton St Mary's.

On the opening of the new Sports Ground in 1923, Stony Stratford Town was renamed Stony Stratford Sports. For a time they played in the North Bucks League, in the late 1920s enjoying some success, joining the South Beds League and winning it. But they were soon back in the North Bucks League, so continuing until 1939. During the war there was no competitive football, but post-war, Stratford became members of the North Bucks Minor and Senior League with the first team in the South Midlands League.

Between the wars Stratford fielded a mid-week team called Stratford Thursdays. This team competed in the Mid-Beds League and comprised mainly shop assistants whose only opportunity of a game was on early closing day. Two of the 'Thursday' players, Austin Birdsey and Charlie Lawman, had trials for Northampton Town.

In 1929 a group of Stratford men formed another football team. Initially they were unable to find a field in Stratford, so they played on the Black Horse field at Old Stratford, making the Swan their HQ. On their first game, an Old Stratfordian called Ratcliffe met them walking to the field and said 'Coming here from Stratford and playing on our pitch you're nothing but a lot of Pirates!'. Thus they became Stony Stratford Pirates. After playing a couple of seasons at Old Stratford in the North Bucks League they managed to find a field in Stony. This was Docker Downing the blacksmith's field and was at the bottom of the Sports Ground. They carried on until 1939.

Wolverton Town was the premier side, although different Bradwell teams have challenged this. Formed in 1886 as Wolverton L & NWRAFC, it competed in the Southern League Division 2, becoming champions in 1895-96, and promoted to Division One, playing teams like Tottenham, Chelsea and London Caledonians.

For a short time the team was called Wolverton Trinity but, in 1902, it became Wolverton Town and the senior side as semi-professionals competed in the South Northants League, the reserves in the Buckingham League. The senior team became champions of the Northants League in the 1913-14 season. After the Great War the Club continued in the South Northants League, the reserves in the North Bucks League and a junior side in the Junior League. In 1932 the Club entered the South Midlands League to become champions in the 1938-39 season.

Reforming after World War II they joined the Spartan League with the reserves in the South Midland League. The first team found immediate success as runners-up on goal average to Huntley and Palmers. The following season saw them in the Premier Division of the Spartan League and they made history by progressing to the 1st Round proper of the FA Amateur Cup.

In 1948 they reached the 3rd Qualifying Round of the FA Cup, defeated by Bedford Town in the Park in front of over 4,000 spectators. The Club finished runners-up to Briggs Sports in the 1951-52 season. In 1957 they reached the Qualifying Round of the FA Cup. 1961 saw them in the United Counties League, but they rejoined the Spartan League for one season in 1982. In 1987 they prefixed the team name with MK.

The Club entered the Athenian League for one season the following year, competing in Division 2 of the Isthmian League. After five seasons in this competition, three of which saw them at the bottom, they once again entered the South Midlands League where they are today (1990).

Over the years Wolverton Town produced first-class football and first-class players and won many honours; Jimmy Frost went to Chelsea, George Henson to Wolverhampton Wonderers, Ernie Fenn to Aston Villa and Bert Russell to Northampton. When Ernie Fenn went to Villa, a cheque for £100 was paid and the Villa first team played Wolverton in an exhibition match down the Park.

Just as the youths of Stratford formed the Pirates so some young men of Wolverton got together to form a side. Among them were Frank Gabell, Sid Willett, Bert Willett and C. Glave, all members of the Congregational Church.

Rev Coltman allowed use of the chapel kitchen as a changing room and for their first season they played friendlies, using Wolverton recreation ground as their pitch, and calling themselves Wolverton Congs. The team joined the North Bucks League, with its HQ at Old Wolverton in the

Locomotive Inn, playing in the field opposite, now the Galleon Estate, but came the war and, like their contemporaries at Stratford, they ceased activities, never to start again.

New Bradwell St James Football Club was founded in the 1890s, its HQ the Foresters Arms. The 'Jimmies' won the North Bucks League for five consecutive seasons up to 1901, when they brought the Berks and Bucks Junior Cup to the north of the county for the first time. The following year they made history by reaching the final of the Berks and Bucks Senior Cup.

The 'Peters' were first named Stantonbury St James, formed by members of St James Church on the Newport Road. Soon after, they were renamed Stantonbury St Peters after the church at Stanton Low. However, up to 1926 their supporters always referred to them as the 'Jimmies'. The ground was on Red Bridge, complete with dressing room and stand.

In 1946-47, they changed their name again when the New Bradwell Corinthians Football Club found themselves in difficulties and merged with the Peters, thus the change from 'Stantonbury' to 'New Bradwell St. Peter'. People make Clubs — trainers like George Odell, Ted Ireson and Tommy Goodger. Behind them were stalwarts like P. Gaskin, player-turned-secretary, Mrs Scragg who did the laundering and for years sold 'penny on the ball' tickets for fund raising, the Dutton family, George Kirk, chairman, followed by Harry Olney and Jim Penman and presidents H. Faithfull and Derricut.

After the Second World War the Club moved from the Red Bridge field to the Mutual Meadow on the Newport Road. At the same time it was asked to vacate its HQ of 50 years, the Foresters Arms, and welcomed to the Railway Tavern by Mr Foddy, and the next landlord, Tom Inwood, until the pub closed down. A Supporters' Club was formed, leaving Reg Pateman secretary of the Football Club and Lionel Turvey secretary of the supporters, which held weekly functions and an annual fête. The team won the Leighton and District Challenge Cup, 1949/50 season and the following year the minor team won the Berks and Bucks Minor Cup. In the 1969/70 season the reserves won the North Bucks League Division 3, and the North Bucks Division 3 Shield, a satisfying double. Then there came a change of ground from the Mutual Field to the Bradwell Road Recreation Ground, using the New Inn for training, then the Progressive Club.

At the time, the Football Club invited the Cricket Club to join them in an effort to build a sports pavilion on the Bradwell Road Recreation Ground. After lengthy discussions with the local council, the venture came to fruition and the New Bradwell Sports Club was officially opened by Councillor Dr Love.

The Club captured the services of Brian Gibbs as team manager in 1975, and under his guidance won the South Midlands League in 1976/77 and 1977/78, the reserve team having a similar success. In the early eighties the 'Peters' were granted senior status.

The predominant figure for thirty years was John Booden, who has worked in every capacity and still found time to be groundsman. The Club's colours are still claret and blue and they are still amateur. The Club's most faithful supporter and worker, who still checks the ground and premises every day, is Bill Callow.

In the mid '30s ladies' football teams were formed. The townships of Stony Stratford, Wolverton, Bradwell, Olney, Bozeat, Wollaston and Bletchley all had teams and played charity matches during the summer months. Mrs Martha Draper formed the Bradwell ladies' football team to provide funds for the Stantonbury Hospital Fund Effort at a meeting at the Newport Road Recreation Ground in 1936; the HQ were at the Morning Star. These teams, complete with their own trainer, (Ernie Lane for Bradwell) played in full kit with leather boots and regulation size football, attracting some 2,000 spectators. The Berks and Bucks FA soon made it known that they objected to any members getting involved, but the Cobblers at Northampton actually enquired about staging a game at the County Ground for charity, though this did not come to fruition. Like many things, these teams ceased to function after 1939, and were not recommenced after the war.

Cricket at Wolverton is recorded first played in Mr Battam's Big Field, which ran parallel with and the length of Green Lane, the cricket square located at its eatern end, approximately on the site of the Elms, a house built for Dr Harvey. Then Mr C.A. Park came to Wolverton as Superintendent of the L & NWR Carriage Department at Wolverton Works in 1885. He was a keen cricketer and a capable bat, and through his exertions Wolverton obtained a fine ground. He was also instrumental in persuading the Directors of the L & NWR Co to build a pavilion. On 18 may 1901, he opened the New Cricket Ground with a game between Wolverton Trinity CC and Stantonbury CC (Trinity won by five runs). The town side supplied seven players to Bucks County during the twenties, these being Bill and Frank Adams, Jack and Frank Whiting, Dave Mackey, E.T. Brocklehurst and H. Jennison. Also Jonah Brown and Jack Timms both played for Wolverton before gaining their places in the Northants County side, the former becoming its Captain.

In the decade leading up to the last war, Wolverton Town Cricket Club's 1st XI fixture list included an annual day match with Northants County Cricket Club at Wolverton. All proceeds went to Northampton General Hospital. The county's side always included a number of well-known county players and the home team had its own stars, E.T. Brocklehurst, Nigel (L.N.) Smith, Frankie Brown.

The match took place in glorious weather on Saturday 16 September 1933, before a good crowd. Duncan Wills, the Wolverton captain, won the toss and elected to bat. Things went well, Brock reached his fifty and lunch arrived with the score at 128 for two. At about 2.45pm Brock reached his century and at the mid-point Wills declared at 246 for eight. E.T. Brocklehurst was not out 143, L.N. Smith made 35, C.H. Piper 20 and F.H. Brown 17. Northants' opening pair, F.G. Watts and N. Grimshaw, began cautiously against the bowling of Johnny Eales and Syd Goodridge. The first wicket fell at 100 after 70 minutes. There was obviously some concern about the run rate in the visitors' camp. The new batsman appeared keen to rectify this. He had not been at the crease many minutes when Wills, from the rec end, bowled a no-ball. The batsman went for his shot, middled it and up it went. The crowd gasped at the height it reached. 'Six' some cried without fear of contradiction. On it went, easily clearing the boundary in front of the tea pavilion, then down, down it sped, landing smack on top of a little boy's head. Horror. Silence.

Someone screamed. The boy, Ted Ellery, eight-year-old son of Mr and Mrs C. Ellery of 34, Church Street, Wolverton, yelled and everyone, including the players, moved to console him. Fortunately, Dr P.B. Atkinson of New Bradwell was on the ground. He took the Ellerys to Northampton Hospital where Ted was admitted, suffering from concussion. He was kept in hospital for several days.

The game, scarred by this accident, continued. The scoring rate improved. Another wicket fell. With 25 minutes to go the county still needed 50 runs to win. They eventually won with a few minutes to spare, and 259 for four wickets. It had been a wonderful day's cricket. 505 runs were scored. Brock made a century; F.G. Watts nearly did. On a good batting wicket and against first-class opponents, Goodridge bowled brilliantly (finishing with one wicket for 32 runs). The weather played its part. All in all it was a memorable day's cricket yet, few people remember it but they all remember the little boy being hit on the head by a cricket ball.

That little boy later won a state scholarship to Oxford University. He did not gain a cricket blue, or play for Merton College or play for anyone else, as far as I know. Edward Ellery MA was probably just too busy.

Cricket at Bradwell was played on the Red Bridge field until after the Second War. In 1947 the Club moved to the Bradwell Road Recreation Ground. Before the Club entered League cricket in 1982, all its games were friendlies. These friendly games were not without incident. It was in the mid-twenties and Bradwell were playing away to Crawley, travelling in Derricutt's charabanc, with Derricutt as driver; he was also Bradwell's umpire. The game started but, after an hour's play, a swarm of bees settled in a nearby hedge. Now Derricutt was a keen beekeeper and always carried his kit with him in case of such an occurrence. He stopped the game, collected the swarm, put them in the chara and then started the game again. There was hardly room to fit eleven men in the chara, but on this day on the way home only the bees had ample room. Stony Stratford's cricket team only played friendlies and in the 1980s they too entered League cricket.

Wolverton and District has always been proud of its allotments. Flower and horticultural shows were an annual attraction. All the clubs ran shows as did one or two public houses, the Printing Works and the Railway Works. The Wolverton and BR Horticultural Society first met on 21 October 1953, and held its first annual show on 14 August 1954, and its last in 1987.

The North Bucks and BR Chrysanthemum and Dahlia Society was formed in 1947, holding its first show in 1948. When the Railway Canteen was no longer available, the society held its last show in October 1989. A century earlier, the Wolverton Horticultural, Floral and Beekeeping Society was founded in 1890, and held an annual show down the Park, midweek, for many years.

In the early twenties special seed peas were being grown in a field at Stacey Hill Farm, some eight to nine feet high. One young man took home a handful of pods to show his father, reputedly with twelve to fourteen peas *per pod*. His father saw the potential and went to collect enough for seed; on his second trip he was caught by the farmer and locked in a stable tackroom until the police arrived. While in the tackroom the man, Webster by name, was in such a temper he began slashing the harness. For this offence and pea stealing he was charged and convicted, but the peas survived and were grown all over the district under the name of 'Webster's Downfall'.

Then there was the camaraderie of the Cubs and Scouts and Brownies and Guides.

The first Guide Company in the area was started in Wolverton in 1919 by Miss Sylvia Harnett of Wolverton Vicarage, later Commissioner Harnett. This was quickly followed by York House School Company, Stony Stratford with Miss Enid Walton as Captain (later Mrs H.E. Meacham).

By 1922, 1st Wolverton Rangers had been formed, again with Miss S. Harnett as Captain. On November 1928, *The Bucks Herald* reported on the service of dedication of the County and District Commissioners' standards of the Buckinghamshire Girl Guides. The standards were made the previous year for the county competition by Guiders and Guides. Wolverton District's original banner is still paraded at this Annual County Banner Service. When it was made, every Guide and Guider in the District did a stich towards it. Wolverton District also still have their original Union Jack (1919/1920).

The Rangers organised dances in the Science & Art Institute, Wolverton, where one raised £20 for St Dunstans. An annual good turn was to clean the Wolverton War Memorial prior to the Remembrance Day Service. A Scout and Guide Club flourished for some years at Wolverton and produced its own magazine *Pow-Wow*.

The District has had only two Presidents from the 1920s to the present day, the first being Mrs. H.E. Meacham; she was succeeded by Mrs Mary Webb (née Jakeman) who can recall, when as a Brownie, they met in the eerie Apple Loft at St George's Vicarage.

After all the difficulties of four years of the Great War, scouting in the urban area was strong in youngsters, particularly in Stony Stratford and Wolverton. They lacked leaders because most had been in the Forces. Gradually those returning from the war once again took up scouting. Eventually a district was formed in 1920, covering a larger area than the Urban District, from Deanshanger to Newton Blossomville. This was under Oswald Hamilton as District Commissioner, 'Pa' Holloway as District S.M. and Bob Fisher, Secretary. Mr T.G. (Tommy) Dicks was a member of the Committee. This team stayed together until the early '30s, when the District was re-drawn.

Wolverton also gave charitable concerts in the winter with their Concert Party, The Gilwellians, and summer displays. In the 1920s they acquired the use of an old quarry between Old Stratford and Cosgrove. They worked hard on this and in 1928 the then owner, Mrs Ager of Cosgrove Hall, gave it to the Scouts for their own District Camp Site.

Baden-Powell, the Chief Scout and founder of the movement, visited the District Rally in 1923 at Old Wolverton and was overwhelmingly received by hundreds of Scouts in camp. He also visited Gayhurst in 1933, the house of their County Commissioner, Sir Walter Carlile Bt, a personal friend, and inspected the 1st Wolverton Scouts in camp.

For many years both 1st Stony Stratford and 1st Wolverton had been raising money to build their own HQs. Eventually 1st Stony Stratford was opened in 1937 and 1st Wolverton in 1939. Both halls have proved a boon to both town's inhabitants.

After the Second World War, scouting again took off, with R. Saunders and W. Coxhill at Wolverton and T. Dicks and his son George at 1st Stony Stratford. At Stony Stratford Mrs C.M. Campbell formed a new group, the second group to be numbered the 2nd, succeeded by Ken Edwards (Boy Scouts) with Joy Small and Audrey Waine (Wolf Cubs). Dick Saunders was then the District Commissioner and had been for some years — he was also Assistant County Commissioner, and was in charge of all Cubs in the County. 2nd Stony Stratford ran their own Gang Shows for several years in the 1950s.

There was a Group at New Bradwell from the early 1920s under the leadership of Rev J.H. Walton. When he left the area in the late '20s, various leaders from Wolverton kept the Group functioning. There has always been a Cub Pack but Scouts had difficulties until World War II. They were reformed as a complete Group in 1947 with F. Bird as Scoutmaster. In 1963 this lapsed, re-starting in 1964.

Eventually, owing to the loss of Gayhurst to the Wolverton Scouts, the Quarries, under the wardenship of G. Dicks, became the District Camp Site and Training Ground. Wolverton had a successful year in 1956, winning the International Shooting Connaught Shield, open to all Scouts worldwide and they won the County Rifle competition for many years under the expert leadership of Tom Smith (ASM). Father Tommy Dicks and son George Dicks of 1st Stony Stratford were both awarded the Medal of Merit.

Fred Beales in his canoe *Zephyr*.

ABOVE: The Barley Mow bathing place, Stony Stratford c1930; on the extreme left is Joan Nicholls; third from left, front row Alice Coles and Molly Atkins centre, behind the first row, wearing a white bathing hat. LEFT: The White House, Stony Stratford was the pre-war residence of the Moss family, with its semi-circular drive, and the Scala battlements showing through the trees. RIGHT: Standing alongside the Scala Cinema, the Palace and Scala advertising car had a removable box which encased the vehicle; upon it was advertised the week's programme. This travelled around the district weekly.

ABOVE: The Empire Cinema, Wolverton pre-war, and BELOW: post-war.

120

LEFT: The Railway Tavern, closed in 1960, and demolished soon after in 1961, seen here as it was in 1922, with the then proprietor Mr B. S. Garrett and his cousin from Australia who was visiting him. RIGHT: The Morning Star, New Bradwell c1935, prior to the re-aligning of the Newport Road in 1938. This establishment closed in December 1970 and was demolished some twelve years after. BELOW: The County Arms Inn at Corner Pin c1919, still a Hipwell's Brewery house; the Olney Brewers sold out to Phipps of Northampton in 1921.

ABOVE: The New Inn (known as the War Office) as it was between the wars under the tenancy of Tommy Squires. It was also the HQ of the New Bradwell Whippet Club. BELOW: The New Inn darts team c1955 — standing: Vic Ewens, Arthur Godfrey, Frost, Bill Preston, Mick Emerton, George Odell; sitting: Odell, Bill Taft, Sam Tuckey.

ABOVE: The Morning Star darts team c1957 — standing: Jeff Lines, Reg Howe (landlord), Frank Owen, Alec Levitt, Arthur Godfrey, R. Shrimpton, ?, Ede Howe (landlady); sitting: Vic Ewens, George Hedge, Jack Smith and Slogger Burnell. BELOW: Stony Stratford British Legion Darts League Committee of 1950, photographed with the trophies of that year: Fred Cox, Edgar Tyler, Bob Lake, Bert Preston and Billy Lamb.

124

OPPOSITE ABOVE: Children's party at Stony Stratford Workmens' Club c1957 — lady organisers: Mrs Blair, Mrs Pearce (stewardess), Mrs Gregory, Rita Westcott, Mrs Webster, Mrs Shakeshaft, Mrs West and Mrs Nichols. LEFT: Stantonbury Working Mens' Social Club, c1919. RIGHT: The Galleon Inn lounge as it was from 1938 until the early 1960s. BELOW: The Bradwell Social Club 'cycle club line up for their photograph before going off for a spin. ABOVE: The founder members of the Bradwell Progressive Club outside their first premises at No 2 Queen Anne Street. BELOW: One of the Bradwell Social Club's winning quoits teams.

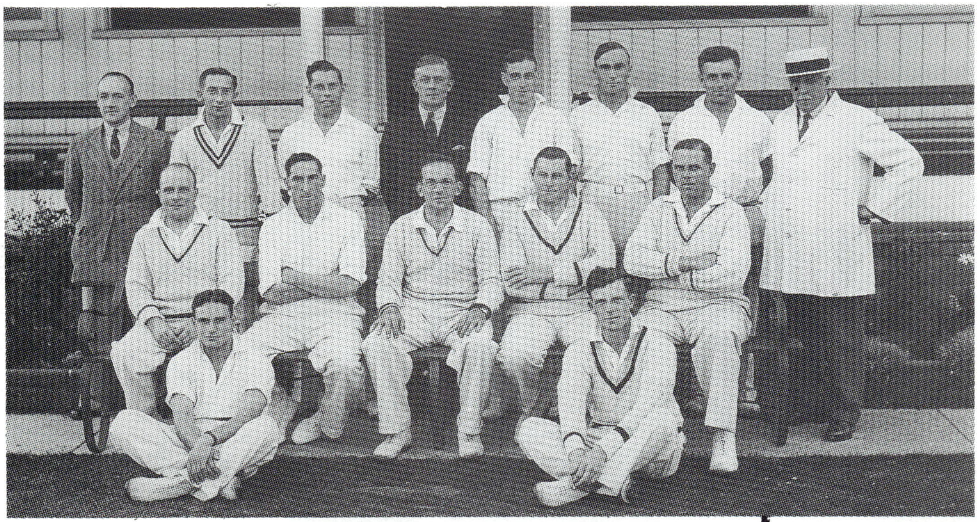

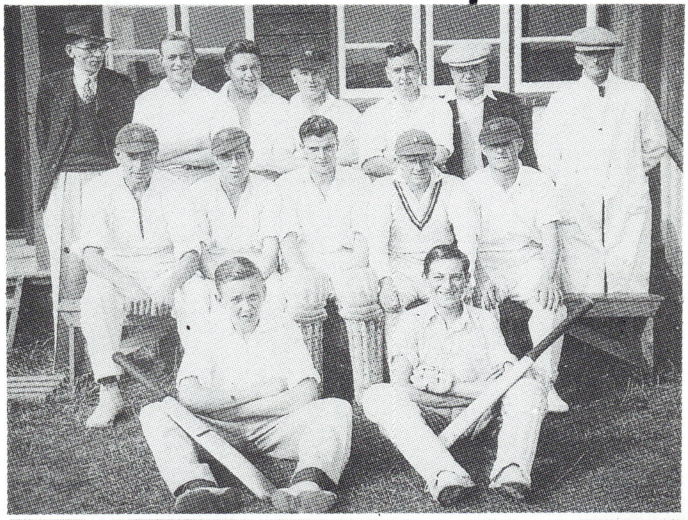

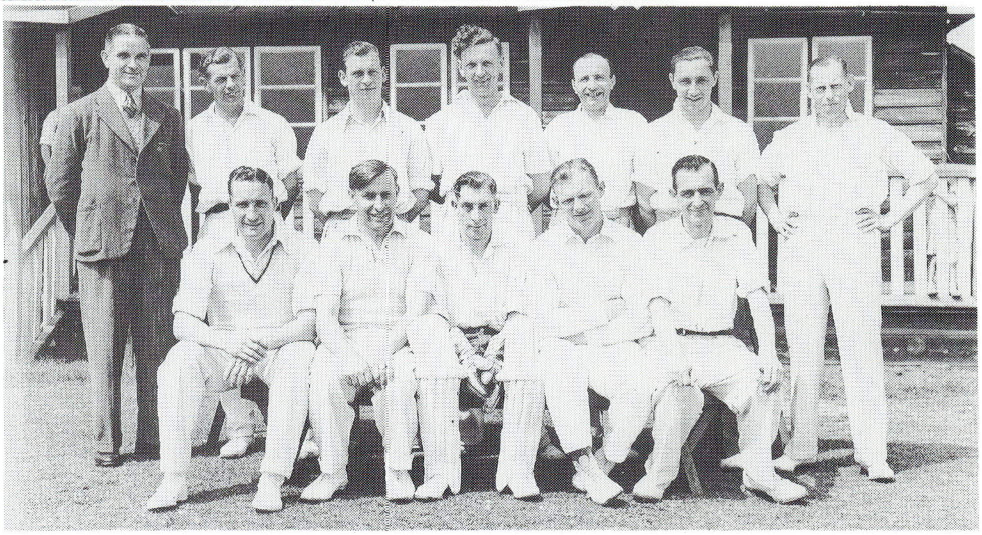

OPPOSITE ABOVE: Wolverton Cricket Team, c1933 — standing: Paul Wills, Syd Goodridge, Harry Culver, ?, Johnny Eales, Ernie Brocklehurst, John Davis, ?; sitting: Cyril Piper, E. T. Brocklehurst, Duncan Wills (Captain), Frank Brown, L. N. Smith; front: Frank Brown and Cyril Dormer. CENTRE: New Bradwell CC, c1937 — standing: Ted Bennett, Eddie Dillon, Frank Chapman, Bill King, George Wood, George Odell, Fred Lane; sitting: Bill Tapp, Ernie Cook, Boughton, Jack Pimbley, Vic Gray; front: Norman Lloyd and Fred Lane. BELOW: The McCorquodale Printing Works Team c1950 — standing: Len Squires, Percy Shouler, Albert Kightley, H. Lloyd, Les Sims, Reg Russell, Harry Culver; sitting: R. Hillesden, Harold Russell, F. Kightley, George Sterman and H. Walker.

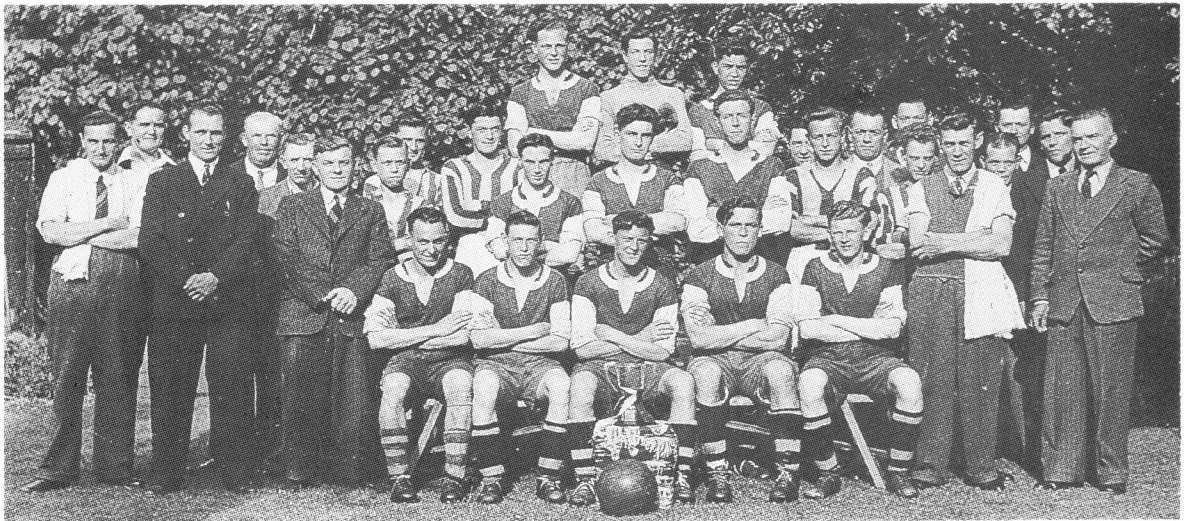

ABOVE: Stantonbury St Peter's AFC season 1923-24 winners, Leighton and District Football Competitions, Stantonbury Hospital Cup, Runners-up North Bucks League (Div 1), Leighton and District League — back row: A. Cole, J. Scragg, P. Markham, F. Scott, E. Old, C. Coleman, P. Clamp, H. Blunt; second row standing: G. Boughton, J. Ager, C. H. Scott, P. Lines (Capt), W. Boughton (Capt), H. Lewis, C. Jakeman, C. Atkinson, C. Lister, W. Green, R. Barton; 3rd row sitting: S. Coles (Sec), G. Odell (Trainer), C. Eakins, F. Strong, L. Eakins, W. Wildman, B. Nash, F. Massey (Asst Trainer), F. Fancutt (Chairman); front: F. Haynes, P. Walker, A. Watson, C. Brice and C. Wood. BELOW: Stantonbury St Peter's Minor Team, winners of North Bucks Minor League 1946-47 — back row: Tony Hillyer, Rex Atkinson, Tony Stobie; second row: Mowy Dix, Den Lockwood, Den Willett; front row: Pete Riley, Ron Kelly, Bob Varney, Brian Poynter, Ken Coast; reserves in stripes: Lionel Stobie, Ted Parker, D. Gibbons, Tim Atkins, Rob Atkins; officials: Walt Haynes, Len Clarke, Harold Bates, Ted Kirk, ?, Harry Olney, Ted Glenn, Ron Smart, Pete Royce, Tommy Goodger, Dick Herbert, George Jones and Dick Jones.

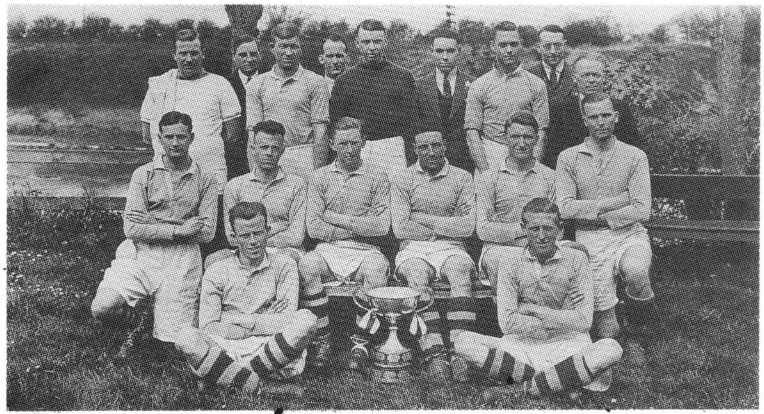

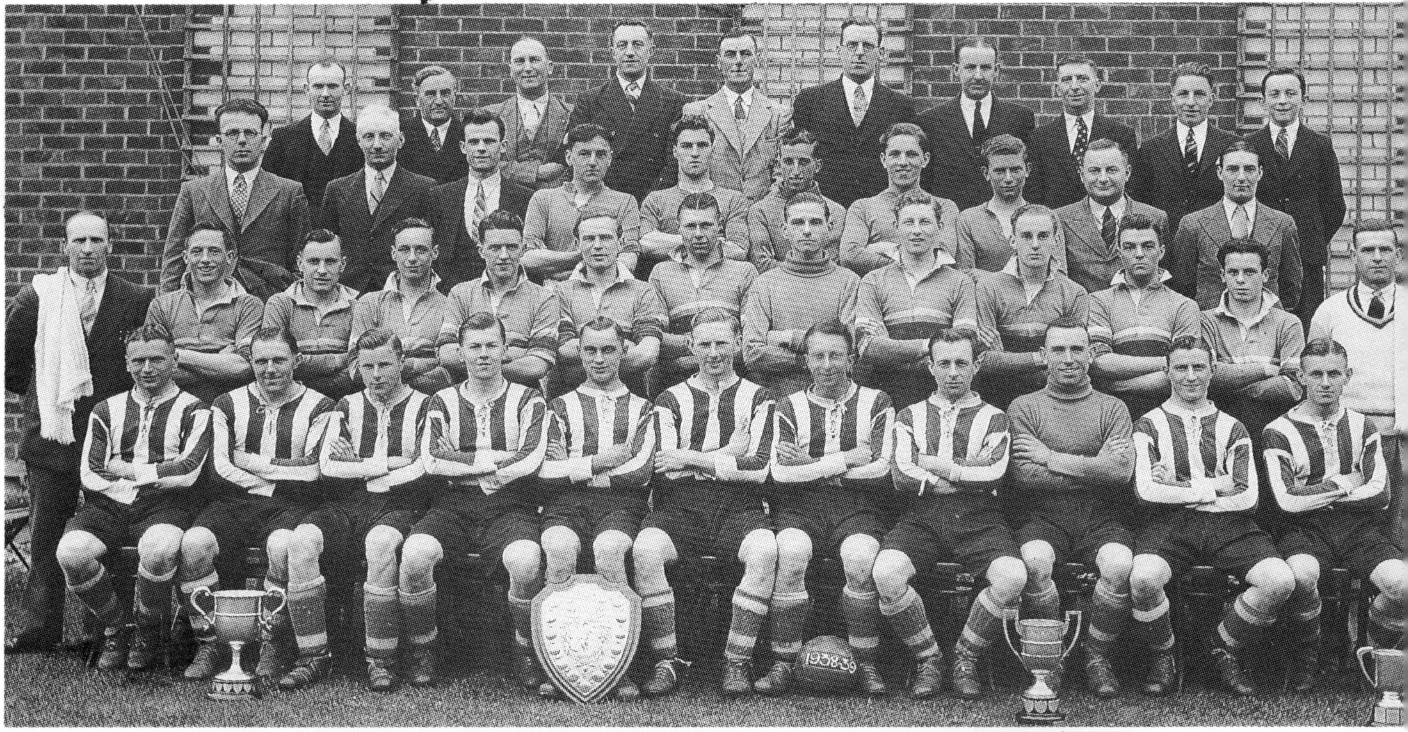
1938-39

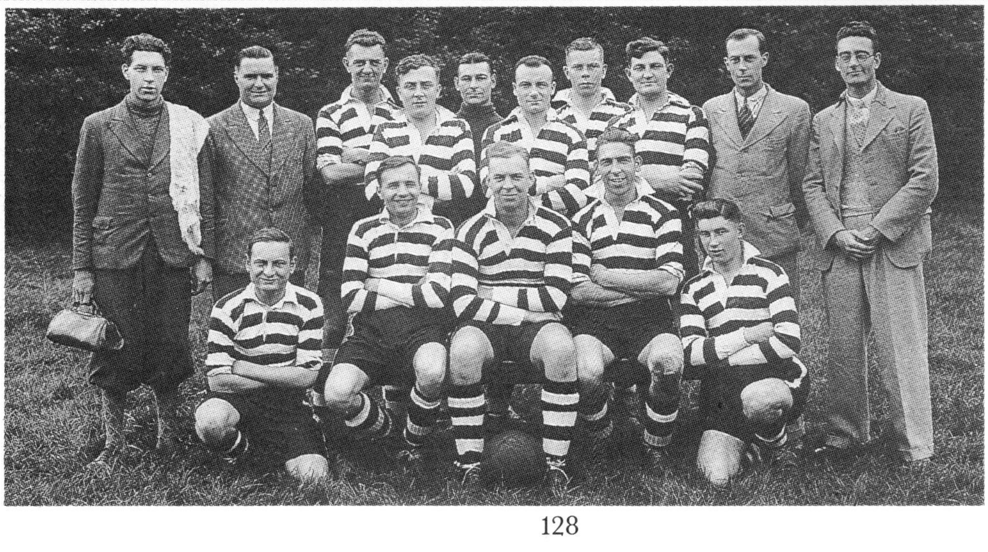

ABOVE: Wolverton Congregational Juniors FC Season 1935-36, Winners of Bletchley Hospital Cup, Stantonbury Hospital Cup, Runners-up North Bucks League (Div 1), and Divisional finalists in the Berks and Bucks Junior Cup — standing: S. Tuckey (Trainer), Rev Claude M. Coltman (President), C. Glave, J. Jones (Committee), E. Bull, S. Willett (Committee), E. Reynolds, H. Willett (Chairman), B. Henson (Linesman); seated: G. Frost, V. Gee, J. Cooper (Capt), H. Franklin, O. Tole, E. Hall; front: L. Gee (Hon Sec) and F. Miles. CENTRE: Wolverton Town 1st and 2nd Teams, Officials and Committee, 1938-39 season — back row: Walker, J. Tearle, J. Smith, R. Eales, S. Morley, J. Durdin, C. Goodridge, A. Crook, M. Brock, Pratt; 2nd row: C. Harding, J. Atterbury, J. Dormer, Gregory, P. Henson, M. Emerton, J. Williams, C. Nichols, D. Frost, R. Brown; 3rd row: J. Atkinson (Trainer), R. Dicks, W. Russell, G. Pollard, R. Frisby, D. Andrews, H. Brooks, J. Westley, S. Yates, D. Parker, W. Cheney, K. Dormer, Ratcliffe (Trainer); front row: Evans, F. Sayers, S. Tubbs, C. Lawman, A. Russell, J. Cowper, G. Eales, G. Dicks, W. Cook, C. Morley and J. Smith. BELOW: Stratford Pirates, c1938 — standing: Sid Andrews (Trainer), Ted Southam, Les Clarke, Fred Key, Wilf Canvin, Jack Fawson, Bill Clarke, Ted Waine, Bill Andrews, Bill Wyatt; seated: Les Sims, Buff Rogers, Dick Holland; kneeling: Bill Watts and D. Lancaster.

ABOVE: New Bradwell Ladies' Football Team — standing: Mrs Draper, Muriel Coles, Betty Draper, Violet Dowdy, Stella Bowdler, Vera Owens, Mary Spencer, Mrs Walton; front row: Doris Cook, Jean Sanders, Norah Levitt, Rene Martin and Lily Sayell. CENTRE: Danny Roberts far left and senior scouts of the 2nd Stony Stratford troop in their *Gang Show* of c1953 held at St Giles & St Mary's School: An Hawaiian scene, singing the Hawaiian song, *Bambazulian Way* — back: Pete Roberts, Bill Barby, Brian Taylor, Arnold Richards, Ken Jelley, Dave Brown; front: Geof Fulcher, Ken Savage and Tony Henson. BELOW: Stony Stratford 1st Scouts at Camp at Clacton, 1937.

ABOVE: Up the quarry — all shoulders to the development of the site; Oswald Hamilton (Hiawatha) talking to a young local scout, and Walt Parker (Wanbeek) next to Hamilton, holding the thumb stick. BELOW: York House School Girl Guides of 1919; third from left middle row, Miss Edith Walton, later Mrs Meecham.

Community Spirit

Community spirit has always been strong in the district. Before the introduction of the National Health Scheme, hospital, doctors' care and fear of being sick and off work were perhaps the main concern.

In 1872 the Bradwell Good Samaritan Society was formed, its HQ the Foresters Arms. For one penny per week membership, this covered the cost of hospital treatment as an in or out patient for the member and his family. Later it became the Bradwell and Wolverton Good Samaritan Society, until the NHS in 1945. After this date, for an annual subscription of one shilling, members were able to borrow if need be, sick room requisites, such as bath chairs and commodes. After 115 years' service this Society was dissolved in 1987.

Backing this local society up were the larger societies of the Ancient Order of Foresters, the Oddfellows, Hearts of Oak and National Deposit. But locally the one with the largest membership was the L & NW Railway Provident Society to which belonged most of the men in the Works.

New Bradwell were to the fore in support of the Northampton Hospital: in 1904, the Stantonbury Hospital Fund was founded. The main event of the year was the Whit-Monday Fête, held in the Newport Road Recreation Ground. Perhaps the most outstanding feature was the carnival. In 1939, the 25th annual effort for Northampton Hospital, 150 children and young people presented a non-stop revue, *Picturesque and Burlesque Scenes at Home and Abroad*. The Carnival Queen was crowned, in the presence of the Indian Prince and his Indian Princess, who had jointly held office during the previous 12 months.

During the cross-country race, the Bradwell Band toured the streets and collected for the hospital. A crowd of over 600 congregated near the Post Office in the High Street to see the finish. The winner was Frank Stephenson, second was his brother George, closely followed by Ron Tilley and Lionel Exley. Miss Edna Lindon was appointed Carnival Queen by popular vote. All the equipment was owned by the Hospital Committee and stored in an old railway carriage body alongside the Morning Star fence.

Wolverton Hospital Fête began on the square with all the decorated floats in readiness for the parade down to the Park and the main attraction was a sports meeting for all age groups. Before the building of Marina Drive and Gloucester Road, the fêtes were held in the Stacey Hill Recreation Ground.

Midway through the sports, the Wolverton Works Fire Brigade did their party piece. This consisted of the erection of a mock-up house, with scaffolding within. The house was set afire, the whistle sounded and the horse-drawn fire engine (until 1934 and thereafter a motor fire escape) galloped on, the escape went up, for within the building were two firemen dressed in night shirts; these were rescued, one by fire escape and the other by safety net, amid cheers.

It was not until 1920 that Stony Stratford formed a Hospital Committee and set their sights on a spectacle as good as or better than Wolverton or Bradwell. Fête day began with a carnival parade headed by both Stratford Scouts and Town Bands. The Fête itself was held in Toombs' field. The main attraction was a detachment of mounted troops from the Military Equestrian School at Weedon, who gave displays with lance and sabre. Horse-drawn gun teams simulated action, ending their show with a musical ride. Pack mules belonging to the Mountain Artillery also figured plus the ominous figure of the recruiting sergeant. Stony's first effort raised some £700. Stratford kept this theme for many years as did Wolverton with their 'house fire'; Bradwell were more versatile, changing their topic annually.

When the military were not available, Stony held fêtes at three other venues, the Sports Ground, Colonel Hawkins' garden but mainly in Dr Habgood's field at the rear of his house along the Calverton Road.

Other events were held at all three townships to support the Hospital Fund. Mrs Draper of Bradwell ran weekly whist drives in her house along St Mary's Street. Both Wolverton and Bradwell ran knock-out football tournaments annually, called the Wolverton Hospital Cup and the Stantonbury Hospital Cup.

When the National Health Scheme came into being in 1948, the Hospital Fund ceased to function. Bradwell continued its Whit Fête for quite a few years after this but not on such a grand scale as pre-war. The two Hospital Cups are still competed for in the guise of Charity Cups.

When the Bradwell branch of the British Legion held a discussion in 1946 as to what would be a fitting memorial to the fallen, it was decided to build a Memorial Hall. Dances and whist drives were held to raise funds and a suitable location was sought. The fund-raising kept going apace but an appropriate site was not so simple. Then it was agreed to erect a Clock Tower. The UDC was approached and this resulted in a strip of land between the old and new Newport Roads being designated for the tower and memorial gardens. The Council prepared the flower beds and the British Legion supplied rose bushes. Bradwell Band donated two teak seats for the memorial garden. The tower was quickly erected by Tarrant and on Sunday 2 September it was dedicated; Dr Love unveiled a plaque. The total cost was some £1,700, the British Legion also donating a cheque for £200 to the UDC, to be invested towards maintenance costs. In October 1962, the Bradwell British Legion also purchased and fitted a memorial wrought-iron gateway for the Memorial Hall at Old Bradwell.

Perhaps the most controversial and long-running subject (after housing), that the WUDC dealt with during its time, was the swimming pool. The river was declared unfit for bathing in 1937. Rev Claud Coltman failed to gain re-election to the Council in 1938 due to his progressive ideas and views on the swimming pool issue. Through his insistence the UDC applied in 1938 for a 50 per cent grant for a pool from the National Fitness Council. Plans were agreed along with the grant and it was only the oubreak of war that stopped it.

For the first five years after the war, housing was the priority. In the '50s noises were again made for a swimming pool. Stony Stratford Chamber of Trade asked the Council for £6,000 to build a learner tank for children. This brought forth protests both from Wolverton and Bradwell residents. The Council then had second thoughts and reversed their decision, this resolution backed by Stratford Councillor P. Cosford, which pleasantly surprised the Wolverton and Bradwell protesters.

It was shortly after this that Wilf Amos of Bradwell read in the *Northampton Echo* of a similar situation at Daventry. Wilf and Reg Pateman phoned the man who had organised Daventry's fund-raising, who told them all the steps they would have to take, one of which was to apply to the Home Office for permission to make street collections.

The next step was to call a public meeting. In a packed Labour Hall the motion to seek weekly subscriptions was passed and a committee formed. The Bradwell Labour Party gave the Bradwell Swimming Pool Organisation free use of its printing facilities and made no charge for the Hall, which became its HQ for meetings, plus a donation of £100 to get the fund off the ground. This was followed by all the other organisations contributing. The schools put on plays and raffles and the committee of twelve were allocated so many streets each.

After nine months, the Committee was approached by Harry Winsor and J. Cornwell of Wolverton, so Wolverton could make a similar effort. They then called a Wolverton public meeting which achieved a similar response to Bradwell. The Wolverton Swimming Pool Association got under way.

On 17 November 1963 work began on the Open Air Heated Swimming Pool at Wolverton, culminating in its official opening on the 1st day of August 1964. The man who inspired the WUDC of his day to go ahead with a swimming pool, was chosen to open it — Rev Claud M. Coltman. Among the guests were the committee members and voluntary collectors of Wolverton and Bradwell Swimming Associations who subscribed over £4,000 between them. The chairman of the New Bradwell Swimming Pool Organisation handed over a cheque for £1,544-14s-4d, for the Chairman of the Wolverton Swimming Association could not be present. Mr G Taffs handed over a cheque for £1,400 from weekly collections; donations and other receipts amounted to another £1,200 and another £112 were also in hand, a total of £2,560 8s 3d. The first three swimmers in the pool (all off the top board) were Ted Cowley of Bradwell aged 75, Frank Bates of Wolverton aged 74 and Bill Alderman (56) of Bradwell. This was followed by a gala arranged by the North Bucks Amateur Swimming Association.

The Wolverton Area Grand Carnival Parade and Gala Fête came into being in 1963; organised by the Wolverton Freedom from Hunger committee, it attracted over 2,000 onlookers and proceeds were £370. In March 1964, an independent committee was formed with forty members, chaired throughout its fourteen years by Frank Atter; R. Staley was secretary for eight years, Mrs Hewitt one year then Dennis Young for five years. In 1966 an advisory committee was set up to decide the allocation of funds.

The start to carnival day was a morning parade through Bradwell by the Bradwell contingent, a like parade by the Stratford section around their town, then the two portions joined Wolverton's formation at Wolverton for the main procession. As the years progressed this magnificent spectacle got bigger and better. It supplied a mini-van to the local RWVS meals-on-wheels service and help toward a second one; a replacement ambulance for the Wolverton St John Ambulance Brigade, guide dogs for the blind and assistance toward the Red Cross appeal for the elderly. The 1976 Carnival was the last; as no new blood came forth to assist the veteran organisers, it was agreed to call it a day.

Aubrey Barby, mine host of the White Horse, Stony Stratford for forty years was also perhaps the most popular landlord of his period. A native of Wicken, he became the inn-keeper in 1933 and from then on, it was always referred to as 'Barby's'. He had a unique way of calling time; 'Come on Whiting the puddings done!' which went back to his early days and one Sunday lunchtime when Stratford's Teddy Whiting was enjoying his Sunday lunchtime appetizer; on the stroke of two o'clock (then closing time), Teddy's wife put her head around the door and shouted, 'Cum on Whiting the pudduns dun'.

In the mid-1950s the White Horse organised a Flower Show in aid of the Renny Lodge Hospital patients. This developed into an annual event and continued until 1974, through the White Horse Sports and Social Club; it was always held on the first Saturday in June and called 'Charity Lane'. This organisation of young workers raised funds not only for Renny Lodge but presented three electric wheel chairs and a collection of equipment to Stony Stratford Health Centre, made donations to the Red Cross, Stoke Mandeville Hospital and the Jubilee Appeal.

During 19 and 20 May 1973, the White Horse Sports and Social Club got themselves into the Guinness Book of Records for pram-pushing. A sixty-strong club team covered the greatest distance in pushing a pram, 319 miles in 24 hours, on the 'cycle track at the Wolverton Park. The Club discontinued in 1985, but three of its members transferred their enthusiasm and experience to the Stony Stratford Association, an off-shoot of the Stony Stratford Chamber of Trade. In the late 1960s a town meeting was called in the old Fegans Homes gymnasium, to voice the concern of the town at the many adverse proposals that the MK Corporation wished to implement.

The response to the meeting by the residents was overwhelming and a committee was formed under the chairmanship of John Lane; Maurice Howell was elected secretary. Its first task was to pressurize the MK Development Corporation into retaining the character of the place. The first confrontation concerned the Health Centre, which was originally planned to be on one of the new estates, thereby leaving Stony Stratford without a doctor. After strong representation, the Health Centre was built in the town.

In 1972 under the leadership of Peter Cosford the Stony Stratford Town Fayre was formed, to raise money for a town community centre. This Fayre was held on the Green and stallholders split any profits 50/50 between themselves and the community hall appeal. After a while this agreement was changed to a charge of £5 per stall plus a prize toward the day's raffle. In April 1976 the town acquired a large community hall, converted from the Church of Wolverton St Mary, that had closed in 1968. In 1989 The Town Fayre was a joint effort between the Stony Stratford Association and the Stony Stratford Lions. This same year saw the association registered with the Civic Trust.

The Wolverton Corps of the St John Ambulance Brigade has been in existence since before 1900. In the beginning its HQ was at the Science and Art Institute. In the 1950s a ladies' section was formed.

In 1926 Wolverton St John Ambulance Brigade obtained a motor ambulance by public subscription which was built, maintained, and manned by Wolverton Works personnel. The Works paid all expenses. This service was open to anyone living in the Wolverton Urban Area. The entrance fee was 2s 6d (12½p) and thereafter sixpence (2½p) per year, for which a card was given. This entitled the member and his immediate family to the use of the ambulance. The service continued until the introduction of the Health Service. During 1926-46, three ambulances were built and maintained at the Wolverton Works.

All three communities had at one time strong branches of the Toc H movement. This trio gave an unsung service in many forms to the community, but sadly only one remains today, that of the Wolverton Branch 13. Stony Stratford's branch began in a room at the rear of Callows tailors' shop at 78 High Street, moving to more suitable premises down the George Yard. New Bradwell branch stemmed from its Wolverton neighbour and held its meetings in Dr Miles' stables. It was on 15 December 1922 that the Wolverton branch received its petition and lamp maintenance from the Prince of Wales at the Guildhall.

This branch has been involved in countless projects over the years: the running of the Wolverton Area Transport Association, a door-to-door bus service for elderly and infirm people, initiated by Dr Hall and assisted by a grant from WUD Council, the Wolverton Area Christmas Cheer Organisation, variety shows and car outings for the elderly and mentally handicapped.

OPPOSITE: The Peace tableau of 1939, the closing scene of New Bradwell Hospital Fête that year. LEFT: Olive and Olwen Sapwell ready for the Bradwell Hospital Fête parade in 1938, and RIGHT: Mrs Walton of Bradwell dressed for her traditional role of John Bull. BELOW: New Bradwell's Carnival Queen and her attendants, 1946 — Amy Wood, Vera Clarke, Kathleen Lane, Molly Adams (Queen), Dorothy Crawford, Daphne McLeod, ?, in front, Doreen Clarke.

ABOVE: Charlie Scott's Pantomime Party of 1927 — back: B. Hood, P. Phelps, S. Heap, M. Alderson, V. Brooks, L. Fisher, B. Pikesley, E. Procter, W. Dearn, K. Pikesley, C. Ellis, H. Dowdy, Mrs Dowdy, Mrs Leether, C. Pidgeon; 2nd row: Mr Tapp, Mrs Pidgeon, C. Watts, Millard, B. Foxford, M. Alderson, J. Procter, J. Ellis; 3rd row: ?, Mr Kightley, F. Miles, H. Bates, B. Robinson, ?, S. Tapp, ?, L. Packer, W. Ellis, E. Pidgeon; 4th row: ?, A. Labram, H. Dowdy, W. Pidgeon, Mrs Scott, Mr Scott, Mrs Ellis, J. Bates, E. Knight; 5th row: O. Anstee, D. Dunkley, ?, ?, ?, V. Dowdy, D. Knight, K. Barton, H. Knight, G. Seals, L. Ellis, J. Pidgeon, ?, B. Wood, L. Hollis and S. Blunt. BELOW: Stratford Volunteer Fire Brigade in the mid-1930s — standing: S. Holland, Kirk, W. Dunkley, G. Glenn, J. James, G. Goodger; front: F. Whitehead, ?, Crow, W. Yates, R. Roberts, W. Goodridge. RIGHT: The mock-up of the house that was fired purposely at the Wolverton Hospital Fêtes.

ABOVE: A charity pageant organised by the Stony Stratford Conservative Club and held in St. Marys' vicarage garden in June 1930 — back row: P. Philpotts, ?, ?, Dave Haseldine, W. Stevens, Joe Ayres, George Shurmer, ?, Les Sims, Jim Pratt; 2nd row: Sister Stretton, Payne, ?, ?, Claude Bailey, Doug Dunkley, Ron Buswell, Billy White, Horace Newman, Tony Clewett, H. Johnson, 4 witch doctors, Smith, H. Ayres; 3rd row (standing): Mary Phillips and Sylvia Clark, ?, Edna Hurst, Kath Stretton, Miss Sibthorpe, Arthur Tite, L. Odell, Bill Rowledge, R. Odell, Clark Sisters; 4th row (sitting): Phyllis Phillips, Dorothy Smith, ?, Mrs Page, E. Meakins, Mrs Gammage, Marg Crofts (Britannia), Daisy Hurst, Marjory Clewitt, Mary Lunn (girl kneeling in white), Mrs Mackerness, Mrs Dunkley, Louie Waine (later Mrs Rowledge); front row (sitting on grass): (small girls were butterflies and fairies) Joan Tomkins, Daphne Phillips, Eileen Goodman, Muriel Lancaster, Nora Adams, Pearl Gammage, ?, Eileen Lovesy, Eileen Dunkley, Mary Waine, ?, ?, ?. BELOW: Stratford Welfare Carnival entry c1933 — 'The Wedding Party' — back: Cyril Brown, Cyril Stimson, Betty Scragg, Audrey Richards; front: Eric Stimpson, Barbara Morris, Beryl Castle, Trevor Brown, Taylor, Alan Bowdler, Bill West. (Centre five ladies unknown).

ABOVE: The New Bradwell Swimming Pool Committee — back row: Wilf Amos, Charlie Morley, Abbott, Charlie Huckle, Jim Cook, Reg Pateman; front row: E. Alderman, C. Jeffs, S. Hammond, Boddy, M. Morris and Hawkins. BELOW: McCorquodale's contribution to the Wolverton Carnival of 1968, *Up Pompeii* — standing: Teresa Rice, Bert Coleman, George Green, Dick Westcott, David Goldsmith; sitting: Judy Mynard, Carol Pointer, Janice Jones.

ABOVE: A group of Toc H No 13 Wolverton on 26 August 1928 — back row: Jim Whyte, Thompson, Ben Cahill, Len Dewick, Jack Constable, Tom Elmes; centr row: Ron Odell, Stan Kettle, Pa Holloway, Rev Eric Steer, Harry Trow, Bro Rose, Goodger; front row: Bert Holland, L. Odell, Blossom Rich, Harold Brown and Sookey Taylor, BELOW: Wolverton Toc H celebrates its 50th Anniversary (December 1972): Sydney Swain, Stephen Ingham, Bob Fisher (founder member), David Stimson (Chairman) and Tim Bellamy.

ABOVE: St Giles Church, showing the chancel exterior before its alteration in 1928. CENTRE: New Bradwell St James Church Choir of c1948 — back row: H. Tapp, Bill Scott, Malin, B. Welch, M. Brock, P. Baines; 2nd row: W. Oldam, C. Scott (Choirmaster), D. Savage, B. Whitehead, J. Welch, B. Kirk, Frank Pell; 3rd row: Colin Clamp, F. Craddock, John Bull, Dave Pell, Fred Warner, Arthur Clarke, ?, John Palmer, George Cobley, Bill May; seated: Eric Coles, P. Millard, B. Church, Ron Frost, Rev H. T. Trapp, J. Osborne, G. Godfrey, Barry Kimble; front: ?, John Doddington, John Heap, John Foster, Tony Guntrip, Allen Shinwell. BELOW: Stanton Low Church of St Peter, showing the entrance porch that was on its northern side.

Mind and Soul

There were in 1919 some twenty places of worship in the Urban District. At Stony Stratford there were two Anglican churches, St Giles and St Mary the Virgin. St Giles was reconstructed in 1776, except for the tower, which has eight bells; the chancel was rebuilt in 1928. The Church of St Mary the Virgin was erected in 1864. The Baptist Chapel is in Horsefair Green and was built in 1625, rebuilt in 1657 and again in 1823. Other places of worship in the town were the Methodist Church, the Congregational Church, the Chapel of Mr Fegans Homes, the Christian Science Institute and the Salvation Army chapel down Bulls Yard, (sometimes referred to as the Cross Keys Yard) and the Primitive Methodist Chapel along the Wolverton Road.

By 1974 Stratford had lost fives places of worship; St Mary the Virgin closed on Palm Sunday 1968 after the morning service, later in the day St Giles Church was rededicated the Parish Church of St Mary and St Giles. The Fegans Chapel was closed in 1962, the Salvation Army Post in the late 20s and the Christian Science Institute. It gained one — the Roman Catholic Church of St Mary Magdalen, built in 1958 on the site of Oswald House. In the early thirties the Primitive Methodist Chapel closed its doors, purchased by Mr H. Meacham for £10, later converted to a Diagnostic Clinic, now used by the Red Cross. The Church at Calverton has stood since the twelfth century and was first dedicated to All Hallows. In 1818 it was rebuilt as All Saints Church. At Middle Weald stood a chapel that was a branch of the Fegans Chapel at Stratford.

At Old Wolverton some evidence suggests that there was a church here before the tenth century as there is indication of Saxon work in the vicinity but no proof to substantiate this. The Normans, however, certainly built a church at Wolverton. After the Black Death the church fell into decay. The Radcliffe Trustees built a new one complete in 1815, which is the present Holy Trinity.

At New Wolverton by 1844 the Church of St George the Martyr had been built. The Parish of St George the Martyr was created in 1846. Other places of worship were the Salvation Army Post, the services held in the Scout Hall, Kingdom Hall of Jehovah's Witnesses, the Methodist Church, the West End Methodist Church, the Congregational Church and St Francis de Sales Roman Catholic Church. Over our period two of these ceased to function, namely the Salvation Army and the Jehovah's Witnesses.

New Bradwell or Stantonbury's places of worship were the Methodist Church, the Baptist Church, the Salvation Army Citadel, the Mission Hall, St James Church and St Peter's at Stanton Low. Two of these were destined to stop operating during the Urban District's period; the Salvation Army Citadel and St Peter's Church.

The New Bradwell section of the Salvation Army began its operations in Bradwell in 1893 in premises known as the Old Mill in the Thompson Street area. In the early 1900s this was sold and they moved into a building on the site of where Telfers DIY store now stands. In 1915 a new citadel was built further along the Newport Road. During the 1930s a wooden hall was built on brick piers behind the 1915 citadel at a cost of £120.

New Bradwell was the main Corps in the area, with outposts at one time at Newport Pagnell, Stony Stratford and Wolverton. New Bradwell was quite strong in numbers, up to, through and for a few years after, the Second War. Its membership then began to dwindle and the Citadel closed around 1967. The Citadel was sold to another religious order in 1987.

St Peter's Church at Stanton Low was built in the Norman style. It stands close to the River Ouse on the battleground between the Newport Roundheads and the Wolverton Cavaliers.

In 1908, there came to New Bradwell as Vicar of St James, the controversial Rev Allan Newman Guest. The vicar was not the type of man whom one would expect to have personal difficulties with his parishioners. He was a big, burly and genial Irishman who could make a joke and take one and he could even laugh at himself. He was an accomplished musician, a composer of many pieces of music and a first class athlete, but his ecclesiastical views were at sharp variance with those of the parish.

In a circular he distributed to his parishioners he flouted the Nonconformists thus:

'Unchristened Nonconformists are like good jews or virtuous Chinamen, excellent Pagans.'
'Christians who assemble for worship outside the church organisation are nothing but clubs.'
'Chapels are voluntary societies broken away from the Vine and destined to perish like the Pentecostal Roller Church in America.'

That was not the language that English people had been accustomed to hear from the Established Church, and it was evident that at Stantonbury they would not listen to it.

He was taken to court on two occasions. The first was reported in all the daily papers and *John Bull* with the headline of 'Religion by Assault'. According to evidence given at the Newport Pagnell Petty Sessions, Guest had two obsessions, one a love of Ritualism and the other a hatred of Nonconformity.

On one evening about seven o'clock a girl of fourteen, whose practice it was to attend the local Methodist Chapel, was standing outside her home with some friends when the Vicar came up and said to her 'You must come to church tomorrow morning at a quarter past eleven; never mind the Primitive Methodist Chapel.' The young girl answered that she would never leave the chapel and the vicar retorted 'There is only one church in England; that is my church' and after further insistence and further refusal on the part of the girl he struck her across the face 'and the marks were visible the next morning'. The mother appeared and asked the Vicar if he had struck her child. 'Yes', responded the Vicar. 'I did hit her and I will hit you too.' After much dialogue, some of which questioned the sanity of the Vicar, he was fined £3.

His second appearance was for using insulting language in the public streets, for which he was fined one pound or in default fourteen days' imprisonment.

In his church services he celebrated the Roman High Mass, for which he was attacked from all sides, but some eleven surrounding C of E churches were implementing similar services. The press both locally and at Northampton carried regular features of his activities with headlines like 'Stormy Scenes at Bradwell', 'Lively Stantonbury Vestry Meeting'. Such was the feeling that a petition was sent to the Bishop of Oxford.

The Bishop came to Bradwell for 'laying on of hands', at a confirmation one Sunday afternoon and to meet the parishioners and those who had signed this petition. Over 1,000 people attended the meeting in the evening held in the Council School. The Bishop's address called for 'Give and Take' and sided with the Vicar.

After wild scenes and disorder, police were called from Newport Pagnell. There was general uproar and confusion when the Bishop and Vicar made their way out of the building and so left the parishioners to continue the meeting as they pleased.

The confrontation with his church council and some of his parishioners carried on, but in 1922, he made a statement of 'Fair Offer' as he called it and was willing to shake hands with everybody.

He said he was prepared to organise the service on Sundays and have a choral service (to which the parishioners were used) and re-organise the services on a Low Church basis, providing that his own service, which did not include evensong, was left alone.

For a time he retained a fair congregation, but he was still strong in his views and interpretation of the *Book of Prayer*. There was still also a large body of ardent and devout church people in Bradwell who continued to resent what they described as Romanish practices.

Throughout the '20s and early '30s, when there were many men tramping the country searching for work, Rev Guest would invite many to the vicarage; many a time he gave a hungry traveller his own dinner, going without himself. Mr A. Brown of New Bradwell was a high official at the Bradwell Baptist Church and held a post that is today's equivalent of Personnel Manager at Wolverton Works. It was in the mid-'30s, when the Works began setting men on again, and Brown was of course sympathetic to the followers of his church. Rev Guest was aware of this and one Sunday evening he arranged his own service to finish early. He cycled round to the Baptist Chapel and accosted Brown on his emergence, with the exclamation 'Brown, now you have got all your flock back in work, how about starting on mine!'

Even at 76 years of age in 1944 he was still hitting the headlines with his confrontations at the annual Easter Vestry and Parochial Council meeting — at this he threatened to eject his Warden. He continued in office until 1947 when he retired; he died later the same year in a nursing home.

The state education system between the wars was based on the Education Act of 1870 which had established elementary schools, the Act of 1902 which created state secondary schools and the 1918 Act which raised the school-leaving age to fourteen. Educational matters throughout the period saw great progress and many changes. At Stony Stratford there were no less than five schools, two of them private, two church schools and the council school. St Mary's church school (now the Plough Inn) was built in 1873; originally a mixed school, it changed its function in 1908 and became a girls' and infants' school. In 1819 St Giles (now 30 High Street) was also opened as a mixed school, it was enlarged in 1858, in 1908 it became a boys-only school, its girl pupils transferring to St Mary's, the boys at St Mary's changing over to St Giles. The council school in Russell Street opened in 1907 and was mixed.

The two church schools closed with the opening of the St Giles and St Mary's Senior School in 1937. This was a mixed school, both by sex and denomination, as non-conformists also attended. The old Council School became a County Junior School.

The first of the two private schools was that of the Misses Stockings that operated from High Street, now Willis' the greengrocer; this closed in the late 1920s. York House School, the second of the private schools, was founded at Hanslope in 1853. Later it became a boarding school in Linford Place, Great Linford, a lovely house with a ballroom and terraced garden. From great Linford the school moved to the White House, Stony Stratford (afterwards the Moss residence, then from 1953 the bus depôt, now the site of a new estate, Emerton Gardens); it was at this house that founder Mrs Slade died. Her daughter-in-law, Mrs Edward Slade, continued the school at premises in the High Street that now house the Conservative Club. York Road was named after this school, which stood at the corner.

After some years here, in 1902 Mrs Slade moved to a building in London Road, which was originally known as Clarence House and from which Clarence Road received its name. Mrs Slade's daughters, Miss Agnes and Miss Dorothy Slade, continued the school until it was taken over by Mrs Ogilvie in September 1933; she was the daughter of Mrs Slade's half sister. The school finally closed its doors in 1953, its school colours of navy blue, saxe blue and white, its motto 'ALTIORA PETO' (Seek the Highest) gone from the Stratford scene for ever.

At New Bradwell there was only one place of learning; this was the Council School. These premises were opened the same day as the church in December 1860, and extended in 1892 by Messrs Kemp and Son. The Bounty Street School was opened for boys in 1913, these premises being enlarged in 1974.

The Wolverton Schools began as Railway Schools, the first premises in Creed Street, built and opened in August 1840, and extended in 1891. A Boys' School was opened in Church Street in 1896, the Creed Street school kept for girls and infants. The new elementary school in Aylesbury Street was completed in 1906 and the Creed Street School was closed by 1907, then taking on the role of Market Place.

A scheme for secondary education was prepared in 1901 by Mr Soames, the vicar of Lavendon and Chairman of the County Education Committee, with Mr Woollard of Stony Stratford, Mr Wylie of New Bradwell and others in Wolverton. The first class of the Wolverton County Day School was of thirty-two pupils on 14 January 1902, and held at the Science and Art Institute, under the Headmastership of Mr L.N. Leadley. In 1907, a new school was erected on the old Three Bush Fields; called Bucks County Secondary School, it was later renamed the Wolverton Grammar School.

Wolverton has a proud tradition of technical education. Those far-sighted men in 1840 set aside a room for the London and Birmingham Railway Institution for Moral and Intellectual Improvement at Wolverton Station, the precursor of technical and further education in Bucks.

Three years after that, evening classes were arranged and lectures delivered on various subjects. In 1860, classes in connection with the Science and Art Department commenced and 12 months later the Railway Company provided a piece of land for building a mechanics' institute.

The opening ceremony of the Wolverton Science and Art Institute took place on Monday 16 May 1864, and when the City and Guilds started their examinations in 1879, Wolverton claimed one of the first successes, a second-class pass in gas manufacture by J. Plant. The Institute had to be enlarged in 1891, and in 1909 the volume of evening classes was such that the appointment of a part-time principal was justified.

Daytime classes were started in 1925, the first full-time principal, Mr A.G. Milner appointed and a Junior Technical School opened. The next year, the Institute was given the status of Technical College by the Board of Education and in 1929 commercial courses were started at the Junior Technical School. Mr R.S. Anderton took over from Mr Milner as principal in 1944, and was himself succeeded in 1947 by Mr T.J. Davies, who became the first principal of the renamed Wolverton College of Further Education in 1954. The first phase of the new college buildings along the Stratford Road was opened in 1955 and Mr Davies handed over to Mr Sharp in 1959.

For over a century, Wolverton-trained men ensured railways throughout the world learned that, for skill and knowledge, North Bucks craftsmen and engineers were hard to beat. From India to Argentina, from Canada to Australia, Wolverton men have been a byword for all that was best in railway loco and carriage building. In July 1958 the Technical College amalgamated with the Grammar School (Radcliffe Grammar/Technical).

The Radcliffe School is a co-educational Comprehensive School built in Aylesbury Street West, Wolverton. It was formed in September 1968 by combining the Radcliffe Grammar/Technical with the County Schools of Wolverton, Stony Stratford and New Bradwell.

In 1954 the Wolverton BR Apprentice School opened. Perhaps the greatest single feature in the training of young men as skilled craftsmen of the future was the introduction of this training school.

Before 1953 boys were allocated to one of the eighteen trades without any real reason for selecting a particular trade, except that perhaps it was the boys's own choice or it was one in which there were a number of vacancies. With the Apprentice School system every boy had a chance to 'have a go' at every trade before he was asked his preference.

This school continued on these lines until September 1984, when BREL Headquarters decided to cease taking apprentices at Wolverton. However, after twelve months this decree was reversed and a new training school opened in August 1985 in the Old Finishing Shop. In August 1986 it was again decided to end apprenticeships at Wolverton Works and in 1987 the school closed. It was announced in March 1988 that apprentice training would recommence in Wolverton Works. These apprentices do their first year off-the-job training at the Milton Keynes Training Centre.

ABOVE: The interior of the Stony Stratford Baptist School Room in 1934. CENTRE: A view of the main entrance from the south of the Orphanage, Stony Stratford, before the fire on 30 March 1938 that destroyed the spire shown here. BELOW: The War Memorial and the Congregational Church, the latter demolished in 1970, Square, Wolverton.

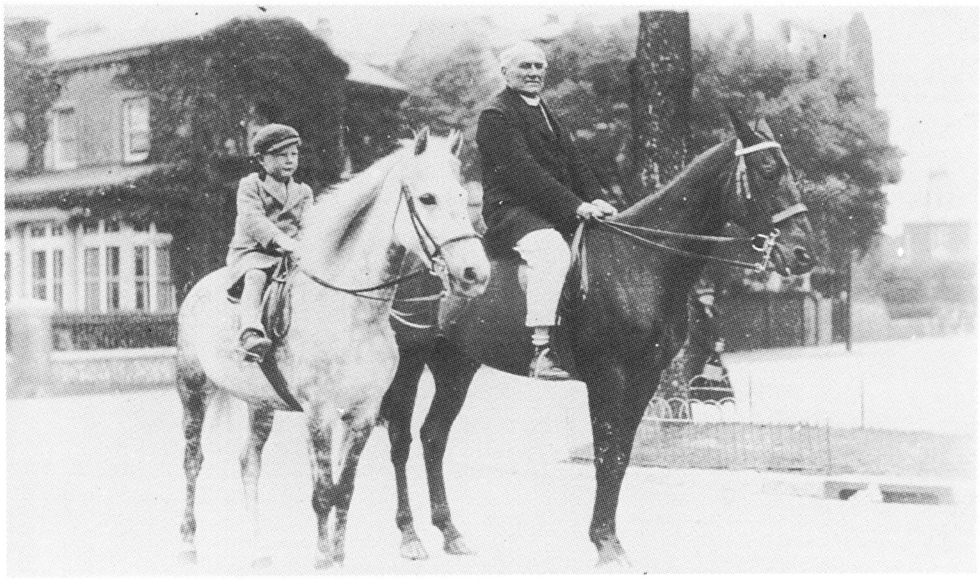

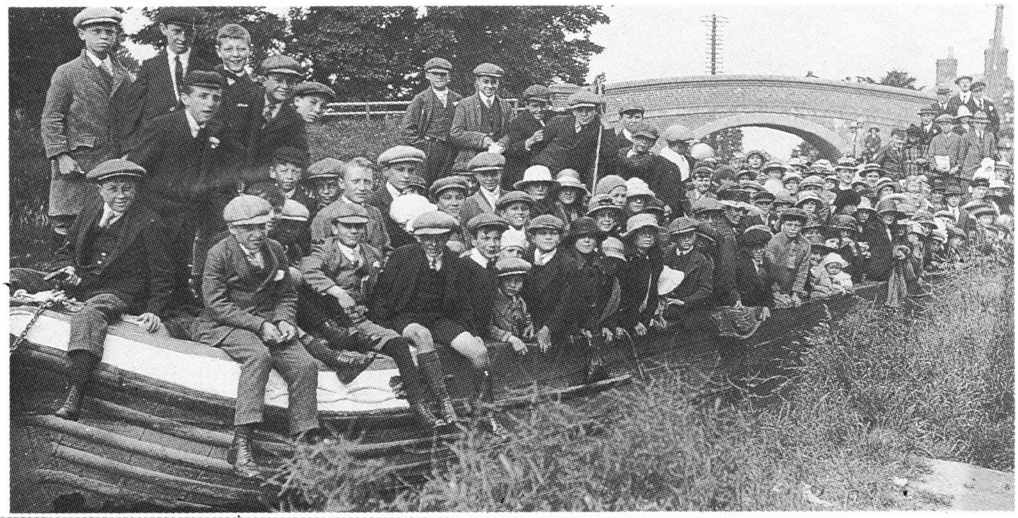

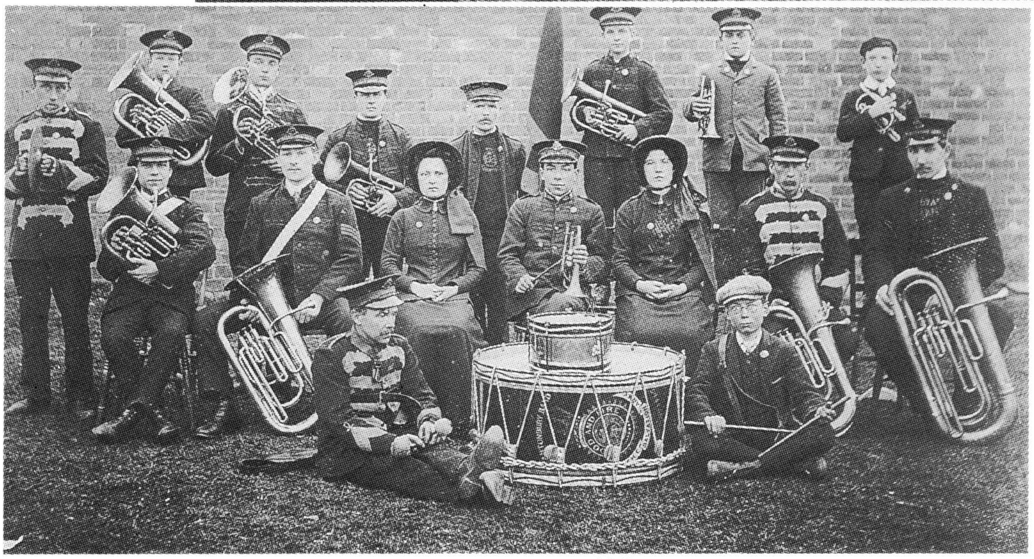

OPPOSITE ABOVE: Rev Allan N. Guest and his son, Newman, on holiday at Bournemouth. CENTRE: The Bradwell Salvation Army Sunday School outing, a trip up The Cut by horse-drawn barge. BELOW: The Bradwell Salvation Army Band, c1920. ABOVE: Stone-laying ceremony, 19 June 1915, New Salvation Hall, Stantonbury. BELOW: The Salvation Army Life Saving Guards of New Bradwell — standing: M. Noble, L. Blunt, Q. Philips, E. Norwood, K. Willison, Fielding, R. Smart, M. Dimmock; sitting: L. Sayell, Mrs Noble, Ensign Thurman, Mrs Blunt, Lt Pearce, M. Willison, L. Kightley; front: V. Wilcox, E. Meakins, E. Cox and D. Curtis.

ABOVE: New Bradwell schoolchildren, c1920. BELOW: Bradwell Bounty Street Boys' School, c1948 — back row: Bob Barnet, Graham Riley, John Varney, Derek Booden, Peter Webber, Alan Rose, Keith Turvey, Ray Brown, Alan Alderman; 2nd row: Michael Mumford, Thomas Bird, Jefferey Wood, Raymond Foster, Leslie Tarbox, Peter Levett, William Axtell, Sydney Smith, Kenneth Stobie, Anthony Cave, Michael Brazier; 3rd row: Kenneth Brown, Roland Carpenter, E. J. Wilson, Ralph Short, Arthur Taylor, Kenneth Alderman, Michael Nash, Derek Savage; front row: Colin Palmer, Thomas Cleary, Gerald Stimpson, John Bull, John Haseldine, Geoffrey Huckle, Sidney Nicholls and Derek Birdsey.

ABOVE: Wolverton County Secondary School Hockey Team of c1937 — back: Ivy White, Joan Preston, ?, Gladys Tilley, Freda Swell, ?; sitting: Marjory Andrews, Barbara Barnell, ?, Marjory Page and Mary Cloverly. BELOW: Stony Stratford Russell Street School football team of 1961 — standing: Derek Daniels, Michael Evans, Steve Chipperfield, Mr Bentley, Ian Rahn, Roy Baxter, Graham Brown; sitting: Chris Weller, Pete Eglesfield, Malcolm Rose, Malcolm Tapp and Des Smythe.

LEFT: 'Yorky' (Bill Williamson), the well-known wanderer, seen here earning a shilling sharpening a knife on his portable grindstone, a fixture attached to his 'cycle. RIGHT: A view of the Hawthorns, one of the six railway villas that stood alongside the canal to the south of the present station. Four of these were built in 1838, and two in 1845. Two were demolished to allow the first paint shop to be built in 1894; the remaining four were demolished in 1974. BELOW: View of the Square, looking north-east, pre-Agora.

New Town Blues

Almost as soon as the celebrations of the war's end had died down the problems started. With foresight the Council had, during the war, laid plans. In 1944, a London architect (Mr G.A. Jellicoe), was employed to prepare a Town Planning Scheme for Wolverton and the neighbouring area.

Among its main points were a civic centre at Wolverton, housing development on its south side and new schools at the west end. At Old Wolverton there were to be a lido and outdoor recreation area, with the whole of Wolverton surrounded by a green belt, and the Stratford Road lined with trees and flower beds to screen the Works wall, plus an English garden laid out at Stacey Hill. At Bradwell a garden of bridges and winding paths would occupy spare land between the old and new roads that had been part of the old fair field. By-passes were to be built for Stony Stratford and Wolverton.

In 1938 a by-pass had been surveyed and started for Stony Stratford. This began at Oakhill Lane and continued on the western side of Stony Stratford, crossing the Calverton Road near the pumping station, then over the Mill fields to skirt the western side of Old Stratford, rejoining the A5 *via* the Black Horse field. The war stopped this project but not before a large area had been cleared of trees at the Oak Hill end.

The lack of any new housing for six years had created a desperate accommodation situation for men returning from the war and setting up home and family. In the 1945 landslide election, for the first time Labour won the North Bucks seat — Aidan Crawley was elected.

In early 1945, the Council had asked for and been allocated ninety prefabricated houses. These were constructed in New Bradwell forming Abbey Way, Bradvue Crescent and Bridle Crescent, the first tenant moving in on 1 June 1946. Thirty conventional houses were built at Althorpe Crescent. At Wolverton fifty-nine homes were erected at Furze Way. Private enterprise acted and one hundred and fifteen homes were built at Haversham and Kingston Avenue at Stony Stratford.

When in 1946 the Council wanted to build at Stony Stratford the Ministry raised difficulties over costs. This was the Debbs Barn Estate and it was mid-1950 before the first tenants moved in. In the same year the Council prepared to build a further two hundred homes at Wolverton — Southern Way, Woodland View and St John Crescent.

The bitterness of the winter of January-March 1947 brought desperate hardship. The Railway Works virtually closed down and men were stood off or sent clearing snow from the main line and keeping points free from freezing. Supplies of coal failed to get through to the power stations and for domestic use. Current for domestic use was cut off between nine am and noon and again for two hours in the afternoon. Every piece of wood lying in the fields for miles around was removed for fuel and many trees sawn down for the same reason. There were long queues at the Wolverton and Stony Stratford Gas Works for coke. Snow was still lying across the fields in May.

In those days Sunday newspapers were still taken around the villages of Beachampton, Nash, Whaddon, Thornborough and Thornton on foot, by Jack Cox of Stony Stratford, an elderly gentleman who worked for Becketts, the Stony Stratford newsagents.

At the beginning of the cold spell Jack set off one Sunday morning. His customers were concerned for his welfare and he was proffered many hot drinks and much home-made wine. He usually reached his last customer at five thirty; Mr Harding was a local man and retired ex-Metropolitan policeman, employed on part-time work as an assistant gamekeeper, living alone in one of the Thornton Lodge gate cottages. He called Jack in and said 'You are running a bit late Jack [around seven o'clock], come in, sit down and I will get you a drop of whisky'. After two or three more Harding added 'You had better have a bite to eat and stop the night and go home first thing tomorrow morning'. Meanwhile at Stony Stratford Mrs Cox was getting worried. She went to see police sergeant Bob Rollings who cycled up Silver Street and enquired in the Royal Oak, then carried on to the top of Beachampton Hill. Returning to Mrs Cox he said he would look again first thing in the morning, which he did, and met Jack coming up the hill out of Beachampton. 'Come on Jack, hurry up, where have you been? Your wife's worried and they have had a collection at the Oak for you'. The old boy replied: 'Oh thanks very much, how much did they get for me?'

On 1 January 1948, the Wolverton Works became part of the newly nationalised British Railways. On 11 March HRH Princess Elizabeth and the Duke of Edinburgh visited Wolverton to view two coaches converted for their personal use on the Royal Train.

The water supply for Wolverton and Bradwell came from the wells at Old Bradwell, now owned by BR who, with little warning, told the Council this could not continue. The Bucks Water Board took over but the water had worms in it; they blamed the pipes. As there had never been any worms with the old supply, this argument was not convincing. The worms were supposedly not harmful, but they were visible. Even so the Medical Officer advised consumers to boil all water. It took two years of constant pressure from the WUDC before the Water Board took action and the worms disappeared. The Board announced that they were spending £33,000 a year on special filters to produce odourless and tasteless water — and the water charges would go up by about twenty five per cent.

When water was piped into Calverton an elderly gentleman who had been drinking his own well water all his life refused to have tap water. After much cajolery by Council members, he was persuaded to send two samples to the county analyst, one from his well and the other from a neighbour's tap, both sealed in his presence. The analyst's report was duly received — Frank's water was declared fit for human consumption and the tap water labelled 'This horse is not fit for work'.

Another large and much-needed undertaking was the new sewage system and disposal scheme which got under way in the early 1950s; by the end of the decade it was complete. The Calvertons were excluded and still had the 'night cart' in 1973.

There were setbacks for the Council in its efforts to get new industries into the area; when the long-awaited town map appeared in 1955, the planners had ruled out any new industry at Wolverton and any new population apart from natural growth from 13,000 to 15,000.

Further plans for light industry were put forward but the Ministry explained that the water and sewage systems could not support industrial expansion, or the inevitable population growth. There were similar worries at fifteen other railway towns and a meeting was called by Eastleigh in Hampshire to support a conference with constituency MPs, trade unions and the British Transport Commission on how to get new industry into these areas. Wolverton and most others agreed to the proposal. And then everything changed, Wolverton Works was given a large new build programme, which included new electric stock, which in turn necessitated more men being recruited and the relaxing of the retirement rules.

More or less simultaneously the Ministry performed a complete about-turn by approving a town map which showed positive expansion for Wolverton both in industry and housing, indicating the Ouse valley in November 1959 could cope with the water and sewage problem.

Travelling round the district there was a 'milestone inspector' of some individuality, known as 'Yorky'. With his portable grinding machine, he was well-liked and each week he walked down Stony Stratford High Street, calling at food shops where he collected scraps of bacon and cheese and stale loaves, enough to last a week. His diet was supplemented with rabbits and vegetables, and nuns at Thornton also supplied him with a certain amount of food. Yorky was also a regular customer at local hostelries, telling tales of his father being a millionaire and of his exploits in the Great War. In fact his name was Bill Williamson and he was related to Chief Inspector Williamson of the Northamptonshire Police.

When he came to the district c1948, he lived in a tent in the Silver Spinney between Deanshanger and Wicken. Then he moved to a hovel at Cattleford Bridge along the Buckingham Road. He kept himself clean by bathing in a stream that ran through the field. He was joined by another wayfarer called Brown and his wife, who roved the locality pushing an old perambulator accompanied by an aged black dog, making their living by trapping and selling rabbits. All three ended their days in the hovel; first the wife died, then Yorky and finally Brown. All were interred in Thornton Churchyard.

In the 1950s improvement grants eased the housing shortage, by prolonging the life of old properties. This also provided work for small building firms; the main alteration was that of adding a bathroom. Before that, Friday night was 'marmy night'. This entailed bringing a 'bungalow', or tin bath, into the kitchen or living room. One local wag used to say that when all the kids and Mum and Dad had a bath, and the dog's turn came, the water was like mud. Wolverton people enjoyed the use of the Railway-owned Public Baths, opened in 1855 in Ledsam Street and from 1891 until the early 1970s along the Stratford Road. This establishment opened every day except Sunday, until eight o'clock at night, with special times for ladies. At Bradwell the Progressive Club supplied a similar service, with its baths upstairs on two evenings a week, Thursdays for men and Fridays for women.

The early 1960s saw the beginnings of major upheaval in the area as the Beeching axe fell on the national railway system. In 1962 this threatened the closure of Wolverton Works and the Council saw its chance to channel new industry to cushion this threat. The Works itself won a new future as a repair depôt at the expense of 2,000 jobs. New industry arrived in the form of R. Daleman, a plastics firm, in 1962, followed by Copperad Ltd, later to be merged with Ideal Standard in a £500,000 factory on the new Old Wolverton Road industrial estate and followed by other large employers such as Rank Hovis and the Electricity Board.

Then came a bombshell that dwarfed all of North Bucks' local problems: a plan for a new town of a quarter of a million people. A few years earlier, the authorities had opposed industrial expansion because the River Ouse could not take any more industrial effluent. Now Mr F.B. Pooley, the County Architect and chief architect of the Bucks plan, stated it would be a 'New Town' and nothing less. Bletchley's hopes of big town status were dashed aside. Wolverton was assured that, along with Stony Stratford and Bradwell, if they welcomed the plan their future would be bright.

Meanwhile Wolverton carried on with its own building plan. The Council, having bought the 'Little Streets' at Wolverton (Creed Street, Ledsam Street, Young Street and Glyn Square) for £18,000, started demolishing these houses and rebuilding, including an eleven storey block of flats to be called the Gables, after a large house on the site. Also planned were other flats, maisonettes, houses and a block named Orchard House, specially designed for the elderly. The Gables flats were opened in 1965; thrown open to public view, they attracted 3,200 visitors.

Before the decade was out, a similar scheme for Bradwell was started. Both schemes had a common basis, the clearance of old railway houses, but here the plan differed, inasmuch as the Council envisaged a new settlement 'over the hill', spreading over thirty-six acres, adjoining Althorpe Crescent.

The Council went ahead, but hit major costs; sewage alone was some £20,000. So attention was switched to Newport Road, New Bradwell, simultaneously negotiating with MK Development Corporation for the sale of the Althorpe Crescent land.

Estimated at the time to cost £1,100,000, the plan set out to provide homes for 1,150 people then living in the old railway houses and prefabs, but without building high-rise flats. Instead the flats would be two- and three-storey buildings and there would be bungalows and houses, the whole to be built in three phases. The first was tenanted in 1971. On completion of this estate the Council cleared most of what was considered unfit housing at Bradwell, Wolverton and Stony Stratford, replacing them with good quality homes.

In 1960, the first tenants moved into the Ousebank estate at Stony Stratford, housing families from Oxford Street, Silver Street, High Street and Bath Terrace. The newly built Radcliffe School opened to accept pupils on Tuesday 13 September 1960.

In November 1960, the M1 motorway was completed and this had a marked effect on Stony Stratford. Lorries were diverted on to this new road as were coaches and many private cars by choice. It caused the closure of two transport cafés, the one at the London Road garage and Ken's in the High Street. Hotels, public houses and restaurants suffered a great loss of trade.

The Council built two-storey flats in Queen Anne Street, New Bradwell. Then, during March 1961, a whirlwind struck New Bradwell, causing severe damage to property. Stony Stratford lost another public house, the Royal Oak on the Green, and in July 1961, the Fegans Homes Orphanage closed. It had been sold in May 1961 by Fegans to a Mr G. Allen, a Kent paper merchant, who intended to use it as a depository for furniture. But within a few weeks it was resold to the Franciscan Friars who ran St Bernardine's Roman Catholic College at Buckingham. They had tried to buy the buildings when they were first offered for sale but were told by Fegans that they did not want the Friars to have them as it had always been a Protestant Home. Exactly one hundred years since it was first built as a public school, the former orphanage was officially opened in 1963 as the first Franciscan Preparatory School in the country, dedicated to St Anthony of Padua. The old orphanage buildings had been transformed both externally and internally.

Up to this time there had been no Catholic School in the Wolverton district. The building was originally opened as St Pauls College in 1863, by Rev W.T. Sankey, vicar of St Giles, Stony Stratford, at a cost of £40,000. Sankey was the foremost of Stony Stratford's three building parsons, responsible for clearing the slums of Ram Alley and building New Street, the Parish Room and Church Infants school on its site; also building a new Vicarage, Vicarage Walk, Russell Street and Swan Terrace. The college was closed in 1895, after falling into the hands of sadistic masters. In 1896 it became a cigar factory, but this venture failed.

It remained empty for four years, when in 1900 it was bought for £4,500 by F.W.C. Fegan, for use an an Orphanage, for his 'bold and pert and dirty London sparrows'. For the next sixty-one years it remained an orphanage, Fegans Evangelical Chapel, and was prominent in the religious life of the district. The Roman Catholic School closed in 1972 and the building was then taken over by the Société General, an international finance company. It now embraces a restaurant, sheltered housing, a housing estate and apartments.

During 1962 and 1964, more than half the workforce of Wolverton Works was made redundant: 2,000 men were affected. Most of them found other employment at Luton, Bedford and Bletchley. In 1964 the Newport Pagnell branch line from Wolverton closed to passenger traffic. The works and way consisted of a single track four miles long that crossed the canal at Wolverton, parallel with the main line.

Newport Pagnell had a siding that was an extension beyond the platform. There was a goods shed in the yard with the usual roads for coal and goods wagons. Shunting horses were used there until after World War II. Just before the station a line went to Coales Mill. There was also a line parallel to the platform line which enabled the engine to run around the coaches and wagons. In 1900, at the Wolverton end and a quarter of a mile from Wolverton Station a spur was constructed to connect with the up slow line, and this triangle was used until its closure for turning the Royal Train and/or its engine.

In 1955, the decision was made to close the engine shed at Newport and supply engine and loco men daily from Bletchley Shed. Then Dr Beeching swung his axe and the Newport Line carried its last passenger on 5 September 1964. A daily freight ran for a while and, with the closure of Wolverton's Goods Yard in 1966, traffic ceased on the Newport Line. After 99 years of existence the line was lifted and became a public walkway. At its peak in 1910, it was carrying eleven down and twelve up trains daily (the line was closed on Sundays), reduced to nine each way Monday to Friday and twelve each way Saturdays by 1955.

On 4 April 1966, HM the Queen and HRH the Duke of Edinburgh visited North Bucks. Wolverton itself has a close connection with the Royal Family. Since 1865, the Royal Train has been built, maintained and manned by Wolverton men at the Wolverton Works.

The Royal Tour began at Buckingham, travelled to Stony Stratford *via* Thornton and Beachampton, then visited the Railway Works, the WUDC showpiece development at East Wolverton and Wolverton Station, where the Royal Train was parked on platform five (the old Newport line bay). After lunch the Royal Party left for Newport Pagnell, travelling through New Bradwell, and finishing at Bletchley.

On Wednesday 10 July 1968, a severe cloudburst brought New Bradwell its worst flooding for many years. The main cause was a fifty gallon water butt which blocked a culvert just when the canal men opened the sluice gates to save the canal from overflowing its banks, in a possible repeat of the 1939 disaster.

Abnormal rainfall of 4.7 ins was recorded in 24 hours at Wolverton sewage works; at 8.15 am on Thursday 11 July canal officials ordered the opening of the sluice gates. The water poured into the brook that then wended its way through the allotments towards the river. The brook had twelve right-angled bends and the water took the short cut. Unfortunately the water butt became jammed in one of the relief culverts at Corner Pin. Debris piled up and cut the culvert's efficiency to less than twenty per cent. Within two hours the water was in Caledonian Road and Wallace Street, flooding kitchens. Then at 10.15 am a garden wall in Wallace Street collapsed under the pressure and a wall of water a foot high raced down the street. Houses in Newport Road were inundated as the torrent swept on its way through Corner Pin to opposite St James Church. Over one hundred houses were flooded up to two feet deep for over twenty-four hours. Several elderly residents had to be rescued, other people were marooned in upstairs rooms and Dr M. Coster went on his rounds in his son's boat. Council workmen cut holes in another wall, dredged channels in Corner Pin turf and dug through a footpath to try to divert the flow. It was not until the canal sluice gates were closed at 9 pm that the water began to recede. With the co-operation of the Fire Brigade, who supplied four machines, the flood had gone by early Friday morning.

Other parts of the Urban District were little affected. The nearest any houses at Stony Stratford came to be flooded was when water lapped the doorsteps of Temperance Terrace. There was, however, considerable flooding at Deanshanger and Newport Pagnell.

British Waterways justified their action in opening the sluices when Area Engineer, Mr K Newham explained that this was 'normal good housekeeping', and had been done ever since the canal was built. 'If after abnormal rain the water in the canal rises to such a level that it has to be relieved then the flood paddles are pulled' he said. 'It is a question of making sure that the canal does not get to such a dangerous level that it overlaps.'

In the early days, the District Council had given full support to the Development Corporation but by the '60s, this enthusiasm had somewhat cooled and the Corporation was challenged on many occasions.

By March 1970, the Development Corporation unveiled their master plan for the new City centre, the estimated cost of which soared to £700 million.

The WUDC was disturbed about its likely influence on the area and was among the first objectors. Altogether one hundred and twenty-two objections were raised when the public enquiry opened in June that year. The Council attacked the plan on the basis that one main town centre on Bradwell Common was too big, too dominant and too comprehensive. Councillors feared that an all-embracing shopping centre so close at hand would do untold harm to the Urban District's commercial and industrial development.

The Council still sought the improvement of the railway town in commercial terms with new offices, showrooms and a hotel. There was the old Science and Art site awaiting development. What Wolverton received was the 'Agora', which cut Wolverton in two, and in so doing effectively isolated the original shopping centre on the Square. To the majority of local residents it is an eyesore. Apparently no alternative was offered.

At Stony Stratford they got Cofferidge Close, with the approval of the Council; whether it enhanced the town's appearance or augmented it commercially is a matter of opinion. There was nothing in the Corporation's plans for New Bradwell at all and that is exactly what it received — nothing.

Initially, the Development Corporation told the 250 residents of Old Bradwell it would retain its character. Five years later they planned 49 houses in the centre of the village, so Old Bradwell ended up being surrounded by new houses and roads plus an estate right in the middle, completely destroying its character. At a protest meeting the villagers were told by the Development Corporation that the scheme had already been approved, and that the major decision about the way the village was to be developed was made when the new town was designated; said Corporation spokesman Mr Lane, 'The village as you know it will change'. How right he was.

Perhaps the last amenity introduced by the Urban District Council was that of the riverside walk opened in April 1973, part of Jellicoe's long-term plan presented at the beginning of 1945. This consists of five miles of pathway meandering alongside the Ouse, beginning along the Calverton Road, Stony Stratford and emerging onto the road at Corner Pin, New Bradwell.

With the whole area one vast building site, the WUDC ended its fifty-five year reign on 1 April 1974. In its place came MK Borough Council. Milton Keynes now stands on what was once farmland. The population of the old District must now be content with their pleasant memories of the rural bliss of yesteryear.

ABOVE: The White Swan Scooter Club of Stony Stratford, seen here on a spin out at Chackmore, on the green, c1957. OPPOSITE ABOVE: Down come the old (the little streets of Wolverton) and up go the new. (JT) BELOW: The WUDC members at the time of the Queen's visit to North Bucks in April 1966 — back row: Jack Clamp, Mr Howe, Dr Love, Nevill Crook, Bill Hilton, Donald Morgan; middle row: Jim Dewick, Clem Lister, Dr Hall, Nurse E. Wakefield, Aileen Button, Robert Eyles, Brooks; front row: Reg Wesley, Peter Cosford, Frank Atter, Fred Cornford (Chairman), Frank Canvin, Mrs Johnson and Len Causer.

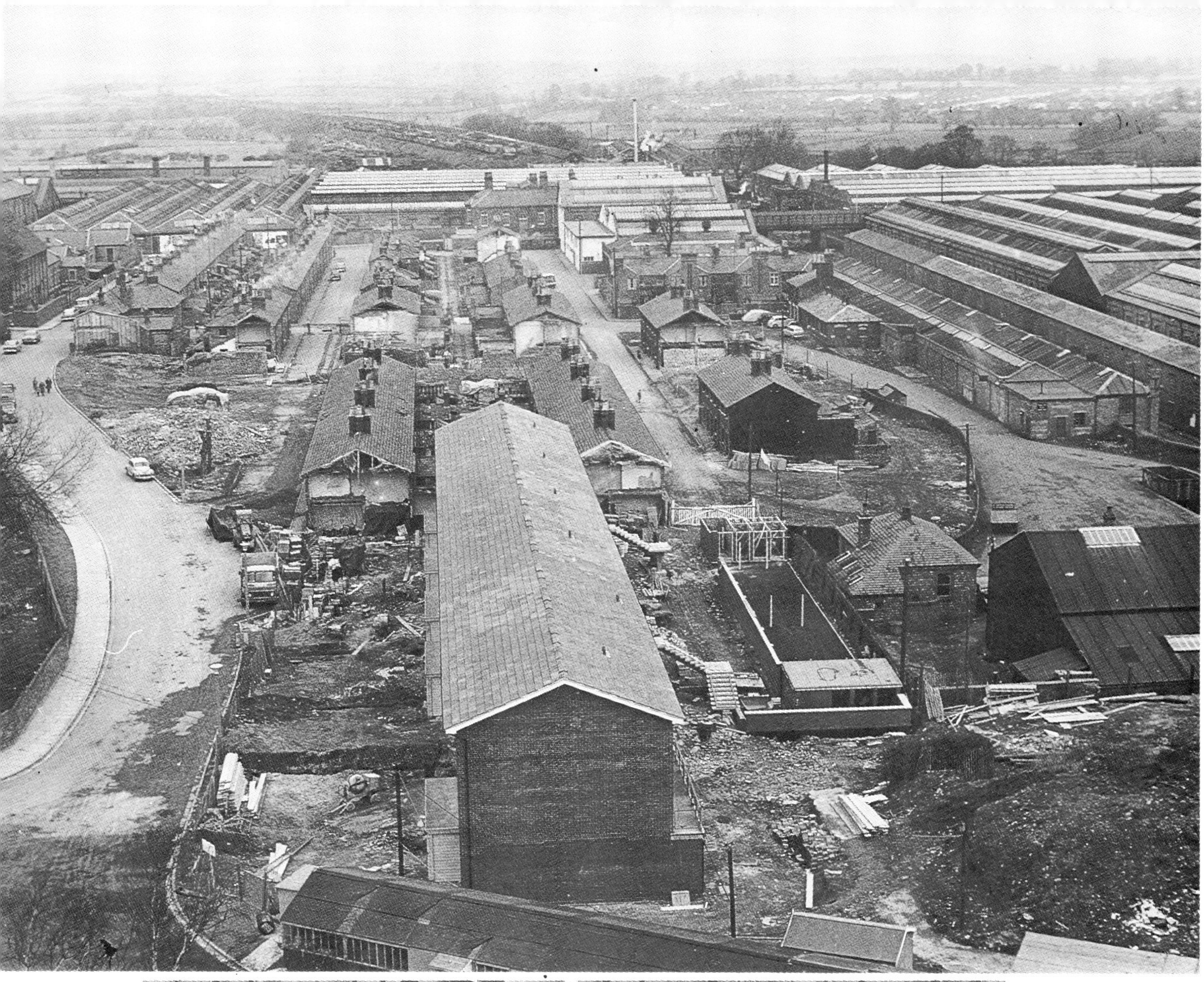

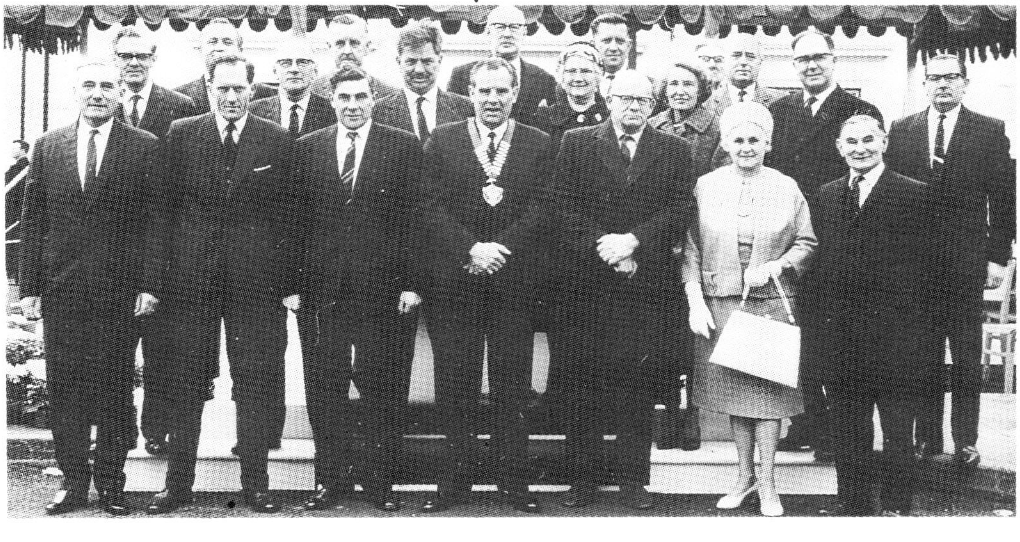

The end of an era: ABOVE: The bunting out and decorations up for the last passenger train from Newport to Wolverton on Saturday, 5 September 1964.

BELOW: Demolishing the Wolverton Congregational Church in 1970; on its site was built the Budgen's supermarket. (JT)

Index

All figures in italics refer to illustrations

Abbey Farm 64
Adams, Bill 116
   family............................11
   Frank............................116
   Len................................*29*
Airships R100 ....*39*
   R101...............................22
Ager, Mrs 117
Aggutter, George 89
Agora 156
Akeley 66
Alderman, Bill.................133
Althorpe 11
Alvrie 12
Amos, Wilf 132
Ancell, Mr.......................108
   Trust..............................113
Andrews, A. *26*
   Harry 91
Ansell, Major 77
Appleton, John 64, 66
Applin, Cliff......................89
Archer, Mr 66
ARP 75, 77, 80, *81*
Ashby, John 11
Aston Sandford 12
Atkinson, Dr P. B. 116
Atter, Frank 133
Axby, Bill 89
Aylesbury.........................14
   Philip de 11
Backlog, Thomas..........24, 25
Baden-Powell 117
Badminton Club 88
Bailey, Tom 64
Baldwin, Stan 90
Bands
   Barry Ward and his
     Rhythm Boys..............88
   Bill Axby and his Night
     Owls............................88
   Blue Bird Mouth
     Organ Band 88, 90
   Bradwell Drum and Fife ..85
   Bradwell Salvation
     Army....................85, *146*
   Bradwell Silver Band 85,
     94, 131
   Bright Knights 88, 98, *99*
   2nd Buck Batt. HG
     Band 85, *95*
   Cecil Stone's Accordion
     Band............................88
   Doug Blunt's Band 88
   Gay Nineties 88
   Harold Battison's
     Band......................88, *98*
   Harold Hood's Futurist
     Band............80, 88, *100*
   Jack Durdin's Band 88
   Jack Pooles Band............88
   Jock Jamison's Trio.........88
   Joe Lovesey's Old Tyme
     Dance Orchestra ...88, 90,
     100, *101*
   Luton Red Cross Band 86
   NUR Band 86
   Potterspury Silver Band ..86
   Stony Stratford Scout
     Band........*31*, 85, 87, 131
   Stony Stratford Town
     Band...........85, 86, *94*, 131
   The Ambassadors 88
   The Carlton Players 88
   The Collegian Swingers ..88,
     91, *99*
   The Embassy Trio 88
   The Lyric Orchestra..88, 89,
     97
   The Marina Trio.............88
   The Rhythm Aces65, 88, 89,
     90, 91, *96*, *97*
   Tommy Clarridge's
     Amazons 88, 90, *98*
     Orchestra...............88, 90
   Wolverton Home Guard
     Military Band 86
     Orchestra.........87, 91, *105*
     Scout Band 85, *95*
     Town Band......85, 86, 87,
     90, *93*
   Works Wonders.........90, *100*
Bannister, Bobby 22
Barber, Alderman 111
Barby, Aubrey 133
Bardell, G........................79
Barley, Fred 24
Barnes, Adam 21
Barr, Geo 113
Barra..............................*68*
Barre, Ralph....................11
   Robert..........................11
Barrett, Daniel................64
   R. J................................69
   T....................................66
Barry, William 11
Bates, A.D........................68
   Frank............................133
   J.H..................................50
Beachampton ..20, 21, 78, 107,
   151, 152
Beals, Fred 108, *118*
Bears Watering 78
Beeching, Dr 153, 155
Beckett, Tom 113
Becketts.........................151
Bedford 12, 14, 49
Belgium 76
Bennett, Mrs J. 21
   Simon 12, 21
   Sir Thomas 12
Bent, Bert 89
Betts and Faulkner, Messrs ..26
   Jimmy 26
Billings 107
Bird, F. 118
Birdsey, Austin 114
Blackburn, Bill..................86
Bleharies 76
Bletchley Park..................80
   Shed 155
Blitz 79
Blitz 79
Blue Boar Garage..............68
   Bridge...........................77
Blunt, Jim 75, 76
Bolbec, Hugh de 12
Booden, John 115
Boswell, Jack 87
Boult, Sir Adrian 88
Boveton, Hugh 11
Bradwell.........................158
   Good Samaritan Society..131
   Labour Party 132
   League 110
   Priory of 11, 13
   Social Club *124*
   Station 26
Road Recreation
   Ground 115
Brampton 109
Brawnhill Staunch 109
Brentford.........................67
Bristol..............................67
Brittain, Roy 89
Brooks, Frank 86, 88
Brocklehurst, E.T. 116
Brown, (Mr) 153
   A. 143
   Frankie 116
   Jonah 116
   Nigger...........................17
   Willis............................14
Bryan, Frank 52
Buckingham 12, 21, 24
   Arm 63, 67, 107
   Duke of 14
   Market 18
   Town Hall...............88, 92
Bucks Water Board.........152
Bull, Amos 17
   Billy 78
Bunce, Norman................*83*
Burrows, Jack 64
Burt, Harry *61*
Busby, Bert 17, 113
Bushell, Mr 68
'bus accident *58*
   timetables *55, 56*
'buses, 1914 ....*4*
Buses & Bus Coys
   AJS Pilot.......................50
   Black & White 17
   Blue Belle.......................*61*
   Brown's Super
     Coachways 50, *61*
   Blue Coaches.................50
   Cream Line Coach
     Services......................50
   Chevrolet................50, *57*
   City of Oxford Motor
     Services.....................51
   Crossley Alpha..........50, *58*
   Eastern National 49, 50,
     51, 52
   Humphrey, R.J.E.............50
   Lancia motor coach 56
   Leyland Cub 50, *57*
   Lioness...................50, *57*
   London & General Omnibus
     Co...............................49
   Midland Red 17
   Milton Keynes Shuttle.....52
   National Omnibus &
     Transport Co. ...49, 56, 59
   National Steam Car Co....49
   New Central Omnibus
     Co...............................49
   Parlour Coach................56
   Reo.........................50, *57*
   Pullman 50
   Star Flyer *58*
   Seldon....................49, *53*
   The National Co. 49
   United Counties 49, 50,
     52, *61*
   Westley, Percy 50
'busman's supper c1950......*59*
Calais 76
Callendine, Mr 19
Callow, Bill 115, 134
Calverton.....12, 13, 18, 20, 21,
   30, *93*
Campbell, C.M. 118
   Major 77
Cambridge 21
Canal c1933....................*44*
Canvin's, butcher *16*
Cardington 22, 109
   Bridge.........................129
Carlile, Sir Walter............117
Carrs Mill 20
Carter, K.D......................66
Cartland, Barbara 65
Cassel 76, 77
Cecil James 12
Chalfont St. Giles 12
Chambers, Fred *34, 46*
Chapman, Archie 77
   Alan *61*
Charity Pageant *137*
Choulesbury 12
Churches & Chapels
   All Hallows
     (All Saints) 141
   Baptist.......66, 141, 143, *145*
   Christian Science...........141
   Congregational .141, *145*, *159*
     Juniors FC.................*128*
   Fegans Homes 141, 154
   Holy Trinity 12, 141
   Kingdom Hall of Jehovah's
     Witnesses 141
   Methodist, Deanshanger ..89
   Methodist, West End.93, 141
   Mission Hall 141
   Primitive Methodists 141, 142
   Salvation Army 141, 142,
     146, 147
   St Frances de Sales 141
   St George the Martyr.....141
   St George's Concert Party ...
     103
   St Giles........26, 89, *140*, 141
   St James 91, 115, *140*,
     141, 142
   Amateur Dramatic
     Society 91
     FC 115
   St Mary Magdalen 141
   St Mary the Virgin 141
   St Peter. Passenham 22
     Stantonbury......11, 20, 141
     Stanton Low *140*, 142
     Tyringham 91
     Wesleyan 92
'Cinder Billy' 18
Cinemas
   Empire (Stony Stratford) .24,
     54, 111
   Empire (Wolverton) ..87, 111,
     120
   Palace *31*, 51, 52, 91, 111,
     112, *119*
   Scala.......87, 91, 92, 111, *119*
Circus 107
Clarence House 143
Clarke, Mr.......................17
Clarridge, Tommy 90
Cleveland, Earl of..............14
Clock Tower 28, 132
Clubs
   Bradwell Liberal &
     Radical 110
   (Progressive)................*125*

159

Milton Keynes AC 113
Savings....................19
Sick & Divi............19, 109
Stantonbury Progressive ..75,
 80, 91, 92
 Social....................110
 WMC..................*60, 124*
Stony Stratford Conservative
 Club......................111
 Rugby Club................79
 Town FC..................113
 WMC..........80, 109, *124*
 Top Club..................92
 White Swan Scooter
 Club.....................*156*
 White Horse Sports &
 Social...................*133*
 Whippet Club.............111
Wolverton Amateur
 Athletic.................112
 Central WMC.............110
 Social WMC...............19
 Zetters Social Club......112
Cobham, Sir Alan ...22, 23, *39*
Cobham's team..............*39*
Cofferidge Close *156*
Cold Ashby.................12
Colbrook...................69
Coles, Sid................113
Collingtree................50
Coltman, Rev C........108, 114
Comforts Fund..............75
Compton, Amy..............18
Cook, Jim..................23
 Mr.......................111
Co-opediens...........92, *102*
Cornell, J................*133*
Corner Pin 27, 28, 155
Coronation Parade, 1937 ....*46,
 47*
Cosford, P................*132*
Cosgrove..........*16,* 21, 107
 Hall........67, 88, 89, 117
 Lock......................*28*
Coster, Dr M..............155
Council Villas.............*36*
Coventry...............22, 79
Cowley, Arthur.............*45*
 H........................*61*
 Ted..................*61, 133*
Cox & Robinson.........18, 86
 Jack................151, 152
Coxhill, W.................118
Cranfield...............14, 79
Crawley, Aidan............151
Cricket...............115, 116
Crisp, Alf.................*40*
Crispin, Milo..............11
Crystal Palace.............86
Culworth Gang..............20
Cunliffe, C................65
Curlew...................*67*
Currie, Horace............109
Curtis, Charlie............*56*
Dagnal.....................50
Daleman, R................153
Dance Halls
 Bedford Corn Exchange ...91
 Church Institute.......88, 91
 County Arms..............90
 Drill Hall................88
 Dunstable Town Hall......91
 Labour Hall..............90
 McCorquodale's Reading
 Room....................88
 Randolph Hotel...........91
 SKF Works Canteen
 (Luton).................91
 St Giles Parish Room 88

Towcester Town Hall 90
Victoria Hotel.............91
Watford Town Hall 90
Westcott Atomic Research
 Centre...................90
Wolverton Scout Hall 91
Wolverton Works
 Canteen..............88, 90
darts teams...........*122, 123*
Davis, Vic.................79
Deanshanger.......21, 22, 107
 Feast....................22
Debbs Barn.................*77*
 Estate..................151
Denver....................109
Derricutt, Mr........*60*, 115, 116
De-Vere....................12
Dewick, Hugh..............13
 Major P..................*77*
Dicks, George.............118
 Tommy..............117, 118
'diddlem clubs'............19
Domesday...............11, 12
'Donkey Hall'..............*41*
Dormer, Eileen.........87, 92
 Madge..................*102*
Draper, Martha......115, 132
Drayton Beauchamp.........90
Dunkirk................76, 80
Durdin, Jack..............91
Dytham, Doug......*65, 85, 86,
 89, 90*
Ecclesfield, Jack *28*
 Sid......................*28*
 Ted......................*28*
Eaglestone, Mr............20
Eales, Johnny............116
 shop....................*35*
Eastleigh................152
Eden, Mr..................*77*
Edinburgh, Duke of....152, 155
Edward, K................118
Edwards, Tom............109
Eglesfield, Chirp..........50
Eleanor of Castile.........14
 Cross...................14
Elizabeth, Princess
 (Queen)............152, 155
Ellery, Ted..............116
Ellesborough..............12
Elliott, Connie...........87
Ellis, John...............92
Elms, The................115
Emberton Gardens.........143
Emerton, Mrs..............25
Eridge, R.................68
Exton, John..............91
fairs.............107 et seq
Faithfull, M.............115
farm machinery............*43*
Faulkner, Ron............93
Fegan, F.W.C.............154
Fenn, Ernie..............114
Fenny Stratford......20, 50, 107
Field Names
 Barley Mow Field 108
 Battams Field 112, 115
 Black Horse Field 79, 114,
 151
 Burry Field 113
 Canvin's Field...........113
 Dr Habgood's Field......132
 Hassell's Field 113
 Jimmy Knight's
 Paddock............77, 78
 Luckett's Field 111
 Mutual Meadow..........115
 Red Bridge Field......111, 115
 Shoulder of Mutton

 Field...............21, *30*
 Toomb's Field 107, 131
 Windmill Field.....21, *30*, 79
Fielding, Bill..............91
 Robert..................93
Finmere..................79
Fire Station..............65
First Aid Post 75
Fisher, Bob..............117
Fleet Prison..............11
floods................*35,* 155
Foddy, Mr...............115
football...........113, 114, 115
Fowler, Mr...............20
Franklin, John.....108, 111
Friendly Societies..........109
 Ancient Order of
 Foresters..............131
 Hearts of Oak...........131
 L&NWR. Provident
 Society................131
 National Deposit........131
 Oddfellows.............131
Frost, Doug..............89
 Jimmy.................114
Fry, Mr..................*56*
Gable, Fred.............114
Gables Flats............153
gaffs...................110
Galitzine, Prince........89
 Princess................89
Gallop, Bill.............86
Gammonds...............50
Gardener, Ron.......56, 57
Garner, Doug............*61*
Garrett, C.K........91, 92
Gas Works............*37, 38*
Gaskin, P................115
Gayhurst................117
General Strike...........17
Gibbs, Armstrong........93
Girl Guides........116, *130*
Glave, Ron..............89
Gledhill, Cyril..........78
Godfrey, Evelyn.........23
Godwin..................12
Good Samaritans Society 65
Goodger, Tommy........115
Goodridge, Mrs..........18
 Syd....................116
Gorricks Spring......18, 21
Grace, Reg..............91
Graf Zeppelin............22
Grafton Regis...........14
Grand Union Canal....11, 12
 Junction Canal 13, 14,
 63, 67
Gray, John..............91
Great Linford.......50, 143
Green, E.W.............112
 family.................18
 Green, Porky..........18
 & Son..................*41*
Griffith, Derick........113
 Joseph.................11
Grimshaw, N............11
Guest, Rev A.N......143, *146*
Habgood, Dr.............80
Hagley, Col..............*77*
Hamilton, Oswald......117
Hamon................12, 13
Hancock, Mr............66
Hanslope.........29, 78, 87
 Park...................80
 Working Men's Club.....93
Hardie, Jacqueline......93
Harding, Mr............152
Hardwick, Charlie.......89
Harnett, Sylvia........117

Harris, Jack............111
 R.......................66
Harrold.................109
Harvey, Dr..............116
Haseldine, bakers........18
Haversham....20, 23, 24, 25,
 29, 79
 Bridge..................*34*
Hawkins, Col. L.C......23, 25,
 66, 80
 Miss...................25
Hawthorns, the..........*150*
Hayes, E............*62, 69, 70*
 Wharf............*62, 67, 69*
Hazenbrouck...........76, 80
Health Centre..........134
Helpasthorpe............12
Hemel Hempstead.........50
Henson, George.........114
 Monty..................89
Herbert, Eva............89
Hewitt, Mrs...........133
Hill Farm..............20
Hill, Lord..............90
Holland.................76
 D.....................66
Holmes, S.J............69
Holloway, 'Pa'........117
Home Guard.......77, 78, 80,
 81, 82
Hood, Henry............89
Horwood................79
Hospital of St. John the
 Baptist................13
Howe, W................17
Howell, Maurice.......134
Huguenots...............14
Hull....................67
Huntingdon.............109
Inwood, Tom............115
Ireson, Ted............115
Iron Trunk, the.......*106*
Isenhampstead Chenies ...12
Jackson, Mr........66, 111
Jellicoe, G.A..........151
Jelly, Malcolm.........50
Jennison, H...........116
Johnson, Mr............85
 Brian.................85
 Frank..............49, *56*
Jones, Arnold.........92
 Arthur................87
 'Coddy'...............17
Kaiser, H..............67
Keech, Clive..........85
Key, Sandy............*26*
Keynes, Robert de......11
Kightley, Margery.....23
Kings
 Edward I.........13, 14
 IV...................14
 V....................14
 George V Jubilee.....*46*
 Henry II.............11
 III..................13
 Richard III..........14
 Stephen..............11
 William the Conqueror 11
Kings Langley..........50
Kingstone Hippodrome....89
Kingston, Rhubarb ...112, 113
Kirk, George..........115
Knight, Major J........*77*
 Jimmy............*77, 78*
Ladies football teams..115
Lake, Mr..............20
Lamb, Bill............*56*
Lamport...............12
Lancastrian............90

Lane, John 134
Latimer, Lord 12
Lawman, Charlie 114
Lawrence, Dr. 78, 80
Leadley, L.N. 144
Leckhampstead 21
Le Havre 76
Lesdain 76
Levis, Carol 90
Linford 20
 Place 143
 Wood 78
Little Loughton 12
Littledale, E. M. 68
LM&SR Company 27
Local Defence Volunteers 77
London County Council 68
 & North Western Railway
 Co 11, 20, 116
 Road Garage 68, 154
Longueville de, family 13
 Sir Edward 13
Loughton 11, 19, 20, 50
Lovatt, Charlie 26
Love, Dr. 115
Lovesey, Joe 90
Lucas, Sir Jocelyn 89
 Paddy 89
Ludlow Castle 14
Lunn, Bert 93
Lunn's School Choir, 1927 .*103*
Luton 22
 AC 113
 FC 85
M1 154
Mackey, Dave 116
Maids Morton 21
Maidwell 12
Maigno the Breton 12
Manchester United 85
Manfelin 12
Manor cottages *30*
 House 11
Manning, Thomas 67
Marlborough, Duchess of.....11
Marshall, David 93
Martin, Pete 8
Mansell, J.C. 67
Mazzonne, Ralph 92
Maclean, Mr 19, 86
McConnell, J.E. 67
McCorquodale, G. 64
 H. 65
 Mrs H. 65, 89
 Malcolm, Rt Hon 65
 Reading Room 88
Meacham, H.E. ...66, 117, 141
Meakins, Den 86
Mecca 68
Mepal 109
Mercia 12
Mestayer & Gunso 68
Metcalf, Bill 109
Mills
 Haversham (Carrs)..107, 109
 Kempston 109
 Passenham *30*, 109
 Ravenstone 109
 Stratford (Rodgers or
 Catts) 21, *31*, 108
 Wolverton (Woods)....21, 108
Milner, A.G. 144
Milton Keynes 13
 Development
 Corporation 155
Minstrel Troupe *104*
Morris, Bim 91, *99*
Morton, Frank 78
Moss, T. 111

Nash 18, 151
 Mrs *36*
New Bradwell ....11 passim, *36,*
 39, 45, 46
 CC *126*
 Hospital Fête *134, 135*
 Ladies' Football team *129*
 Wolverton 13
Newbury Racecourse 76
Newman, Rev Allan 142
Newport Pagnell 11, 12, 14,
 17, 21, 78, 91, 154
 Road Recreation Ground .22
 Workhouse 24
Neville, Katherine 12
Newton, Billy 52
Nichols, 'Darby' *34*
 Fred 89
 Stan 90
 T. (Sooty) *28*, 113
Nigellus 11
Northampton 27, 50
 Electric Light & Power
 Co 65
 Town FC 114
Northumberland, Earl of 12
North Bucks Guides 116
Nutt, Harold 88, 92
Odell 109
 George 115
Ogilvie, Mrs 143
Old Bradwell 11, 12
 Stantonbury ....11 passim
 Stratford ....11 passim
 Wolverton ....11 passim
Olney 14
 Harry 115
Orphanage 108, *145*, 154
Orphean Singers 93, *104*
O'Rourke, Mrs 79
Oxford 20, 22
 Earls of 12
Padbury 12
Page, Ron *61, 69*, 111
Paget, Lord Alfred 67
Pankhurst, E. 66
pantomime party *136*
Park, C.A. 116
Parry, Capt. 76
Passenham 21, 79
Pateman, Reg 115, 132
 Wilf 132
Paveli, William de 13
Pavenham 109
Payne, Bert 17
 Rev 25
Pearce, Charlie 112
Penman, Jim 115
Penn, family 66
Pettifer, A. 50
Petts, Bert *46*
Phelps, bakers *35*
Philpotts, Snr 18
Pimpo the Clown 107
Piper, C.H. 116
Pittam, Arthur 78
 Gerald 78
Plant, D. 144
Pooley, F.B. 153
Poplars 108
Porteus, Mr 66
Portsmouth 51
Post Office 21, 24, 66
Potterspury *15*, 19, *19*
PoWs 79
programmes *105*
Public Houses
 Angel 110
 Barge Inn 28

Barley Mow...17, 26, 27, 50,
 108, 110, *118*
Black Horse 78
Bridge Hotel 50
Bull Hotel 17, 49, 79, 80, 110
Case Is Altered 110
Cock Hotel *4*, 17, 49, *59,*
 88, 110
County Arms Hotel ..28, 90,
 121
Crauford Arms 88, 89, *96*
Cross Keys 21, *94*
Crown Inn 80, 86, 110
Duke of Edinburgh 110
Foresters Arms,
 Bradwell 115, 131
 Stony Stratford............110
Fox & Hounds 63, 110
Galleon Inn 20, 78, *124*
George 110
Greyhound..........20, 24, *29*
Locomotive Inn 20, 115
Mill Inn......................109
Morning Star......19, 28, *121,*
 123
New Inn 19, 89, *122*
Pig & Whistle 109
Plough *16*, 110, 143
Prince of Wales 110
Radcliffe Arms 11
Railway Tavern 115, *121*
Red Lion 110
Rising Sun *34, 35*, 110
Rose & Crown 14
Royal Oak 110, 152, 154
Saracen's Head 11
Shoulder of Mutton...18, 20,
 21, 110
Victoria Inn 80, 88
White Horse 110, 133
White Swan 110
Pyne, Psyche 93
Quarry......................117, *130*
Queen's Oak *15*
 Farm *15*
Radcliffe, Dr John 13
 Trustees 11, 13, 19, 25,
 64, 141
Randle, Mr 86
Ratcliffe, Harry *28*
 Teddy 19, *44*
Reading 79
Reading Room 65
Regents Hall 75, 79, 88, 89,
 90, *97*
Renny Lodge 92, 133
Rhythm Club *96*
Richardson, Dick *40*
Rickett, Mr 67
Rifle Butts 20
 Volunteer Corps
 (Territorials) 20
Rivers
 Bradwell Brook 27
 Cam 107
 New Bedford 109
 Nile 68
 Ouse 12, 13, *30*, 77, 107,
 108, 141, 153
 Thames 67
Riverside Café 109
Roberts, Edwin 63
 Dan 91
 Henry 63
 ironmonger 18
 John 63
 Tom 63
 Windmill 63
Rollings, Sgt. 51, 152

Rous, Mr 79
Salmon, Mr 66
Sapwell, Mr & Mrs *36*
Sanger's Circus 107
Sankey, Rev W.T. 154
Saunders, R. *118*
Sayell, Archie *16*, 27
 Sarah 17
Sayell's Fish & Chip Shop ...*45*
Schools & Colleges
 Bounty Street School.....143,
 148
 Cambridge 90
 County Junior School.....143
 Creed Street School 144
 Grammar School......88, 144
 Merton College 116
 Military Equestrian
 School 132
 Misses Stocking School...143
 New Bradwell School *148*
 Oundle 90
 Oxford 90, 116
 Radcliffe Grammar/
 Technical.92, 113, 144, 154
 Railway School 144
 Russell Street School.....143,
 149
 Science & Art Institute ...88,
 90, 117, 144
 Secondary School....144, *149*
 St Bernadines R.C.
 College 154
 St Giles Boys School 143
 St Mary's Girls School ...143
 Technical College 112
 Thornton Convent School.88
 University College,
 Oxford 13
 Wolverton Apprentices
 School 144
 Wolverton Boys School....93,
 144
 Wolverton College of
 Further Education .92, 93,
 144
 County Day School 144
 York House School 143
Scott & Co. 26
 Charlie 91
 Tina 91, 92
Scouts 114, 118, *129*
Scragg, Mrs 115
Seabrook, Mr 113
Selby Lowndes, William 12
Sharp and Woollard 66
 Mr 85
 Samuel 67
 William 67
Sharpe, Mr 86
Shenley 11
Shepherds Bush 68
Shirley, Dorothy 66
 Mrs 25
Silver Jubilee *47*
Simpson 12
Sittingbourne 69
Slade, Agnes 143
 Dorothy 143
 Edward 143
 Mrs 143
Small, Joy 118
Smith, Derek 18
 Fred *61*, 77
 James 61
 Len 64
 Nigel 116
Smock Mill 11
Solihull 79

161

Southam, Fred..............86
South Midland Div (48th)...76
　　League.....................114
Spartan League...............114
Sparteolus....................68
Spencer, Earl.................11
　　John........................11
Square, the...................*150*
Stacey Hill Farm........25, 112,
　　　　　　　　　　　117, 131
Stantonbury...........11 passim
　　Fête.......................131
　　Hospital Fund....85, 115, 131
　　New Salvation Hall.......*147*
　　St. Peters F.C..........115, *127*
　　Theatre..................92, 93
Stantonians, the.................91
Stanton Low........11, 20, 21, 23
Steer, Rev E..................25, 51
Stephens, Colin.................86
Stephenson, R...................20
Stewkley, R......................50
Stoke Bruerne....................28
St Germains Sluice..............109
St John Ambulance
　　Brigade...................134
St Nazaire......................90
St Neots........................109
Stoke Hammond...................12
Stonebridge House...............11
Stones, Ernie...................26
Stony Stratford.........13 passim
　　Ambulance..................*15*
　　Association............133, 134
　　Comforts Fund.............*84*
　　Gas Works.................151
　　Lions.....................134
　　Pirates...................*128*
　　Town Fayre................134
　　Volunteer Fire Brigade...*136*
　　Water Tower................*36*
Stowe............................12
Stowell Brown...................14
Streets & Roads
　　Abbey Way............151, *158*
　　Althorpe Crescent.........151,
　　　　　　　　　　　153, 154
　　Augustus Road..........26, *36*
　　Aylesbury Road.......18, 144
　　Bradvue Crescent..........*158*
　　Bath Terrace..............154
　　Beachampton Road....22, 26,
　　　　　　　　　　　　　　77
　　Bradvue Crescent..........151
　　Bridge Street..........*32*, 85
　　Bridle Crescent......151, *158*
　　Brookfield Road............79
　　Buckingham Street..........64
　　Bull Yard..........26, *37*, 141
　　Caledonian Road.......26, 155
　　Calverton Road....18, 26, *36*,
　　　　　　　　　77, 108, 132, 151
　　Canal Hill.................*32*
　　Church Street.....24, 26, *38*,
　　　　　　　52, 66, 85, 144
　　Clarence Road..........25, 143
　　Cock Yard..................87
　　Corner Pin.................28
　　County Arms................28
　　Creed Street.........144, 153
　　Frankstone Avenue..........26
　　Furze Way.................151
　　Galleon Estate............115
　　Gib Lane...................21
　　Gloucester Road......26, 131
　　Green Lane.............21, 27
　　Glyn Square...............153

Haversham Ave..............151
　　Road.........20, 26, *39*, 108
High Street....13, 17, 21, 26,
　　　　　　27, *32*, *37*, 79, 134
　　New Bradwell..............18
Horn Lane......................66
Jersey Road....................52
King George's Crescent...26
Kingston Ave..................151
Ledsam Street.................153
London Road........23, 26, 80
Marina Drive........26 *37*, 131
Market Square.....26, *38*, 66,
　　　　　　　　　　86, 107
Mill Lane......................66
Newport Road.....27, 28, *34*,
　　　　　108, 141, 154, 155
New Street....................154
Oak Hill Lane.................151
Old Road.......................76
Osbourne Street................27
Oxford Street.................154
Parkers Yard..............26, *34*
Pin Alley......................28
Queen Anne Street...26, 28,
　　　　　　　　　　110, 154
Ram Alley.....................154
Ratcliffe Street...............52
Russell Street.................26
St John Crescent..............151
St Giles Street................26
St Mary's Street........26, 132
Silver Street..........107, 154
Southern Ridgeway
　　Road................20, 26
　　Way....................151
Spencer Street.17, *32*, *45*, *46*
Stacey Avenue..................26
Station Hill...................*32*
Swan Terrace..................154
Vicarage Road............28, 79
Wallace Street...........26, 155
Watling Street.13, 14, 20, 21,
　　　　　　　　　　26, 67
White Horse Yard........26, 87
White Swan Yard................26
Windsor Street.................26
Wolverton Road....17, 26, *42*
Wood Street....................26
Woodland View.................151
Young Street..................153
York Road..........19, 27, 143
Styles, Ted....................78
Suzette......................68
Swain, Fred...................113
Swimming pools........*106*, 132,
　　　　　　　　　　133, *138*
Tailby.........................66
Tanner, Basil..................69
Tapp, T........................92
Tarry, George..................40
Tattersall, Mr.................86
Territorials..........20, 75, 76
Thenford.......................12
Thomas, R......................66
Thornborough..............12, 151
Thornton......................151
　　Lodge....................152
Thornycroft, Oliver............89
Thursday League...............114
Tilley, Fred..................112
Timms, Jack...................116
Toc H..................134, *139*
Toombs, Edgar.................111
Tore............................12
Towcester.............20, 77, 90
Tower of London................14

Traffic Act....................51
　　Commissioners..............52
Tram Co......*48*, 49, *52*, *54*, *55*
Tunningley, Bill...............90
Turvey........................109
　　Lionel...................115
Ultra..........................80
United Dairies, London........66
Vache, the.....................12
Vauxhall Motors............50, 91
V-E street party..............*84*
Waine, Aubrey.................118
　　Audrey....................*30*
Wahagnies......................76
Wakefield Camp.................79
　　Lodge.....................23
　　Sir Charles...........22, 23
Walton, Rev J.H...............118
War Memorial........86, 87, 117
Ward, Harry....................89
Warren, Mr.....................66
Waterfield, R..................66
Waterloo Bridge................68
Watford........................90
Watts, F.G....................116
Webb, Cyril....................89
　　George (Senior).......87, 89
　　George (Junior)...........91
　　Jack......................89
　　Mary.....................117
　　Nancy.....................22
Websters Downfall............117
Weedon........................132
Welcome Home Dinner..........*84*
Wells & Son....................45
　　outfitters................19
West, Vince................75, 76
West Haddon....................12
Westley, Percy.................79
Westminster Abbey..............14
　　Hall......................93
Whaddon.......................151
　　Hall......................80
Whaddon Chase................80
Whitchurch.....................12
White House....*61*, 111, *119*, 143
White, George.................112
Whiting, Teddy................133
　　F........................116
　　Jack....................116
Whitley bomber................*83*
Whittlebury Forest.............14
Whittlewrong, Sir John.........11
Wicken........................133
Wickens, E.....................19
Wicksteed Park.................51
Wills, Duncan................116
Wilmin, Mr.................85, 86
Wing...........................79
Wings for Victory Parade....*81*
Winslow Market.................18
Winsor & Glaves................*37*
　　H.......................133
Winterbottom, Mrs......88, 89,
　　　　　　　　　　　90, *97*
Wise, Billy....................90
　　Bros......................90
Woburn.....................14, 51
Wolverton Boys School
　　Choir.....................93
　　B.R. Horticultural
　　Society.................117
　　Carnival............92, *138*
　　Choral Society........88, 92
　　Church Institute..........24
　　Co-operative Society...*40*, 64
　　Cricket Team c1933......*126*

　　Drama Society.............92
　　Drill Hall......75, 76, 77, 78
　　Fête...........131, 133, *136*
　　Gilbert & Sullivan
　　　Society..........88, 92, 93
　　Goods Yard................63
　　Horticultural Floral & Bee
　　　Keeping Society........116
　　Hospital Committee.......132
　　Loco Works................67
　　Market................18, 27
　　Mill......................21
　　Orchestral Society........92
　　Swimming Pool Assoc....133
　　Town F.C.................*128*
　　Urban District Council..23,
　　　　　63, 133, 156, *157*, *158*
　　Works Fire Brigade.......131
Wolverton, Ralph..............13
　　Sir John de..............13
Wood, Bill....................78
Woodville, Elizabeth
　　(Queen)..............14, *15*
　　Sir Richard..............14
Woolard, C.P.................108
　　F.W......................67
Wooton........................49
Worker, Tom...................17
Works & Companies
　　Allens (Bedford).........79
　　Bowater Industries plc....66
　　Carriage Works...........17
　　Copperad............69, 153
　　Ltd, Daleman, Richard..68,
　　　　　　　　　　　　　　69
　　Deanshanger Oxide........64
　　Deanox Division..........64
　　Gowand...................79
　　Harcross Chemical Group 64
　　Harrison & Crossfield
　　　plc....................64
　　Hayes, E., Watling Works 14,
　　　　　17, 21, 49, 63, 67, 68
　　Holmes Engineering.......79
　　Ideal Standard......69, 153
　　IRG Plastics Ltd.........68
　　McCorquodale Confidential
　　　Print..................66
　　Envelopes.......64, 65, 66
　　Print Works.......13, *73*, *74*,
　　　　　　　　　　79, *126*
　　Morris Ashby Smelting
　　　Works..................64
　　Myson Qualitair..........69
　　Norton Opax..............66
　　Pressed Steel........50, 79
　　Roberts, E. & H.
　　　Deanshanger Foundry..17,
　　　　　　63, *71*, *72*, *73*
　　Tailby's.................66
　　Vaverusave, J.H..........89
　　Vauxhall Motors.......50, 91
　　Wolverton Works...11 passim
WVS...........................80
Wykhamon......................12
Yardley Gobion.....11, 49, 113
Yates, bakers................18
　　Ted..................17, 19
　　Mrs..................17, 18
York House Guides...........*130*
'Yorky'.................*150*, 153
Young, Dennis...............133
Youth of Britain............22
Yuill, G.H...................66
Zephyr...........108, 109, 118

Subscribers

Presentation Copies

1. Milton Keynes Borough Council
2. Bucks County Council
3. Wolverton Library
4. Stacey Hill Museum
5. Stony Stratford Library
6. Milton Keynes Library
7. Reg Westley

8. Bill & Dorothy West
9. Clive & Carolyn Birch
10. Darrin Lloyd Baines
11. Paul Woodcraft
12. R. Umney
13. Roy Stanton
14. Dave Morris
15. Mrs Rita Bedford
16. J.C.F. Warren
17. Sheila Tompkins
18. Sarah Haycock
19. Sally J. Emerton
20. Craig Samuel Richardson
21. Patricia Ann Whitlock
22. Linsey & Nick Folwell
23. Joy & Dave Beal
24. Elizabeth Gould
25. Nick Torpey
26. Andy Meagher
27. John Parker
28. David A. Smith
29. Peter N. Hill
30. David James Hayle
31. George & Gwen Webb
32. Terry Myers
33. Beno Catalanotto
34. Robert Ayers
35. Robert Parry
36. E. Turner
37. S. Petts
38. R.S. Pulley
39. C.F. Brown
40. K.R. Preater
41. M. Fox
42. Paul West
43. Pamela West
44. Arnold Jones
45. David & Cindy Becky
46. Margaret & Calvin Becky
47. Vicky Brittain
48. John F. Pratt
49. L. Rawles
50. H. Millard
51. Mr & Mrs P. Millard
52. Les Tarbox
53. Gerald Kingston
54. H. Sear
55. William Harry Preston
56. Richard H. Cook
57. Peter Osbourne
58. Vera Danby
59. Colin Smith
60. David Goldsmith
61. Barry Mynard
62. N. & J. Clutton
63. P. Clutton
64. W.J. & N. Larkin
65. R.E. Johnson
66. M. Tapp
67. K. Bird
68. R.J. Hobbs
69. G. Cataldi
70. J.H. Bowler
71. Mrs M.E. Goodger
72. G. Massey
73. J.H. Mynard
74. A.G. Brown
75. J.S. Cummings
76. D. N. Chipperfield
77. M.J. Swain
78. John Osborne
79. J.R. Smith
80. A. Wright
81. Peter Allwood
82. J.F.W. Eales
83. L.C. Baxter
84. Colin Smith
85. Mrs E. Dunkley
86. D.G. French
87. F. & J.E. French
88. D.L. Lidster
89. D.A. Dolton
90. M.D. French
91. M.J. Pearson
92. N.R.G. Webster
93. W.A. Webster
94. J.F.C. Law
95. Philip J. Eaton
96. G.G. Fulcher
97. J. Hawkins
98. R. Holt
99. Edward R. Quinn
100. John Cox
101. Mrs Pamela L. Coleman
102. David App
103. Audrey & Jim Lambert
104. Julie Gillam
105. Mr & Mrs R. Sullivan
106. Mr Cavalot
107. Peter F. Brazell
108.
109. R.J. Atkins
110. P. Easter
111. R.F. Birchall
112. Mrs V.A. Milton
113. Mrs E.M.W. Calvert
114. Mr & Mrs A.H. Kirk
115. Denis A. Chipperfield
116. David Bateman
117. William Prescott
118. Darren P. Gallop
119. W. Coxhill
120. Gwyneth & Eric Howe
121. Mark A. Price
122. Mrs G.M. Williams
123. John Crossan
124. B.E. Nash
125. J.J. Middleditch
126. Michael Derbyshire
127. P. Phillips
128. Olive Wickson
129. Norman John Holman
130. B.G. Tomkins
131. R.A. Holbrook
132. Anthony Tyson
133. J. Johnson
134. J. Grimsley
135. V. Leyshon
136. David Hayfield
137. P.E. Prior
138. Mrs H. Hughes
139. C.H. Mitchell
140. K.J. Shean
141. Mrs Win Blackwell
142. A.R. Kingston
143. W.R. Coley
144. Ian Richard Campion (Benny)
145. F.G. Wright
146. P.E. Dorrill
147. T. Morley (Artist Wheels)
148. Mrs S. Callow
149. W.L. Beeton
150. Mr & Mrs M.J. Addams
151. S.E. Lane
152. Meacham Red Cross Day Care Unit
153. Roger Worton
154. M.J. Hornby
155. M. Hicks
156. Mr & Mrs D.E. Statham
157. Mrs V. Woodley
158. Mrs S. Lewis
159. G. Cloake
160. Arnold Croxall
161. Kenneth J. Woodward
162. John Toogood
163. Keith Mason
164. Peter Norton
165. C. Eden
166. W. Bonham
167. Brian R. Lambert
168. Roger Delve
169. Brian Bailey
170. Stephen James Illing
171. J. Welch
172. W. Griffin
173.
174. Tony Ibell
175. G.J. Roberts
176. Peter Battison
177. Rosemary Dytham
178. Mrs S.K. Hillyer
179. F. Cornford
180. L.G. Markham
181. Reg Westley
182. Julie Neal
183. Chris Waugh
184. David West

185	M.J. & S.R. Chappell	243	Richard Eglesfield	297	William Fuller	358	W.H. Emerton
186	Paul Richard Francis	244		298	Ian T.B. Scott	359	S.H. Light
		245	Christopher Talbot	299	Colin West	360	Bruce Goldsmith
187	H.L. Thomas	246	Leslie Charlesworth	300	Dennis Overton	361	James F.A. Shaw
188	R.J. Palmer	247	Ivor Carter	301	Clive Nichols	362	Ashley Mayo
189	C.J.S. Holloway	248	S.W. Butler	302	Colin Kightley	363	Mrs P.M. Webb
190	R. & C. Holden	249	C.D. Hillyard	303	F.J. Old	364	Mrs Christine Meakins
191	Ray Green	250	Michael Felce	304			
192	Andrew Lambert	251	Trevor Tustain	305	G. Garrett	365	Chris Gravell
193		252	Albert William French	306	Leonard Robert Bailey	366	Patrick G. Atter
194	A.J.H. Ferguson					367	Nicholas J. Atter
195	D.J. Wesley	253	G.W. Hughes	307	R.W. Johnson	368	T. Clarridge
196	Reg Goodridge	254	Amy Allen Rowlandson	308	Michael Brian Barby	369	Stuart Smith
197	J.D. Hedges					370	Neil Davison
198	Dave Rivers	255	Stuart Borland	309	Cyril Webb	371	M. Harris
199	Richard Turner	256	Tom Borland	310	Pat & Kit Walsh	372	G.D. Mitchell
200	Duncan Borland	257	Brian Jones	311	Griselda Gifford	373	Mrs P. McMahon
201	Keith Meakins	258	Neil Charles Jones	312	John Bull	374	Alan Herring
202	Norman Walker	259	Grace Wootton	313	G. Ellis	375	Mr & Mrs J.D.H. Warr
203	Angela Parker	260	Roy Reynolds	314	Iris Day		
204	Diane Groom	261	Mrs W. Shean	315	Sheila Beales	376	A.J. Godwin
205	Graham Crisp	262	Les & May Wilson	316	Betty M.C. Wise	377	M.A. Godwin
206	George Wyatt	263	Roy & Beryl Pateman	317	Sue & Dave Pedley	378	Mr & Mrs J. Goldsmith
207	Delphine Cole			318	Mrs June Axtell		
208	Fiona Smith	264	Royston & Linda Camozzi	319	Philippa Wills	379	Neil John McComish
209	Stephen Dee			320	William H. Gurney		
210	Judith King	265	Doreen & Leslie Cook	321	G.A. Brandom JP	380	Mrs P. Crossman
211	Mr & Mrs K. Henson			322	Eric Mayo	381	Julian Warr
		266	Reg & Doris Pateman	323	J.E. Wearing	382	Alistair Warr
212	Sylvia & Tony Mead			324	John Brandom	383	Hazel Cox
213	Maureen & Eric Higgins	267	George T. Moore	325	Geoffrey Albert Brandom	384	June Burbidge
		268	John Coales			385	Mrs S.L. Stone
214	Bernard Wills	269	Kenneth Stone	326	H.A. Canvin	386	Mrs S. Martin
215	Mrs Hazel Mynard	270	Cecil Stone	327	Clive Boddington	387	Frank E. Atter
216	Alec Whitlock	271	Pearl Ringham	328	R. Coombs	388	R.W. Bunce
217	Derek A. Savage	272	Linda Yourin	329	R.L. Ballard	389	Stella Vigar
218	M.J. Leach	273	Basil J. Dawes	330	M.J. Ballard	390	H.A. Severne
219	Mrs Dorothy Williams	274	Tony Jenkins	331	A.J. Horton	391	Helen & Keith Bailey
		275	John & Joyce McClusky	332	Ms H.J. Crossman		
220	P.I. Wenham			333	W.H. Chappell	392	M. Hayle
221	Peter K.D. Wickson	276	Miss Kathleen Sanders	334	Mrs M.E. Gurney	393	Mr & Mrs W.B.H. Bessell
222	Olive Wickson			335	A. Faulkner		
223	Keith Gooding	277	W.T. May	336	T.H. Wilmin	394	Aubrey Barby
224	Scott J. Booden	278	John Phillips	337	Miss A. Button	395	J.A. Walden
225	A.G. & P. Cook	279	Jane Privett	338	Mrs M.J. Crook	396	Mrs Valerie Holden
226	John Booden	280	Jeff Woolner	339	Mrs B. Tomalin	397	L. Paul Prior
227	Lindsay and Greg Deslandes	281	Nigel Jon Fisher	340	C.H. Brightman	398	Frank Atkins
		282	W.T. Atterbury	341	Raymond Essam	399	Bernard Berry
228	Frank Todd	283	W.C. Hughes	342	P.M. Tomalin	400	P.S. Cleaver
229	W.D. Henson	284	William L.A. Skeats	343	R.L. Tomalin	401	P. Evans
230	Harold Batterson	285	Leslie George Walker	344	John Sprittles	402	David Pell
231	Ernie Johnson			345	Edith Holyhead	403	Pat Mortimer
232	J.C. Herbert	286	G.R. Milton	346	F.G. Beales	404	
233	Julie Borland	287	Linda Smith	347	Mrs P. Derbyshire	405	Edward Legg
234	Gordon Borland	288		348	I. Johnson	406	Sid Savage
235	Alan Hambley	289	R.J. Tite	349	Michael S. Gregory	407	Jim Brazier
236	Mrs Jennifer A. Gee	290	Alan Williams	350	Mrs E. Jones	408	Buckinghamshire County Library
237	Mrs Eve Mynard	291	David Kennedy	351	Mrs D. Stanton	422	
238	Mrs L. Frost	292	Den Willett	352	Mrs J. Nott		
239	S.A. Urwin	293	Gerald Stimpson	353	Edward Reuben Crossman		
240	Phyllis Hutchinson	294	Frank Basil Stimpson				
241	Mrs M. Hansford			354	J.T. Simons		
242	Arthur Reginald Onan	295	Dennis Michael Andrews	355	Stephen Montague		
				356	Mrs D. Morris		
		296	Richard Norwood	357	A. Spenceley		

Remaining names unlisted

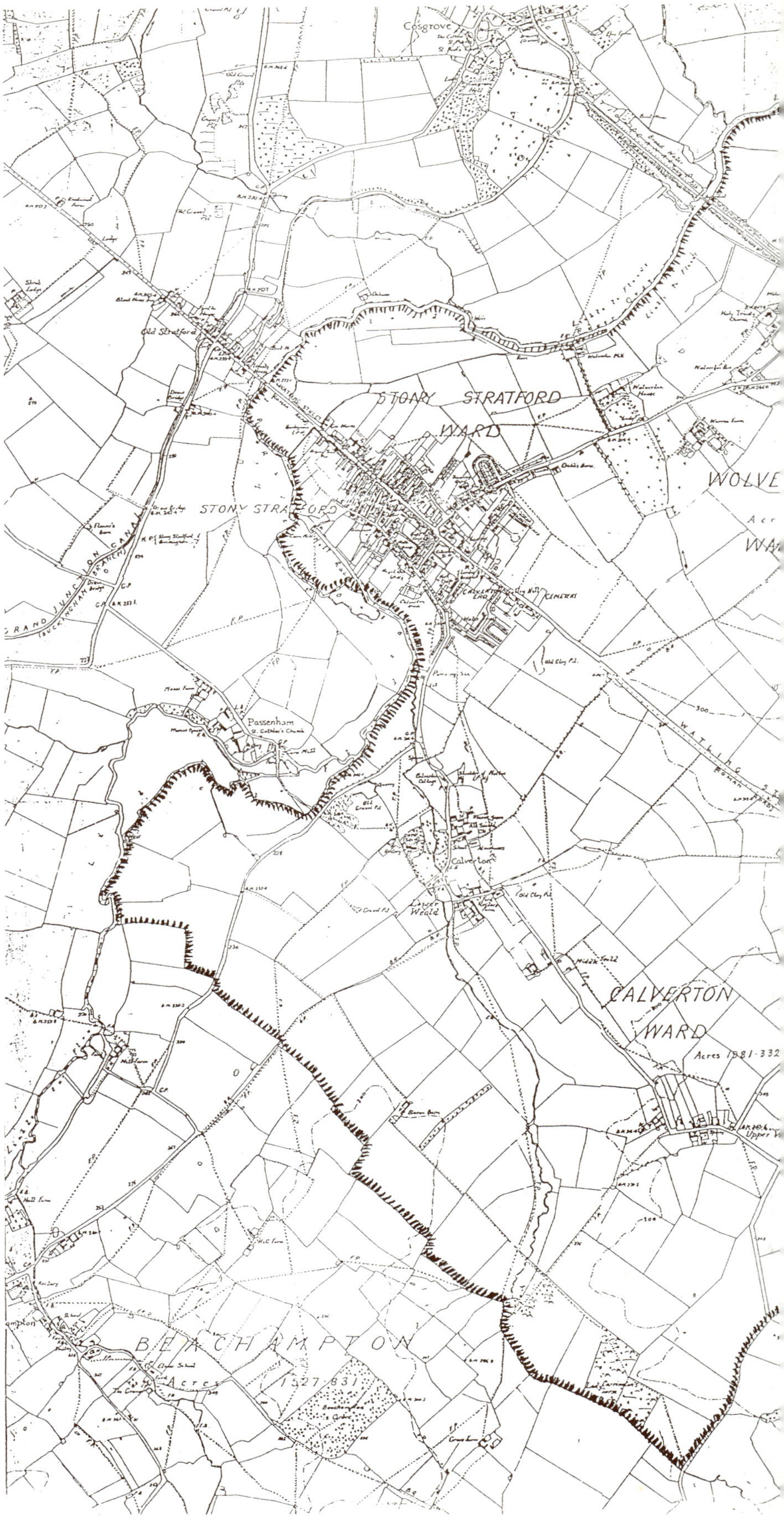

Cosgrove
Old Stratford
STONY STRATFORD
WARD
STONY STRATFORD
GRAND JUNCTION CANAL
(BUCKINGHAM BRANCH)
Passenham
Calverton
Lower Weald
CALVERTON
WARD
Acres 1381·332
Upper
WOLVE
BEACHAMPTON
Acres
1527·831
WATLING